BECOMING
AND BEING
A TEACHER

CRITICAL STUDIES
in DEMOCRACY
& POLITICAL LITERACY

Paul R. Carr
General Editor

Vol. 2

The Critical Studies in Democracy and Political Literacy series
is part of the Peter Lang Education list.
Every volume is peer reviewed and meets
the highest quality standards for content and production.

PETER LANG
New York • Washington, D.C./Baltimore • Bern
Frankfurt • Berlin • Brussels • Vienna • Oxford

BECOMING AND BEING A TEACHER

Confronting Traditional Norms to Create New Democratic Realities

EDITED BY P.L. THOMAS

PETER LANG
New York • Washington, D.C./Baltimore • Bern
Frankfurt • Berlin • Brussels • Vienna • Oxford

Library of Congress Cataloging-in-Publication Data

Becoming and being a teacher: confronting traditional norms to
create new democratic realities / edited by P.L. Thomas.
pages cm. — (Critical studies in democracy and political literacy; vol. 2)
Includes bibliographical references and index.
1. Teachers—Training of—United States. 2. Teachers—United States—Conduct of life.
3. Critical pedagogy. 4. Neoliberalism. I. Thomas, P. L. (Paul Lee), editor of compiliation.
LB1715.B38   370.71'10973—dc23   2012034861
ISBN 978-1-4331-1686-5 (hardcover)
ISBN 978-1-4331-1650-6 (paperback)
ISBN 978-1-4539-0931-7 (e-book)
ISSN 2166-5036

Bibliographic information published by **Die Deutsche Nationalbibliothek.**
Die Deutsche Nationalbibliothek lists this publication in the "Deutsche
Nationalbibliografie"; detailed bibliographic data is available
on the Internet at http://dnb.d-nb.de/.

Cover photo by Galen Leonhardy

The paper in this book meets the guidelines for permanence and durability
of the Committee on Production Guidelines for Book Longevity
of the Council of Library Resources.

© 2013 Peter Lang Publishing, Inc., New York
29 Broadway, 18th floor, New York, NY 10006
www.peterlang.com

Printed in the United States of America

Table of Contents

Acknowledgments

Becoming and Being a Teacher: Confronting Traditional Norms to Create New Democratic Realities began as a proposed single-author volume for Paul Carr's series at Peter Lang USA. Soon after my proposal was accepted, however, I began to feel that this message would have more power and texture if it were a collection of voices. Thus, my opening acknowledgment is to the support and guidance of Paul Carr as this project evolved and then to the authors whose essays are collected in the pages that follow.

If I pull back, I must also thank a long list of influential people in my journey to becoming and being a teacher myself: my mother and father, my teachers throughout all of my schooling from first grade through my doctoral program, and my many wonderful students. To become and be a teacher is a complex and never-ending journey, and I am a fortunate person to be a teacher as well as a perpetual student.

This volume is my first major edited work, and in that experience, I have felt more than ever indebted to Joe Kincheloe (1950–2008). As I have acknowledged often, Joe personified for me a different and rich kind of becoming and being a scholar-teacher-writer. Joe reached out and took my scholarly hand, bringing me into the Peter Lang fold that has led to a scholarly life I could never have imagined, one that began in the early 2000s. Thank you, Joe. You are here, always.

Finally, I want to come back to the many teachers, scholars, and advocates who contributed to this volume. The collaboration on the proposal and drafting process has been enriching for me, and I am a different scholar and teacher on the other side of this project.

Introduction

P. L. THOMAS

Writing on the cusp of the most invasive federal legislation addressing education, known popularly as No Child Left Behind (NCLB), Adrienne Rich (2001) lamented: "Over the past two decades or less, we have become a pyramidic society of the omnivorously acquisitive few, insecure, dwindling middle class, and a multiplying number of ill-served, throwaway citizens and workers" (p. 147). Soon after George W. Bush attained the presidency of the United States, in part as an education-reform governor, he ushered in NCLB to intensify an accountability movement begun under Ronald Reagan in the early 1980s—and then he served two terms while NCLB became not an experiment but a fixture of U.S. public education.

America next chose as president Barack Obama, a bi-racial Democrat offering hope and change. Further, we could speculate that Rich could never have imagined that the pyramidic society she observed in the 1990s has accelerated, and at least one category of the "throwaway" workers has clearly been determined, fueled by the Orwellian educational discourse and policy (Thomas, 2011) coming from the hope-and-change administration. And that group of "throwaway" workers is *teachers.* Thrown away along with teacher professionalism have been foundational commitments to democracy, eroding the political literacy of Americans as citizens and workers.

The modern accountability era in public education began under Reagan as a veiled call for higher standards for students (Bracey, 2003; Holton, 2003), planting the seed for bi-partisan and governor-driven marketing of politicians as education reformers. But these seminal elements of the accountability era—state content standards, high-stakes tests, and school report cards—were merely masks for reinforcing and perpetuating a politically conservative agenda built on neoliberal ideologies committed to technocracy, corporatism, and competition to the exclusion of democratic principles.

"Capital vulgarizes," argues Rich (2001), "and reduces complex relations to banal iconography" (p. 149). For public education, popular and political discourse has reduced teaching and learning to consumer paradigms, initially demonizing U.S. public education and the lazy, internationally incompetent U.S. students. "In the interest of marketing," Rich warns, "distinctions fade and subtleties vanish" (p. 149). Such has been the case for the past 3 decades of ever-increasing educational accountability, and we have now reached a new pinnacle—the public and political demonizing of the teacher.

Traditional education has long suffered the fate of being authoritarian—a structured and state-controlled avenue to assure that children are quiet, still, and receptive, much as corporate America wants its workers to be. "The study of silence has long engrossed me," according to Rich (2001): "The matrix of a poet's work consists not only of what *is there* to be absorbed and worked on, but also of what is missing, *desaparecido*, rendered unspeakable, thus unthinkable" (p. 150). U.S. public education renders students and teachers into that "unspeakable" and "unthinkable" because, as Rich observes:

> Universal public education has two possible—and contradictory—missions. One is the development of a literate, articulate, and well-informed citizenry so that the democratic process can continue to evolve and the promise of radical equality can be brought closer to realization. The other is the perpetuation of a class system dividing an elite, nominally "gifted" few, tracked from an early age, from a very large underclass essentially to be written off as alienated from language and science, from poetry and politics, from history and hope—toward low-wage temporary jobs. The second is the direction our society has taken. (p. 162)

And it is in this context that this volume, *Becoming and Being a Teacher: Confronting Traditional Norms to Create New Democratic Realities*, is born and dedicated.

In the chapters that follow, a diverse collection of voices confronts the neoliberal and technocratic assumptions behind traditional school and contemporary reform paradigms, which I have characterized as "No Excuses" Reform (Thomas, 2011, December 30). Specifically, we seek to unmask and then call for Social

Context Reform that re-imagines teacher and student accountability, teacher autonomy, and the democratic purposes of universal public education. Education reform void of commitment to democracy can only fail, and thus teachers—silenced and denied their political voices—can only fail in their mission as educators.

Becoming and Being a Teacher

It is in this era of "No Excuses" accountability that this volume gathers a collective although not monolithic voice—the *voices* of experience and expertise accumulated by teaching and researching education. The common threads running through the volume's chapters include the following:

- The framing of becoming and being a teacher within the Critical Studies in Democracy and Political Literacy series' focus on democracy and political literacy.
- The identification and confrontation of neoliberal assumptions about American society, universal public education, and education reform.
- A commitment to foundational ideals often associated with America, but ignored or distorted by corporate and neoliberal realities—democracy, human agency, professional autonomy.
- Evidence-based examinations of complex problems and complex solutions facing teachers, education policy, the public, and students.
- An embracing of teaching as a political act and of critical subjectivity as a rejection of objectivity and traditional paradigms of teaching designed to create a compliant teacher workforce.
- A recognition that race, gender, sexuality, class, and a wide and overlapping range of sub-categories of human existence contribute to and suffer under lingering facts of marginalization and oppression that must be named, confronted, and overcome.
- An honoring and celebration of voice as well as collective voice that speaks to and from the inexorable fact of *becoming and being a teacher* as one and the same.

The volume is divided into four broad sections with 21 chapters. Part I, "Becoming a Teacher: Democracy Within a Corporate Norm," opens with "Continuous Becoming: Fieldwork as a Mutually Transformative Experience" (Chapter 1) by Thomas Robertine, who confronts the idea of "continuous becoming" while reflecting on his field experience at the beginning of his commitment to becoming and being a teacher. Ana L. Cruz's "Becoming a Teacher: Fostering a Democratically Conscious Citizenry Through Critical Pedagogy" (Chapter 2) presents a case study that elaborates on the strategies and techniques used in an undergraduate-level Foundations of Education course that employs Freirean principles wherein the professor and students engage in dialogue to analyze traditional norms of schooling and challenge the current modes of teacher preparation. Cruz argues that early integration of critical pedagogy into the Teacher Education curriculum is crucial for the survival of a modern democratic society. In "Teach for America, Urban Reform and the New Taylorism in Public Education" (Chapter 3), Katherine Crawford-Garrett traces the experiences of one cohort of first-year Teach for America (TFA) corps members teaching in Philadelphia in 2010–2011. Using data drawn during methods courses, Crawford-Garrett finds that TFA recruits felt trapped between their personal ideals and the "'moralistic and technical control' exerted within their school contexts."

"Becoming a Teacher in an Era of Curricular Standardization and Reductionist Learning Outcomes: A Poetic Interpretation" (Chapter 4), by Lisa William-White, is a Spoken Word poetic discourse that complements Crawford-Garrett's study by "beckon[ing] teachers to examine their own curricular and professional journeys, while providing a space for their learners to engage in the same process of self-knowledge and inquiry, called the currere, disrupting the traditional norms that undermine schools as sites of democratic learning." Next, Anthony Cody, in "Learning to Teach: Values in Action" (Chapter 5), addresses essential questions about traditional models for teacher education as well as internship programs such as Teach for America and affiliates of the New Teacher Project. Cody examines the state of teacher education in the high-stakes accountability era and considers how those facts impact the current reform movement, including teacher quality and teacher education.

Part II, "Becoming a Teacher: Teacher Education in an Age of Austerity," begins with Brad Porfilio and Lauren Hoffman pulling several threads together from the opening chapters in "The Corporate Takeover of Teacher Education: Exposing and Challenging NCTQ's Neoliberal Agenda" (Chapter 6). Porfilio and Hoffman critically expose NCTQ's agenda for teacher education as well as highlight an alternative vision of teacher preparation and model of assessment to counter the technical, commercial agenda being promoted by neoliberal corporate entities such as NCTQ and *U.S. News and World Report*. Writing from his experiences in Canada, John L. Hoben, in "Right-Thinking People: Becoming a Teacher Educator in the Age of Austerity" (Chapter 7), suggests the need for a particular form of imaginative education that emphasizes the importance of standing in the place of others, even as we recognize the difficulties and dangers of doing so—a critical stance that uses narrative as a vehicle for new forms of agency and resistance that arise out of the articulation of shared forms of loss.

Also raising issues related to the tension between critical pedagogy and teacher education, John M. Elmore's "Neoliberalism and Teacher Preparation: Systematic Barriers to Critical Democratic Education" (Chapter 8) pursues three issues: (1) the nature of neoliberalism and its assault on democratic education, (2) the proletarianization of teachers and teacher work, and (3) the co-opting and capitulation of teacher education programs and teacher preparation faculty. "Too Late for Public Education? Becoming a Teacher in a Neoliberal Era" (Chapter 9) by Julie A. Gorlewski and David A. Gorlewski ends Part II with a historical overview of the neoliberal impact on teacher education and education from the beginning of the accountability era in the early 1980s. Gorlewski and Gorlewski then offer their own experiences for uncovering the hidden curriculum of school reform that has alienated teachers from their labor and worked to silence the next generation of educators.

In Part III, "Being a Teacher: The Mythology of Corporate Education Reform," "Ignorance Is Strength: Teaching in the Shadow of Big Brother" (Chapter 10), by Lawrence Baines, moves the volume into the silenced field identified by Gorlewski and Gorlewski. Baines describes unsettling similarities between the fictional country of Oceania in George Orwell's novel *1984* and the United States today. From the disproportionate distribution of wealth to the peddling of propaganda and disinformation as fact, American initiatives that mirror the duplicitous, misanthropic manipulations of Big Brother are highlighted.

Next, Ann G. Winfield and Alan S. Canestrari's "Beware Reformers Bearing Gifts: How the Right Uses the Language of Social Justice to Reinforce Inequity" (Chapter 11) argues that public education is under attack. They examine language, positionality, ideology, and political economy as a way of understanding current educational reform agendas that place power in professional organizations at the expense of teachers; as well, they suggest the accountability movement is set to move beyond K–12 into higher education. On a broader scale, Gordon Bambrick's "Spotlight on Failure: The Mythology of Corporate Education Reform" (Chapter 12) places the education reform failures within economic and political failures built on neoliberal assumptions. Bambrick calls for addressing the income gap and suggests that a shift in paradigms would result in the education improvement America claims to seek.

Representing the power and authority of experience and collective voice, Amy Flint, Eliza Allen, Tara Campbell, Amy Fraser, Danielle Hilaski, Linda James, Sanjuana Rodriguez, and Natasha Thornton present two lines of inquiry—sense-making and the role of stories—in "More Than Graphs and Scripted Programs: Teachers Navigating the Educational Policy Terrain" (Chapter 13). The many voices of this piece connect their past with an informed understanding of the future for teachers. As a powerful companion piece focusing on the individual teacher, Dana M. Stachowiak's "Not Bound by Stupid Binaries: Dismantling Gender in Public Schools Through a New Consciousness and Claiming of Agency" (Chapter 14) works from three purposes—engaging in performative writing to confront gender binaries impacting teachers, developing a dialogue with the reader to debunk gender binaries in the context of agency, and advocating the need to challenge gender binaries in educational settings. Another teacher narrative, "So This Is America: A Narrative of Becoming and Being a Teacher" (Chapter 15), from Galen Leonhardy, grows from the journals of his experience working against the tensions created between school structures and assumptions as they come up against teacher autonomy.

Part IV, "Being a Teacher: Accountability and the Death of Democracy," begins with Regletto Aldrich Imbong's "Neoliberalism and the Filipino Teacher: Shaking the System for a Genuine Democracy" (Chapter 16), reminding readers: "Not a single country is immune from the effects of neoliberal globalization." This discussion details and rejects the role of neoliberal policies in the Philippines that has reduced the Filipino teacher to a mere commodity and machine. The power of scripted curriculum, coupled with the commercialization of teaching and learning materials, informs Katie Stover and Crystal Glover's "Mandated Scripted Curriculum: A Benefit or Barrier to Democratic Teaching and Learning?" (Chapter 17). In their examination of these dynamics, Stover and Glover conclude: "By participating in the use of scripted curriculum, teachers assist in the manufacturing of failure by following mandates without criticism and question."

Moving from corporate and commercial influences on teachers and teaching, A. Scott Henderson, in "Schools as Battlegrounds: The Authoritarian Jurisprudence of Clarence Thomas" (Chapter 18), confronts the role of the Supreme Court. Often regarded as the most ideologically conservative member of the Court during his tenure, Justice Clarence Thomas has consistently presented himself as an authority on the role of teachers and school administrators, advocating a full return to *in loco parentis* as a guiding principle for public schools. In "Troubling Traditional Notions of 'Prepared': Two Urban Teachers Ignite the Boundaries of Progressive and Critical Theories" (Chapter 19), Melissa Winchell and Patricia Chouinard—one a progressive educator, the other a critical educator—use a metalogue to subvert this polarized status quo and to reimagine teacher preparedness by "igniting boundaries" of progressive and critical theory. The aim is to engender dialogue that resists traditional education and politicized education reform through a pragmatic-critical discussion of teacher preparation.

Dawn Mitchell's "Why Accountability Measures Fail: Practitioner Perspectives on the Role of Teacher Efficacy" (Chapter 20) builds on themes from her work with four teachers—Martha Frye, Emily Perry, Margaret Rosebro, and Jessie Wolfinger. Mitchell's discussion relies on practitioner perspectives to discuss why teacher efficacy is important and to provide practical ways of fostering teacher and student growth in our classrooms. The final chapter, Michael Svec's "Empowerment Through Classroom Cultural Inquiries" (Chapter 21), discusses experiences in a graduate course on the culture of American schools that engaged teachers in an understanding of the role of culture in their profession and their classroom. The changing role of teachers under pressures from state and national agencies couched in neoliberal assumptions is explored before examining student cultural diversity. One of the primary misconceptions challenged is that a culture is static and exists beyond individuals.

•

Freire (1998) describes the tension inherent in the role of "teacher" that grows from a misguided duality:

> It is in this sense that both the authoritarian teacher who suffocates the natural curiosity and freedom of the student as well as the teacher who imposes no standards at all are equally disrespectful of an essential characteristic of our humanness, namely, our radical (and assumed) unfinishedness, out of which emerges the possibility of being ethical. . . . It seems that we have not yet solved the dilemma arising from the tension between authority and freedom. And we invariably confuse authority and authoritarianism, freedom and license. (pp. 59–60)

Further, Freire recognizes that this failed duality is couched in "the lack of respect for education on the part of the constituted authorities" as well as that teacher behaviors have fueled that status through a "refusal to transform our teaching" as a rejection of teaching as a service industry and of teaching as "a domesticating, paternal attitude toward the students" (p. 65).

With Freire's recognition of authoritarian paradigms and professional agency in mind, then, this volume seeks to name and challenge the status quo while also identifying the need to claim teacher autonomy and agency as a central aspect of what it means to become and be a teacher:

Teachers who do not take their own education seriously, who do not study, who make little effort to keep abreast of events have no moral authority to coordinate the activities of the classroom. (Freire, 1998, p. 85)

Becoming and being a teacher is an act of moral authority inextricably linked to our forever becoming and being students.

The chapters that follow examine the tensions among economic, political, and educational goals in U.S. universal public education as well as in becoming and being a teacher. In the context of critical pedagogy/postformalism, capitalism, Western norms, partisan politics, consumerism/materialism, and corporatism, these chapters also argue for a more robust, critical, and meaningful democracy honoring human dignity and agency, including the political voice inherent in teachers and citizens of a free society.

References

Baker, B. (2012, January 7). Fire first, ask questions later? Comments on recent teacher effectiveness studies. School Finance 101 [Web log]. Retrieved from http://schoolfinance101.wordpress.com/2012/01/07/fire-first-ask-questions-later-comments-on-recent-teacher-effectiveness-studies/

Bracey, G.W. (2003). April foolishness: The 20th anniversary of *A Nation at Risk*. *Phi Delta Kappan, 84*(8), 616–621.

Freire, P. (1998). *Pedagogy of freedom: Ethics, democracy, and civic courage*. P. Clarke (Trans.). Lanham, MD: Rowman and Littlefield.

Holton, G. (2003, April 25). An insider's view of "A Nation at Risk" and why it still matters. *The Chronicle Review, 49*(33), B13.

Rich, A. (2001). *Arts of the possible: Essays and conversations*. New York: W.W. Norton and Company.

Thomas, P.L. (2011). Orwellian educational change under Obama: Crisis discourse, Utopian expectations, and accountability failures. *Journal of Inquiry & Action in Education, 4*(1), 68–92. Retrieved from https://journal.buffalostate.edu/index.php/soe/issue/view/11

Thomas, P.L. (2011, December 30). Poverty matters! A Christmas miracle. *Truthout*. Retrieved from http://truthout.org/index.php?option=com_k2&view=item&id=5808:poverty-matters-achristmas-miracle

Thomas, P.L. (2012). *Ignoring poverty in the U.S.: The corporate takeover of public education*. Charlotte, NC: Information Age Publishing, Inc.

Part I. Becoming a Teacher: Democracy Within a Corporate Norm

Continuous Becoming:
Fieldwork as a Mutually Transformative Experience

THOMAS ROBERTINE

At the age of 21, I decided to break from my intention to become a teacher and instead pursue my passion for music. It was during this hiatus from the academic world that I first encountered the idea of "continuous becoming" (Roth, 2002, p. xix). In my quest to reach my potential as a musician I came to realize that my endeavor would never end. There was no goal to be achieved, but rather a series of checkpoints along the way that might ensure that I was heading in the right direction. Since I have returned to the world of academics to complete my degree in hopes of becoming a teacher, "continuous becoming" has become the basis for my educational philosophy.

Most of us enter this field with a desire to help all students reach their potential; however, realities of classrooms can cause teachers to lose sight of this purpose. Echoing struggles in the field of music, educators in the midst of daily challenges can become distracted by unachievable goals and forget why they chose this profession. In both music and education, practitioners must love the *process* as much as—or even more than—the *rewards* they receive as a result of their perseverance. If we as educators fail to think of ourselves as students in our fields, we will become stale and eventually ineffective. We will, in short, stop *becoming*.

As a student seeking initial certification in New York State, I am required to participate in 100 hours of "fieldwork" prior to student teaching. To facilitate this, the college I attend makes arrangements with schools and teachers in the region.

This chapter will focus on the experiences of my first semester of fieldwork and how they altered my preconceptions of fieldwork. I had expected observations to influence my thoughts and feelings towards schooling, but I did not imagine that it would be a mutually beneficial transformation. During this process, my mentor—in being a teacher—was experiencing his challenges. And through the process of becoming a teacher I was able to provide a little insight that helped him to achieve this goal.

My Inexperienced Assumptions

As I entered the classroom for fieldwork, I believed that I would witness pedagogic techniques that paralleled those discussed in education classes. I hoped to gain greater insight into the minds of secondary teachers, as well as confirm that the creative strategies that I have attempted to acquire in my education courses would be reflected in real-world classrooms. For instance, Robert Bain (2005) believes that by "problematizing" historical accounts we can get students to understand different perspectives of authors as well as facilitate critical thinking that is fundamental to historical thought. Entering fieldwork, I was filled with questions and excited for my mentor-teacher and his colleagues to provide the answers I required in order to leave the experience satisfied. I also hoped to observe a sense of community among teachers as they worked together to promote greater understanding not only within individual classes, but also across content areas.

Although my outlook toward fieldwork was generally positive, I also had various concerns that related to the state of the educational environment in the country. Since I have returned to college after a 5-year hiatus, the struggle over the future direction of our educational system has deepened, and philosophies about how to solve current problems (or improve current conditions) are antagonistic toward teachers. Many education majors will be entering our profession during a very tense period and should expect a high level of scrutiny over our success and failure rate (Dillon, 2009). It is disheartening to imagine teachers who enter the field with all the right intentions becoming beaten down by bureaucracy and suffocated by red tape, leaving them apathetic and content with providing students the bare minimum in order to maintain their positions. It was not until the start of my fieldwork that I realized that my concerns, more than my hopeful expectations, would come to define my experience.

My Shattered Expectations

I arrived at my assigned classroom for fieldwork during a transitional phase of the curriculum; social studies classes were concluding a unit on geography. Following this unit was a series of lessons pertaining to various forms of government and their places throughout history. Although these first 2 weeks raised many questions and concerns of their own, my story will begin with the third week of observations. Over the course of my semester, all of my observations took place on Monday mornings. This was significant because the beginning of the lesson, more often than not, was introduced on the following Thursday. Therefore, I never witnessed the beginning of any particular unit or lesson, but instead observed classes where students were working in groups, individually filling out graphic organizers, or watching films pertaining to the topic.

As I began my third fieldwork session, students were going to be watching a History Channel documentary on westward expansion. The worksheet the teacher provided asked questions that required the regurgitation of facts or specific dates rather than promoted any sense of greater understanding. In addition, the video segment made little, if any, reference to the horrors that the Native American people faced as a result of Manifest Destiny. After the film, while students completed the worksheet, one student asked, "So, what happened to the Native Americans?" The teacher's response shocked me: "They moved onto reservations." The content was troubling, but what was even more disconcerting was the offhand way in which he issued this statement. The plight of the Native American people, as Howard Zinn (1980) details with great emphasis, is a stain on our nation's history, and, in one casual statement, their hardships had been completely brushed aside.

In our fieldwork orientation session, we had been advised by our college professors to consider carefully what we wrote in our notebooks to avoid offending school personnel. However, because I was stunned and offended by my mentor-teacher's verbal misstep, I wrote down his comment—along with a sarcastic remark of my own. What happened next would drastically affect my experiences in fieldwork for the rest of the semester.

During the next period's viewing of the film, my mentor-teacher asked if I would make copies of a worksheet for an upcoming lesson. I gladly accepted the task. It was not until I was walking out of the room that I realized that I had left my notes open to the page where I had written my comments about the previous class. As I waited for the copier, I was increasingly anxious. Surely he would not invade my privacy and read what I had written, would he? I tried to force the idea out of my mind, but as the copier neared the end of its job, I felt certain that he was reading my notes.

Sure enough, when I re-entered the classroom, the video had ended, and the teacher was lecturing about the difficulties that the Native Americans had faced during this period of expansion. The remainder of the period was spent examining questions such as, "How would you feel if you were forced from your house and told you must move?" As the students became involved in the discussion, I sat in the back, filled with mixed emotions. On one hand, I was excited to hear the students participating in a discussion for the first time since my observations had begun; on the other hand, I was not looking forward to the confrontation that I expected from the teacher who had clearly read my critical comments.

Just as I had feared, after class he asked if we could talk. However, the conversation involved a justification of his methods rather than a reproach about my notes. The teacher explained that Native American experiences had been omitted from his lesson because he believed that that the earlier class would not understand. What he seemed to be advocating was reminiscent of the concept of tracking, which I do not support (Zimmer, 2003). To avoid confrontation I did not press him for more information; I was grateful that he didn't seem angry and did not want to risk upsetting him further.

Although I did not pry into my mentor-teacher's justification, I was dissatisfied with his response. At first, I wondered if my being there played any role in his mistake. Although he had been teaching for 8 years, he was still relatively young, and perhaps he was not used to having an observer—even if it was just a student. Another possibility was that he did not fully understand the importance, from a historical standpoint, of the material he had omitted. It was also conceivable that he (or the related examination) required students to know only the fact that Indians were removed from their lands and not the details of how they were removed. Finally, I needed to accept the possibility that he was apathetic and disinterested. We have all had teachers like this, and some of them are still influencing aspiring educators.

Another question that this experience raised was whether this superficial approach was typical or limited to this historical era. Regardless of the reasons for the incomplete presentation of information to students, it was a disheartening experience that left me feeling as though I should have raised my hand to ask him to clarify some details about the Native Americans' move. I selfishly kept quiet because I was not sure how he would respond. Knowing that I had 7 more weeks of fieldwork with him, I did not want to make my situation unnecessarily difficult or uncomfortable. In addition, I know that it is not mandatory for schools to participate in this process of pre-service observation, and I did not want to give this school any reason to withdraw from the process—a decision that might affect future teacher candidates.

As I asked the teacher to sign my fieldwork log, he afforded me greater insight, explaining that much of what I learned in education courses did not reflect how things functioned in the real world. I was advised to do what was needed to pass, while at the same time preparing myself for a different reality. He told me that despite his entering the field with the desire to make a difference in his students' lives, the system was not always set up in a manner that allowed him to do so. "There is never enough time," he said. "Sometimes you just have to cover what they expect of you." This conversation led me to believe that the rest of my observations would proceed much as the initial ones had. However, I was wrong.

The following week, the students continued to work on westward expansion, but there was a clear emphasis on the roles and perceptions of immigrants and Native Americans. Before class, the teacher explained that he believed that the students were beginning to understand the treatment that Native Americans had endured at the hands of their white counterparts. They watched *Bury My Heart at Wounded Knee* and then participated in a class discussion that integrated the film with previous lessons. Although I did not witness the discussion, I hoped that my comments might have influenced the approach to this topic. Thus, my initially awkward critique might have had a positive effect on the teacher and, in turn, on the students.

Perhaps one of the most important lessons I learned from this experience was that provoking students' thoughts to promote deep understanding is not extraordinarily difficult. The teacher's new approach did not require extra planning for exercises or assessments, nor did it require extravagant applications of concepts. In fact, all that was needed was a little prompting to focus students on a broader, more critical path. Through the use of essential, thought-provoking questions, the teacher was able to spark a discussion among students who had been previously quite unresponsive. Historian Thomas Holt (1990) argues that too often history is taught as a series of dates and facts to be memorized and that structuring lessons around essential questions creates a narrative that students can challenge. This method, as proven by my experience, provides a far more interesting experience to students.

After witnessing my mentor-teacher's different approaches, I wondered whether this change in perspective would persist. While attempting to answer this question, I began to explore and consider the reasons that might have motivated him to read my notes. I believe that humans, by nature, are curious. I think it is fair to assume that any one of us would be interested in an observer's notes. However, the fact that his curiosity was elevated to action leads me to conclude that either he wanted an unbiased reflection of his teaching, which he believed he could not get by asking me, or he was aware of his factual neglect and wondered if I noticed.

While it is interesting to wonder why he read my notes, what is more intriguing is why he altered his approach after reading them. I have three possible explanations. First, he may not have expected a critique of his teaching at all, and—if he had not read my notes—he would not have received one (since I would never have offered direct criticism). However, after seeing that I was paying attention to the negatives as well as the positives, his omission of important historical information embarrassed him. Second, this criticism may have provided motivation to prove (to himself and/or me) that he was more knowledgeable and effective than he had previously revealed. Third, he might have realized that the reason he had agreed to allow these fieldwork observations was that he wanted to help a future teacher, as well as provide service to the profession. Whatever the reason for this change, it made me begin to think about fieldwork with a different perspective.

Taking Stock of What I've Learned

In the current educational environment, there is a tremendous and increasing emphasis on teacher evaluations for the purposes of holding teachers accountable to their students, their schools, and society as a whole (Jones, 1998). During my time in this placement I learned that administrative observations were more often than not conducted by the principal and were brief pop-ins rather than full-period sessions. I witnessed two of these administrative observations. On each occasion the whole process lasted no more than a minute. This provides the principal with a minimal understanding of where teachers are in the curriculum and whether or not they are on schedule. If several complaints are registered against teachers, they may be subject to a full-period observation either by the principal or another administrator.

When this evaluation process was discussed at a teacher meeting that I attended, all the teachers expressed an adversarial relationship with the administration—a relationship that would certainly affect rapport between teachers and administrators and limit the effectiveness of administrative observations. Fieldwork, in contrast, represents an opportunity for a long-term, non-threatening observation process. In a traditional master-apprentice relationship, the apprentice can teach very little, if anything, to the master. However, I believe that student-observers have the potential to offer a great deal to their mentor-teachers (Hansford, Ehrich, & Tennent, 2004).

For starters, having a young, enthusiastic observer in the classroom can remind teachers of the reasons they chose to be educators. Student-observers are excited to see good pedagogical methods in action and offer creative perspectives. Fieldwork participants can share ideas with teachers who can actually implement them. Practicing teachers can introduce positive methods to apprentices while gaining access to scholarly concepts that apprentices are immersed in through their coursework.

It also allows teachers a chance to reflect on their own practice. Observers, often closer in age to the classroom students, might be able to offer insights into what students are thinking and how they are reacting. This ties in closely with my previous point, but long-time teachers may not quite understand why copying black- or whiteboard notes is causing their students to fall asleep—or, even worse, text in class!

Finally, it seems obvious that there are often massive gaps between what teacher candidates are being taught in college courses and what they observe in classroom settings (Allsopp, DeMarie, Alvarez-McHatton, & Doone, 2006). Participatory fieldwork experiences may be an opportunity for teachers to connect their practice with current concepts in the field of education. As education majors, we are expected to have an understanding of many up-to-date methods. Often incredibly busy with the daily obligations of the profession, teachers may lack time for and access to contemporary research. Participatory fieldwork is an opportunity for student-observers to provide teachers with insights that may help them with their own "continuous becoming."

If participatory fieldwork could be reframed as non-threatening classroom feedback that benefits all involved parties, then perhaps schools would begin to welcome teacher candidates. Rather than rely on punitive tactics to promote teacher success, schools should consider how these pre-service observations might offer possibilities to motivate teachers as well as help defuse the increasing tensions that arise between teachers and administrators.

From Here on Out

While engulfed in my fieldwork experiences, I struggled to understand what I was witnessing. My observations raised questions about whether I had made the right career choice. While many of my peers described idyllic classroom conditions, I gained insight into an aspect of schooling that often goes unacknowledged. Rather than focus on the negative as I analyze these experiences, I use them to strengthen my original philosophy.

In my pursuit of a higher level of musicianship, I have on numerous occasions reached levels of frustration that made me wonder whether I was pursuing the right path. There is no doubt in my mind that I will encounter similar obstacles in the field of education. The act of questioning is itself not a problem. What is critical is how we respond to those questions. When a musician or an educator is faced with obstacles, it is imperative to introduce new concepts and materials into the mix to remove mental roadblocks and continue making progress. It is through the philosophy of "continuous becoming" that teachers can realize the need to strive for self-betterment—not just for their own benefit, but also for the benefit of their students.

Ultimately, there is no way for me to know the impact my actions had on my mentor-teacher. In writing about my experience, I frequently struggled with whether or not I should approach him; however, for various reasons, I decided against it. Despite not having the level of closure that I otherwise might have received, this experience has greatly affected my current perceptions and has contributed positively to my overall growth as I near the end of this particular phase of my life. As I reflect on my experience, I stand by my decision to return to school to finish my education and enter the profession of teaching. As I do so, I will carry the lessons I have learned from these observations as a reminder that obtaining a teaching position is not the end of the journey but rather the beginning.

References

Allsopp, D.H., DeMarie, D., Alvarez-McHatton, P., & Doone, E. (2006). Bridging the gap between theory and practice: Connecting courses with field experiences. *Teacher Education Quarterly, 33,* 19–35. Retrieved from http://www.teqjournal.org/

Bain, R.B. (2005). "They thought the world was flat?" Applying the principles of how people learn in teaching high school history. In J. Bransford & S. Donovan (Eds.), *How students learn history, mathematics and science in the classroom* (pp. 179–214). Washington, DC: The National Academies Press.

Dillon, S. (2009, April 15). Education standards likely to see toughening. *The New York Times.* Retrieved from http://www.nytimes.com/2009/04/15/education/15educ.html

Hansford, B.C., Ehrich, L.C., & Tennent, L. (2004). Formal mentoring programs in education and other professions: A review of the literature. *Educational Administration Quarterly, 40*(4), 518–540. Retrieved from http://eaq.sagepub.com/

Holt, T. (1990). *Thinking historically: Narrative, imagination, and understanding.* New York: The College Board.

Jones, K. (1998, June). *Teacher accountability: High resolution, not high stakes.* Reston, VA: National Council of Teachers of Mathematics. Retrieved from http://www.nctm.org/res ources/content.aspx?id=7814

Roth, W.M. (2002). *Being and becoming in the classroom: Issues in curriculum theory, policy and research.* Westport, CT: Ablex Publishing.

Zimmer, R. (2003). A new twist in the educational tracking debate. *Economics of Education Review, 22,* 307–315. Retrieved from http://www.sciencedirect.com/science/article/pii/ S0272775702000559

Zinn, H. (1980). *A people's history of the United States: 1492–present.* New York: HarperCollins.

2

Becoming a Teacher:
Fostering a Democratically Conscious Citizenry Through Critical Pedagogy

ANA L. CRUZ

The preparation of classroom teachers is the subject of an enduring and intense debate that is often steered by political considerations. The current flare-up regarding teacher evaluation, teacher tenure, and ranking of national Teacher Education Programs is just the most recent chapter in this saga. This chapter focuses on teacher preparation—on becoming a teacher—stressing the importance of early integration of critical pedagogy into the teacher education curriculum. Critical pedagogy promises not only to contribute to a professionally more competent classroom teacher but also to a more competent, democratically conscious citizen. A modern, truly democratic society needs a vigilant citizenry to counter the current streamlining of all aspects of society along neoliberal designs.

Neoliberalism and Education

Education in the United States, and for that matter worldwide, is at present severely influenced by neoliberal ideology. Neoliberalism, also described as free-market fundamentalism (Harvey, 2005), grew out of the writings of Hayek (1944) and Friedman (1962). Politicians—most prominently Thatcher in the United Kingdom and Reagan in the United States—adopted it in the 1970s and 1980s to remedy the economic woes of the time (Harvey, 2005). Neoliberalism as a politico-economic ideology asserts the dominance of the free market, the absence of government intervention, and the importance of deregulation and widespread privatization (Harvey, 2005). Neoliberal ideology, however, has not been restricted to the sphere of economics but saturates all aspects of social life (Harvey, 2005).

As part of the reshaping of the U.S. politico-social landscape, free-market fundamentalism was able to permeate the sphere of education, resulting in significant changes from the K–12 realm to higher education. The assault on higher education involves its corporatization, commodification, and militarization. Higher education is increasingly characterized by linkages with corporations, in part for research funding, and the commercialization of research; standardization of the curriculum and expansion in courses emphasizing business values; abandonment of shared governance and implementation of top-down management; increase in the proportion of part-time faculty; stifling of academic freedom and the erosion of the meaning of tenure; adoption of a business language (e.g., bottom-line thinking; presidents as CEOs, students as consumers, faculty as academic entrepreneurs, etc.) to go with the free-market view of the new nature of higher education; and the deterioration of education to mere job training (e.g., Aronowitz, 2000, 2009; Giroux, 2004, 2007, 2009a, 2009b, 2011; Giroux & Searls Giroux, 2004).

As pointed out by numerous authors (see Gutman, 1999; Wolin, 2008; Giroux, 2009a), there is an abundantly clear connection between education—higher education in particular—and democracy, but the trend of refashioning the meaning and mission of higher education following free-market principles will result in abandoning universities as democratic public spheres and thus undermining substantive democracy. It is important to remember that the threat of neoliberalism eroding the base of higher education—and thereby weakening democracy—is not just a U.S. phenomenon, but has a truly a global reach, as seen in recent news reports from Canada, Britain, Spain, France, and Brazil.

Critical education is fundamental to a functioning democracy because students have the chance for critical thinking, questioning, discussion, and a critical analysis of the nature of knowledge (Giroux, 2009a; Cruz, in press). Education, particularly higher education, is under threat of losing this core function because it is being refashioned by a neoliberal free-market-centered ideology that places no value on a critical form of education. Instead, what might be called "training to be obedient workers" (Aronowitz, 2009, p. x), an education to fit within the system, to conform without asking questions, is becoming the "rule." This development constitutes a serious threat to a substantive democracy (Giroux, in press).

Teachers face a three-pronged assault from neoliberal ideology. First, teachers as citizens have to cope with the daily manifestations of neoliberal ideology permeating the fabric of modern society. Secondly, teachers, in their daily work, are assaulted by political and societal forces fanned by neoliberal ideology. The attack on the tenure system, the push for high-stakes testing, evaluation of teachers based solely on students' test scores, and the blaming of teachers for the state of education in the United States come to mind. Third, teachers, during their formative years at college, experience the adverse effects of neoliberal-driven change to the nature of their higher education preparation,which tries to mold them into "technicistic specialists" (Freire, 1974, p. 35) instead of well-rounded professional teachers.

Critical Pedagogy and Substantive Democracy

Critical pedagogy is rooted in the work of Paulo Freire and Henry Giroux. Critical pedagogy is, according to Kincheloe (2008a), "grounded on a social and educational vision of justice and equality" (p. 6), "constructed on the belief that education is inherently political" (p. 8), "and dedicated to the alleviation of human suffering" (p. 11). It attempts "to link the practice of schooling to democratic principles of society and to transformative social action . . ." (Darder, Baltodano, & Torres, 2003, p. 3). Giroux (2012) posits that critical pedagogy "emphasizes critical reflexivity, bridging the gap between learning and everyday life, understanding the connection between power and knowledge, and extending democratic rights and identities by using resources of history" (introductory section, para. 5). Further, critical pedagogy "must be interdisciplinary, contextual, engage the complex relationships between power and knowledge, critically address the institutional constraints under which teaching takes place, and focus on how students can engage the imperatives of critical social citizenship." ("Classroom Authority and Pedagogy," para. 5)

Fundamental to an engaged citizen is the ability to think critically, to be curious and to question, and to be able to evaluate knowledge. Freire and Faundez (1989) contend that being able to ask questions is essential to a democratic society. Curiosity is embedded in questioning and, in conjunction, both will aid in the construction of knowledge; curiosity and questioning, moreover, require the ability to think critically. For hooks (2010), "the longing to know . . . a desire for knowledge" (p. 7) is vital for critical thinking. Encouraging critical thinking and questioning should be central to education at all levels. Colleges and universities must offer the space in which critical thinking, questioning, and critical analysis of the nature of knowledge—all of which are attributes of a functional democra-cy—are promoted. Kincheloe (2008b) underscores that engagement with the "world of knowledge production" (p. 3) is crucial to any democratic education. Students need to learn to question where knowledge is coming from, how to eval-uate its quality, who produced it, how it was produced, and whose interest it serves (Kincheloe, 2008b). Suppressing questioning for the sake of order, in con-trast, is anti-democratic and typifies authoritarianism (Freire & Faundez, 1989).

Critical pedagogy, then, is uniquely placed to provide the structure for students to acquire the critical knowledge and agency essential to support a substantive democracy. One major tenet of the work of Giroux (2009a, 2010, 2012, in press) is to emphasize this crucial role that critical pedagogy can play in supporting and defending substantive democracy. Educating youth to become engaged citizens, through encounter with critical pedagogy, can ensure that this educated citizenry will oppose the harmful ramifications of modern neoliberalism and fight back any attempts to metamorphose democracy into a form of authoritarianism (Cruz, in press). Freire (2000) again calls attention to the importance of dialogic relationship, curiosity, and questioning for a truly democratic society:

> A dialogic relationship—communication and intercommunication among active subjects who are immune to bureaucratization of their minds and open to discov-ery and to knowing more—is indispensable to knowledge. The social nature of their process makes a dialogical relationship a natural element of it. In that sense, authoritarian antidialogue violates the nature of human beings, their process of discovery, and it contradicts democracy. (p. 99)

Critical pedagogy, therefore, is imperative for negotiating the social, political, cultural, and economic circumstances that shape the life of all citizens during this neoliberal epoch. Freire (1974) contends that "democracy and democratic educa-tion are founded on faith in men, on the belief that they not only can but should discuss the problems of their country, of their continent, their world, their work, the problems of democracy itself" (p. 33).

Democracy is conceived by Dewey (1916) as " . . . more than a form of gov-ernment; it is primarily a mode of associated living, of conjoint communicated experience" (p. 101). Kindling the critical spirit in students and fostering dialogue, including the "interest in learning from all the contacts of life . . ." (Dewey, 1916, p. 418) will lead to critical consciousness (Freire, 1974). Critical consciousness entails the awakening of awareness about the current socio-political circumstances and their historical roots leading to the development of agency to change these socio-political circumstances within a framework of social justice (Freire, 1974).

This does not include enticing students to just rebel: such fanaticized consciousness (Freire, 1974) tends to emphasize emotionality at the expense of reasoning leading to irrational outcomes. Action, as the ultimate consequence of critical consciousness, must be reflective in order to be effective (Freire, 1970; 1974). This action will then be effective in ensuring the survival of a substantive democracy counterbalancing anti-democratic tendencies and developments during this neoliberal epoch.

Critical Pedagogy in the Classroom

What follows is an illustration of how critical pedagogy is incorporated into a teacher preparation course. The goal is to provide students with the opportunity to reflect on who they are, to ponder the relationship between power and knowledge, to critically analyze traditional norms of schooling, and to challenge current modes of teacher preparation through various exercises and discussions. However, many authors, including Paulo Freire himself, emphasize that critical pedagogy is not a method to be copied (Freire, 1970). Critical pedagogy is always contextualized (e.g., Giroux, 2012), and this context will always be different from classroom to classroom. The ultimate aim of critical pedagogy is to develop critical consciousness in students and for them to mature into active and critical democratic citizens.

It is important to highlight that the incorporation of critical pedagogy into this course, to engage with students in what must be considered political issues, does not represent (political) indoctrination; at no time are students presented with only one option or a single way of approaching issues. Indoctrination and "imposing answers on students is a form of oppressive education" (Macrine, 2009, p. 121) and is contrary to everything Paulo Freire stood for (see Freire, 1970; Giroux, 2010). Therefore, students in this course are expected to constantly consider a multitude of perspectives, to reflect, and to make informed choices by themselves.

The Foundations of Education course presented here is a core-curriculum course at the sophomore level in a Teacher Education Program at a U.S. 2-year college. Again, the following illustration of thematic approaches is not meant to provide recipes to be copied and adopted as "pre-packaged" modules for other courses. Rather it is meant as a guide for thought-provoking ideas and reflection about the role of an educator and the preparation of teachers. It is absolutely crucial to realize that the engagement with critical pedagogy in the Foundations of Education course stretches continuously from the first day of class to the end of the semester.

We adopt a popular textbook, and its comprehensive content includes the following chapters/units: (1) Why teach? (2) What is a school and what is it for? (3)

Who are today's students in a diverse society? (4) What social problems affect today's students? (5) What is taught? (6) What makes a teacher effective? (7) What should teachers know about technology and its impact on schools? (8) What are the ethical and legal issues facing teachers? (9) What are the philosophical foundations of American education? (10) What is the history of American education and the struggle for educational opportunities? (11) How are schools governed, influenced, and financed? (12) How should education be reformed? (13) What are your job options in education? (14) What can the new teacher expect? (15) What does it mean to be a professional? The students are required to read the units and supplementary materials on their own, and class time is used for deepening their understanding of their readings and encouraging them to ask questions. Classes are designed to present students not with formal lectures, but with material that can trigger discussion, provide opportunities to share their lived experiences and connect content to real life, and create the possibility of widening their curiosity. Rather than thinking of it as being composed only of separate units, one should think of the course as integrating repeatedly the following themes, which parallel the course content units.

Theme I—Who Am I?

In an environment that fosters critical thinking and that is grounded in critical pedagogy, it is imperative to establish trust, freedom for critical dialogue, and the classroom as a safe space—where issues, ideas, and thoughts discussed will be respected and will remain confidential. I, as the educator, introduce myself to the students, demonstrating how I reflect about myself as an individual within a socio-historical-political-economic context. I position myself within Brazil (my country of birth is introduced through a video) and its history, and contrast this position with my current status as a resident of the United States. This personal reflection not only introduces *"Who am I"* and the importance of self-reflection, but I also emphasize my passion for travelling and my curiosity about the world, as well as my commitment to life-long learning. This introduction also serves as a vehicle to connect with the students, to begin a dialogue, and to build trust between the students and myself, with the hope of establishing a community. Subsequently, every student engages in self-reflection (by writing mini-papers and presenting them to the class), exploring who they are and where they are coming from, paying special attention to what their values and beliefs are. This self-reflection stimulates extensive classroom discussion, and students develop "an understanding of the world in which they live, in its economic, political and . . . psychological dimensions" (Aronowitz,

2009, p. ix). The students are then questioned on how their own values and beliefs may impact their attitude as teachers and their relationship with future students. Even though we reach a certain level of depth, it is not until mid-to-late semester that students reach a more profound critical awareness about how their values and beliefs have shaped their view of the world and, consequently, their motives for teaching.

Theme II—Commitment to the Teaching Profession

This theme touches upon several units covered in the textbook and entails a discussion about the distinction between a true, professional teacher and a mere "skilled teacher." With respect to a progressive professional teacher, Freire (1998) declares:

> …to know how to teach is to create possibilities for the construction and production of knowledge rather than to be engaged simply in a game of transferring knowledge…. [A teacher] should be someone who is open to new ideas, open to questions, and open to the curiosities of students as well as their inhibitions…[and] ought to be aware of being a critical and inquiring subject in regard to the task entrusted to [her/him], the task of teaching and not that of transferring knowledge. (p. 49)

Identification of political pressures that aim to change the rights and duties of teachers emphasizes the importance of staying up to date with local, state, and national news. Several weblinks to news outlets portraying different political outlooks are posted on the electronic Blackboard. Students can then compare and contrast how news items are covered by the media based on different political coloration. They learn to critically evaluate news stories to recognize tendencies and biases, and to identify who ultimately might be initiating the political pressures to change the rights and duties of teachers. Classroom discussions are also used to spark the curiosity of students about such topics, based on the notion that an informed teacher who is able to critically analyze the news will be part of a democratically astute citizenry.

We also work with Paulo Freire's book *Teachers as Cultural Workers: Letters to Those Who Dare to Teach* (2005). Specifically, two letters are selected: (a) "Third Letter: I came into the teacher training program because I had no other options"; (b) "Sixth Letter: On the relationship between the educator and the learners."

The students are required to read the selected letters and to (a) highlight sections they strongly disagree with, (b) highlight sections they strongly agree with, and (c) mark with a question mark sections they do not understand. Note that I intentionally do not reveal any information about the author and the context of the letters; students are given only a reference indicating where the material comes from. The letters speak to several themes, but—as an example—we focus here on the *commitment to the teaching profession*. The Third Letter leads to discussions on the issue of teacher competence and the peculiar responsibilities of teachers who interrelate with and influence students on a daily basis; the still-too-often promulgated view of the teacher as the "coddling mother" versus what it really means to be a professional teacher; the power relationships in schools and how institutional politics might affect commitment to the profession; and the issue of monetary compensation. Discussions about the Sixth Letter deal with the relationship between teacher and learner and the idea that a commitment to the teaching profession encompasses a dedication to justice and protection of the "weak" against oppression; the importance of staying true to one's own words; and respect and understanding of the student and her/his world.

Interesting things happen when students first encounter Paulo Freire. They very often disassociate themselves from the context and the issues presented in the letters—students mention that "these letters are written to teachers in Brazil where they have a lot of problems with education." It is only after a set of lengthy classroom discussions that students start to recognize the interconnectedness of the various educational issues described by Freire in Brazil to other parts of the world, particularly the United States.

Theme III—Diverse Society and Pluralistic Views

Another important theme recurring throughout the semester concerns the multicultural aspect of modern society. A deep dialogue allows probing students' biases, attitudes, and beliefs regarding differences in ethnicity, race, gender, age, religion, class, and cultural conventions.

As part of a service-learning project, students visit the International Institute, a local non-profit agency that helps with the integration of immigrants and refugees into the local community in particular and the United States in general. Students learn the fundamental difference between immigrants and refugees and are exposed to a multitude of ethnicities, religions, languages, and cultures. They experience the struggles involved in learning a new language and trying to establish oneself in a country with radically different customs and cultural norms. Students gain immediate practical experience by trying to bridge the language/communication barrier and by realizing the kinds of foreign students they might encounter later in their own classrooms. Especially important, however, is the written report produced by the students about their experiences at the International Institute, together with the reflective classroom discussions regarding the hardships faced by the immigrants and refugees (both in the United States and their home country); the international political events that lead to refugees and immigrants; and the cultural, ethnic, and religious differences they experience while in contact with the refugees and immigrants at the International Institute. By discussing their experiences in class, students gain a deeper awareness of diversity in society and acquire the moral and ethical behavior of a critical citizen based on their interaction with, understanding of, and respect for people and cultures different from their own, while understanding the impact of immigrants and refugees on the local and national economy. Students frequently express surprise about how many languages are spoken by some immigrants. Once their curiosity about diversity is sparked, students often request supplementary material (articles or videos) to further investigate issues they encountered (e.g., ebonics; tensions between Bhutan and Nepal).

In another exercise intended to open students' eyes toward economic realities, disparity in income and wealth, and resulting social status, students visit and shop at two grocery stores of their choice: one in a more-affluent and one in a less-affluent section of town. Students are required to visit these stores with a very critical and analytical eye toward the product choices available, the employees and customers, and the overall environment inside and outside of the store. Students are exposed to socio-economic realities some of them have never experienced. In-class discussion brings to light the local/national/international causes of such economic disparities and the differences in socio-economic classes. To illustrate the psychological power of social stratification and how it can affect one's self-confidence, one (middle-class) student reported that, despite being treated with respect in a more affluent store, she was trembling at the check-out counter because she felt uncomfortable and completely out of place and intimidated by this particular environment with its overabundance of "quality" products and "well-dressed" customers.

Theme IV—External Influences on Teaching/Schools

A major focus within this theme is an in-class group project that addresses the avenues of school financing, including local, state, and possibly national revenue streams. The students read and analyze the relevant textbook chapter, correlate it to local governance/finance, and provide examples from their personal experience. In addition, current local or national news is consulted to parse out developing changes in the way schools are financed; the political and economic causes for budget decisions; the move toward privatization and charter schools; and the financial motives for private enterprises to be involved in schools. This exercise concludes with a classroom discussion that also addresses the ever-growing influence of free-market fundamentalism on the way schools are run and how teachers are perceived within such a neoliberal framework.

Important to note is that students initially have a very limited awareness of the level of corporate penetration in schools (e.g., advertisement-covered, junk-food vending machines). It is a revelation to many students when they become cognizant of the extent of corporate influence on school financing, the development of curricula, and so forth.

Overall, one often hears that critical pedagogy is too theoretical, too heady a subject. If taught at all, it should be in a graduate seminar. On the contrary, it is vital to integrate critical pedagogy into all teacher education courses, beginning with the freshman year. Not only do future teachers need to be educated to become well-rounded and competent teachers; they also need to be responsible citizens within a democratic society who can provide crucial knowledge regarding democracy to the students they will subsequently teach in their own K–12 setting.

As an educator, I feel constantly rejuvenated and hopeful because of this course and the teaching of critical pedagogy: rejuvenated because of the experience of constantly learning with and from my students—from their questions and their process of personal and professional discovery—and hopeful because the education of the children in this country—in the hands of such "becoming teachers" awakened to critical consciousness—will endow society with a more substantive democracy.

On Becoming a Teacher

Becoming a teacher is both an intellectual and an emotional journey. As one door opens, another one closes. This might cause pain, as exemplified by comments from some students who indicated that their (welcomed) growth in understanding and reading the world caused rifts with family members who did not partake in the same intellectual journey. Du Bois (2006, Chapter XIII) pointed to this dilemma:

> "John" she said, "does it make every one—unhappy when they study and learn lots of things?" He paused and smiled. "I am afraid it does," he said. "And, John, are you glad you studied?" "Yes," came the answer, slowly but positively.

Du Bois (2006, Chapter XIII) also explored the socio-political transformative power of teaching and of education in the story "Of the Coming of John," in which the white-American judge asks John, the black-American teacher," . . . well, are you going to be like him, or are you going to try to put fool ideas of rising and equality into these folks' heads, and make them discontented and unhappy?"

The journey of becoming a teacher can be painful and may sometimes even cause discontent, but it is definitely a journey worth taking, especially when it can be shown to bring freedom, consciousness, light, and "thirst" for social justice. Perhaps a quote from a student on her own journey to becoming a teacher can convey the growth of critical consciousness after being exposed to critical pedagogy in the Foundations of Education course:

> I started to see education in three dimensions. It felt like I was living in a different world. I have never thought to look at education from this perspective. I was living in the dark, and I can see the causes of the problems. . .very clearly. Understanding critical pedagogy freed my brain and removed the veil from my eyes. . . . Now, I have a better understanding of the message of education which is not the grade that the students have on the test, but how to help them solve their own problem and bring social justice to society. (A. Al_Amery, personal communication, April 29, 2012)

Critical pedagogy that frames the preparation of the teacher from the earliest moment in college is the key to both the competent teacher and the competent democratic citizen. Becoming a teacher, then, must be inextricably tied to becoming a full-fledged and capable democratic citizen as well as a consummate professional equipped with the knowledge and critical capabilities to uphold a substantive democracy.

References

Aronowitz, S. (2000). *The knowledge factory: Dismantling the corporate university and creating true higher learning*. Boston, MA: Beacon Press.

Aronowitz, S. (2009). Foreword. In S.L. Macrine (Ed.), *Critical pedagogy in uncertain times—Hope and possibilities* (pp. ix–xi). New York: Palgrave Macmillan.

Cruz, A. (in press). A global culture of questioning to confront neoliberalism: Henry Giroux's clarion call for collective agency to sustain a substantive democracy. *Aula de Encuentro*.

Darder, A., Baltodano, M., & Torres, R.D. (2003). Critical pedagogy: An introduction. In A. Darder, M. Baltodano, & R.D. Torres (Eds.), *The critical pedagogy reader* (pp. 1–21). New York: RoutledgeFalmer.

Dewey, J. (1916). *Democracy and education: An introduction to the philosophy of education.* New York: Macmillan.

Du Bois, W.E.B. (2006). Of the coming of John. In W.E.B. Du Bois, *The souls of black folk* [Kindle ed.]. Retrieved from Amazon.com

Freire, P. (1970). *Pedagogy of the oppressed.* New York: Continuum.

Freire, P. (1974). *Education for critical consciousness.* New York: Continuum.

Freire, P. (1998). *Pedagogy of freedom: Ethics, democracy and civic courage.* Lanham, MD: Rowman & Littlefield.

Freire, P. (2000). *Pedagogy of the heart.* New York: Continuum.

Freire, P. (2005). *Teachers as cultural workers: Letters to those who dare to teach.* Boulder, CO: Westview Press.

Freire, P., & Faundez, A. (1989). *Learning to question—A pedagogy of liberation.* New York: Continuum.

Friedman, M. (1962). *Capitalism and freedom.* Chicago: University of Chicago Press.

Giroux, H.A. (2004). *The terror of neoliberalism: Authoritarianism and the eclipse of democracy.* Boulder, CO: Paradigm Publishers.

Giroux, H.A. (2007). *The university in chains: Confronting the military-industrial-academic complex.* Boulder, CO: Paradigm Publishers.

Giroux, H.A. (2009a). The attack on higher education and the necessity of critical pedagogy. In S.L. Macrine (Ed.), *Critical pedagogy in uncertain times—Hope and possibilities* (pp. 11–26). New York: Palgrave Macmillan.

Giroux, H.A. (2009b). Democracy's nemesis—The rise of the corporate university. *Cultural Studies—Critical Methodologies, 9*(5), 669–695.

Giroux, H.A. (2010). Rethinking education as the practice of freedom: Paulo Freire and the promise of critical pedagogy. *Policy Futures in Education, 8*(6), 715–721.

Giroux, H. A. (2011). Beyond the swindle of the corporate university: higher education in the service of democracy. *Truthout.* Retrieved from http://truthout.org/index.php?option=com_k2&view=item&id=69:beyond-the-swindle-of-the-corporate-university-higher-education-in-the-service-of-democracy

Giroux, H. A. (2012). Dangerous pedagogy in the age of casino capitalism and religious fundamentalism. *Truthout.* Retrieved from http://truthout.org/index.php?option=com_k2&view=item&id=6954:dangerous-pedagogy-in-the-age-of-casino-capitalism-and-religious-fundamentalism

Giroux, H.A. (in press). Higher education, critical pedagogy, and the challenges of neoliberalism: Rethinking the role of academics as public intellectuals. *Aula de Encuentro.*

Giroux, H.A., & Searls Giroux, S. (2004). *Take back higher education: Race, youth, and the crisis of democracy in the post-civil rights era.* New York: Palgrave Macmillan.

Gutman, A. (1999). *Democratic education.* Princeton, NJ: Princeton University Press.

Harvey, P. (2005). *A brief history of neoliberalism.* Oxford: Oxford University Press.

Hayek, F. (1944). *The road to serfdom.* Chicago: University of Chicago Press.

hooks, b. (2010). *Teaching critical thinking: Practical wisdom.* New York: Routledge.

Kincheloe, J.L. (2008a). *Critical pedagogy primer* (2nd ed.). New York: Peter Lang.

Kincheloe, J.L. (2008b). *Knowledge and critical pedagogy: An introduction.* New York: Springer.

Macrine, S.L. (2009). What is critical pedagogy good for? An interview with Ira Shor. In S.L. Macrine (Ed.), *Critical pedagogy in uncertain times—Hope and possibilities* (pp. 119–136). New York: Palgrave Macmillan.

Wolin, S.S. (2008). *Democracy incorporated: Managed democracy and the specter of inverted totalitarianism.* Princeton, NJ: Princeton University Press.

3

Teach for America, Urban Reform, and the New Taylorism in Public Education

KATHERINE CRAWFORD-GARRETT

By the end of September, when the school year is officially underway, the first set of pencils already missing, and the classroom no longer the spotless, childless realm it was just a month earlier, Teach for America (TFA) corps members have begun a task far more challenging than starting a school year for the first time. As they attempt to make sense of what it means to become urban educators, corps members must also navigate unfamiliar urban contexts; attempt to teach across lines of race, class, and culture; and negotiate a complex and confounding political milieu characterized by rigid reform initiatives aimed, in part, at de-professionalizing and disempowering teachers.

This chapter traces the experiences of one cohort of first-year TFA corps members teaching in Philadelphia during the 2010–2011 school year at a time when the School District faced intense pressure to reform. As a result, scripted reading and math programs were adopted district-wide, and the role of charter schools took on increased significance as an unprecedented number of public schools were taken over by local and national charter corporations. By drawing upon data generated during two required methods courses that I taught for corps members at the University of Pennsylvania, I show that many TFA teachers who entered the profession with profound desires to effect educational change found that they had to reconcile their personal convictions with the "moralistic and technical control" exerted within their school contexts. In response to such working conditions, corps members drew upon analytical lenses such as Taylorism to illustrate the extent of their disempowerment.

Metaphors that made reference to factories, efficiency, and technical rationality were pervasive throughout the data set, suggesting that corps members internalized the mandates aimed at de-professionalizing them. Many struggled to reconcile the realities of their teaching environments with their hopes to encourage educational transformation. Further, the restrictive approaches of organizations such as TFA and the Mastery Charter School Network, with whom they were closely affiliated, contributed to their overall feeling of disillusionment. In response, the university methods course I designed and taught aimed to put forth alternate depictions of what an urban teacher could be and, in so doing, explicitly invited corps members to consider how alternative frameworks such as critical literacy and culturally relevant teaching could transform their classrooms. Drawing upon Kincheloe & Hayes (2007), who liken critical urban teachers to "explorers of the worlds of their students," I sought to foreground student voice and experience in my classroom as a way to humanize urban teaching and counteract the deleterious effects of Taylorism.

Teach for America: Background and Critiques

According to its website, Teach for America's mission is "to grow the movement of leaders who work to ensure that kids growing up in poverty get an excellent education" (www.teachforamerica.org). In order to accomplish this, TFA "enlists committed individuals, invests in leaders and accelerates impact." There is no shortage of recent college graduates willing to take on this work. In fact, TFA has become the nation's largest provider of teachers to low-income communities, and the network of alumni and corps members is over 17,000 strong and growing. Moreover, between 2000 and 2008, Teach for America received more than $213 million in grant money, far more than any other single organization (Fairbanks, 2011). Although the reach and prestige of the program has continued to expand, little scholarly attention has been paid to the experience of the corps members themselves, who contend daily with a number of significant challenges, not least of which is a system that extols their virtues as leaders and intellectuals while simultaneously casting them as low-level workers.

Moreover, as alternative teacher certification programs such as TFA continue to capture the national imagination and reinforce narratives of social mobility through education, it becomes increasingly important to consider the ways in which teachers within these programs make sense of their mission. The corps members highlighted in this study, for example, actively sought spaces in which to discuss, complicate, and even critique their roles within urban communities. Thus far, issues of educational equity with regard to TFA have been considered primarily through the lens of testing outcomes (Laczko-Kerr & Berliner, 2002; Darling-Hammond, Holtzman, Gatlin, & Heilig, 2005.How teachers experience, discuss, and make sense of the inequities they encounter remains a largely under-theorized and un-researched area (Popkewitz, 1998; Hopkins, 2008; Koerner et al., 2008).

The Local Context

The 2010–2011 corps members arrived in Philadelphia at a time when the Philadelphia School District was implementing a dramatic new reform initiative aimed at addressing student achievement in chronically low-performing schools. Some of the turnaround schools remained under district control and were referred to as "Promise Academies." In addition to the adoption of a tightly controlled, highly scripted curriculum in both reading and math, these schools instituted significant staffing changes as well as an extended school day and year. Those schools taken over by charter organizations were obviously subject to more drastic changes, depending on the philosophy and mission of the charter company in question. One of the largest charter networks in the city is the Mastery Charter Network, which manages an increasing number of middle schools and high schools within Philadelphia under the motto "excellence: no excuses." While charter schools based on the "no-excuses" model continue to proliferate nationwide, critics have contended that this approach to school reform conceals factors like institutional racism and systemic inequality, making true educational change impossible (Lack, 2009).

Despite the range of approaches and providers, the schools slated to be turned around in the School District of Philadelphia all shared one thing in common: their teaching staffs contained a considerable number of first-year TFA corps members. Nearly all of the TFA corps members taking the methods courses I taught during the 2010–2011 school year were placed in either Renaissance Schools run by the Mastery Charter organization or Promise Academies managed by the district. Thus, all the schools identified as most in need of radical remedies to reinvent themselves were at least partly staffed by first-year teachers who had little or no prior teaching experience. Thus, as Cochran-Smith and Lytle (2006) note, "it is precisely the students in these schools, who have not traditionally been well served by the system who need the best teachers but who often end up with the teachers who are least prepared" (p. 685). As a result, many of these schools relied on prescriptive curricula to accommodate a teaching staff that possessed little formal experience. This is not an uncommon approach, according to Oakes et al. (2002), who assert that policy makers have typically responded to teacher shortages by "adopt[ing] highly 'prescriptive,' 'teacherproof' curricula" (p. 228). However, as the authors conclude, these "'solutions' accomplish little in the short run and will diminish the capacity of the teaching force for years to come" (p. 228).

Moralistic and Technical Control

Although many TFA recruits enter the field with a strong desire to influence the life chances of their students and contribute meaningfully to the broader school reform agenda, the corps members in my courses continually expressed frustration with what Achinstein and Ogawa (2006) refer to as the "moralistic and technical control" exerted by Teach for America, the Mastery Charter Network, and the School District of Philadelphia. According to Achinstein and Ogawa, recent changes in education policy—including the increased emphasis on assessment as well as more prescribed instructional approaches—have led to what they call "a potent control system." Achinstein and Ogawa use the term "technical control" to refer to the ways in which school districts exact control by mandating certain curricular and pedagogical approaches. Moralistic control, according to the authors, describes a policy environment that demands "compliance with institutional norms and values through ideological means that determine what is and is not allowable in a given system, and thus serves to legitimize the system" (p. 32).

Because the 2010–2011 Philadelphia corps members were, for the most part, young and inexperienced, it became easier for the district, Mastery, and TFA to exert both moralistic and technical control. Even from the initial interviews that determined their school placements, corps members struggled to express their misgivings concerning their work environment. First, many teachers did not view themselves as knowledgeable enough in the field of education to assert beliefs or make decisions that countered the culture of schooling that pervaded the district. Second, if corps members did choose to outwardly oppose particular mandates, they would risk isolation and quite possibly censure from both peers and administrators. Abigail, a second-year Philadelphia corps member, detailed her conflict over whether or not to heed curricular mandates. Like many corps members, she had to reconcile her desire to keep her job and continue her work with students with the conviction that certain district mandates were harming the very children she sought to help:

I've had a very difficult year where I went into the year like, "Screw everyone. I'm doing it. I don't care if they fire me," to then very quickly seeing the climate of my school and the incredible shift in the principal and realizing that I couldn't have that attitude or I really was going to be fired. That was really rough. For a while, I just went with the script because I had to, and that was when I wanted to quit. I just realized I would rather be fired than keep doing this stuff that is harming my kids.

In addition to the moralistic pressure to conform to certain instructional approaches, many teachers experienced the technical control exerted by the district as a means of surveillance. In an effort to theorize the ways in which societies attempt to control their members, Foucault (1977) used the 18th-century prison design of the Panopticon as a societal metaphor. Designed by Jeremy Bentham, the Panopticon places prisoners under constant observation, unable to either escape from or to return the gaze of authorities. According to Foucault, "the major effect of the Panopticon [is]: to induce in the inmate a state of conscious and permanent visibility that assures the automatic functioning of power" (p. 201). Within the Panopticon, power was constantly visible but remained unverifiable. In other words, inmates were always in sight of the tower from which they were presumably observed yet could not discern whether or not anyone was in the tower at a given moment. Individuals who are subject to such observation, according to Bentham, will eventually internalize the gaze and monitor their own behavior. Self-discipline will replace coercion as the method of social control. Ultimately, then, "a real subjection is born mechanically from a fictitious relation" (Foucault, 1977, p. 202). Invoking the effects of this kind of surveillance, teachers used course discussions as a way to process the overpowering sense of fear related to the constant observation exercised by school and district personnel. One corps member shared that the constant threat of surveillance decreased her motivation and compromised her approaches so that she was not able to do what she considered to be in the best interest of her students:

I'm having a hard time even motivating myself. I'm so afraid someone is going to walk into the room and see me doing something I'm not supposed to be doing even though it's "what I think is best for the kids," so I'm not motivated to even go there because I'm a first-year teacher. I don't want to get into trouble. Maybe that makes me like a follow-the-rules kind of girl but it's just killing my motivation essentially and that's really bothering me.

In a similar account, Missy noted the overwhelming sense of fear that impeded her desire to experiment with either her curriculum or instructional approach:

> Due to my inexperience with the teaching profession and the fact that we are pressured to do so by the administration, I am one of the teachers that follows the teaching manual religiously. Perhaps as a crutch, but perhaps out of fear of administrative retribution. I rely heavily on the teachers' manual to conduct my literacy lessons. My students' needs, not the curriculum, should drive the literacy instruction, but this is not the case in my classroom. If we have strayed even a hair from the curriculum when someone from the administrative leadership team walks into the classroom, the children will be barked at, any shred of classroom management will be completely usurped.

Missy's use of language in this instance suggests the kind of toll that surveillance can exact on teachers. For example, she noted that she must follow the teaching manual "religiously" in fear of "retribution" from her administration. Further, she contended that any deviation from the script could result in her classroom being "usurped" by angry administrators. Although she acknowledged that her students' needs were not being met, the sense of control exerted through the threat of administrative surveillance kept her from experimenting with her instruction. This form of control began to infiltrate the consciousness of the teachers, since they were never sure when they would be subject to observation and evaluation. Thus, like Foucault's prisoners, they soon began to monitor themselves:

> I don't know what my objective is at the end of the year because I'm not put in a situation where I need to research that for myself. It's like this self-fulfilling prophecy of teachers that don't work hard or care about their job, so just what people try to say about teachers all the time, but you create a situation in which you have a curriculum and pacing guides where everything is done for you. It's begging for you not to work. You're going against the grain by trying to work hard on your curriculum. Spending time on it means you're probably not being faithful. It's kind of insane.

Although TFA teachers are commonly recruited for their diligence and intelligence, within the context of Philadelphia these traits are not honored. The TFA website, for example, suggests that the characteristics they most value in potential corps members are critical thinking skills, perseverance in the face of challenges, and demonstrated leadership capabilities (www.teachforamerica.org). Despite these claims, many corps members find that a premium is placed on following orders, obeying rules, and trusting a curriculum that they find problematic and fallible.

Thus, the corps members' predicament closely mirrors that of their students, who, subject to a "no-excuses" approach to teaching and learning, must conform to a militaristic environment that seeks to regulate and control every aspect of their educational experience (Lack, 2009).

These modes of surveillance are not unlike Antonio Gramsci's notions of hegemony, in which control is not maintained through the use of violence or economic coercion but through the use of "common sense" or popular ideology (Kenway, 2001, p. 51). According to Gramsci, the "naturalization" of certain ideas and ideologies is ultimately what makes them effective as controlling mechanisms. As new teachers are socialized to accept the dominant school reform narrative of "back to basics" and tightly controlled behavior management as the primary remedies for improving urban schools, the proliferation of other, alternative narratives are squelched.

Thus, the corps members found themselves in settings in which "learning to teach" was translated into "following rules." As the corps members began to internalize these curricular and pedagogical mandates, they exerted the same control over their students that they themselves had experienced at the hands of their respective schools and the district at large:

> In terms of teaching philosophy, I think my ideas are very much based around wanting kids to feel like they have agency in their own learning. I want them to feel like they're agents that have power, that they're agents who make decisions and they are choosing different activities and that they learn in the way that fits them and learn to pursue their interests. However, the message I send out every day to my kids is, "Sit down and listen to me. I am the holder of this knowledge. If you sit down, listen, fold your hands and sit up straight up and sit like a star, then you'll go to college and be successful." That's the message.

This corps member, for example, was aware of the dissonance that existed between her desire to impart agency to her students and the pedagogical reality she enacted on a daily basis. While corps members undoubtedly recognized the importance of getting to know both their students and the local context, bureaucratic obstacles often made these encounters impossible.

Taylorism as an Analytical Lens

When asked in an interview about his tenure within the school district and TFA, Cesar, a second-year corps member, used the word "Taylorism" to theorize his experiences:

I am not going to articulate this very well, but there is sort of a move towards cor-
poratizing schools and making schools like little companies and superintendents
and CEOs and they issue mandates that get pushed down. It's almost like
Taylorism, especially with direct instruction, every single minute of the day is
planned. You're a little robot up there reading from the script. There are some very
corporate models. If we just put a lot of money in schools, we will fix them and
we get lots of CEOs opening charter schools or whatever donating money not
knowing what the hell they're doing quite frankly. I think that TFA really sub-
scribes to that sort of corporate model where there's a student and the student is
a vessel. You have knowledge and you have 180 school days to cram that little head
with knowledge, because if you don't, they're going to fall behind and they're never
going to catch up to their more affluent peers. It's a race, it's a race, it's a race.

Taylorism has a long history within the realm of public education and stems
from the work of Frederick Taylor, who coined the term "scientific management"
as he attempted to find ways to increase efficiency and maximize industrial output at the turn of the 20th century (Callahan, 1962). Although his work was originally intended for use by railroads, it was not long before Taylor's ideas were
adapted for use in the public sector. Because Taylor's primary concerns involved
increasing efficiency and minimizing waste, he asserted that systematic, scientific
study would reveal the best method for accomplishing a particular task (p. 25).
Once this method was determined, the responsibilities of the worker greatly diminished, and she/he only had to follow a prescribed set of orders. In other words, "In
[Taylor's] system the judgment of the individual workman was replaced by the laws,
rules, principles, etc., of the job which was developed by management" (p. 28).

Although Callahan's critique of the application of Taylorism to public schooling was written in 1962, it continues to have relevance today as teachers contend
with what Au (2011) refers to as "the New Taylorism." Au argues that the work of
public school teachers is controlled by high-stakes testing and prescriptive curricular programs (p. 1), a notion that resonates with the ways in which Philadelphia
corps members describe their socialization and training. According to Au, for
Taylor, "efficient production relied upon the factory managers' ability to gather all
the information possible about the work which they oversaw, systematically analyze it according to 'scientific' methods, figure out the most efficient ways for workers to complete individual tasks, and then tell the worker exactly how to produce
their products in an ordered manner" (p. 26). Similarly, the classrooms in which
many of the corps members worked were tightly controlled environments in which
teachers had to meticulously track student achievement, monitor behavior through
the use of incentives, and follow a routinized lesson format that included direct
instruction, guided practice, and independent practice.

The Mastery Charter Network further reinforced these aspects of Taylorism within schools through its strict control of pedagogical approaches. For example, one slide in a PowerPoint presentation given by the leadership from Mastery in the fall of 2010 depicted a large red "X" over the words "project-based," "inquiry-based," "text-based," and "student interest-based," indicating that these modes of learning should not be implemented within Mastery's network of schools. The facilitator went on to mention that it was simply more efficient to tell students what they needed to know (personal notes, 10/20/10). Moreover, the *Mastery Instructional Guidebook* says the following about efficiency:

> With limited time to reach breakthrough academic success, classroom routines must be extremely purposeful and efficient. To this end, time should be used to the teacher's advantage when establishing, communicating, and maintaining classroom routines. Consistently *timing routines*—tracking the time it takes students to complete a specific routine—not only communicates to students how important each minute of class time is, but it also drives at efficiency. (*Mastery Instructional Guidebook*, October 2010, emphasis in the original)

It is evident that Mastery's hope in emphasizing efficiency at the expense of experimentation and exploration is for "breakthrough academic success." The model that Mastery promotes may indeed help students achieve at higher levels on standardized measures; yet, as Kliebard (1975) notes, "as in industry, the price of worship at the altar of efficiency is the alienation of the worker from his work— where continuity and wholeness of the enterprise are destroyed for those who engage in it" (cited in Au, 2011, p. 1). Thus, the tension surrounding an emphasis on efficiency invites deeper questions regarding the overall purposes of school reform and the meaning of education.

Numerous corps members, for example, shared disdain for their summer preparation conducted during the TFA Institute, believing that teaching was reduced to a formulaic prescription and its complexities and nuances elided. With only 5 weeks allotted for formal training during the summer before they were to begin teaching full-time, many corps members felt that TFA focused on the most efficient means of training possible:

> And I felt like that's how all of institute was—this is the most executable way to teach a bunch of non-experienced people how to be a teacher in five weeks and you can take this and you can do it and maybe it's not the most thought-provoking and maybe it's not the most successful way to teach but it's the most efficient for the amount of time we have and now off you go. And when you're working with a corps of teachers that you're really expecting to be there for two years, you

don't have to be thinking about, "these need to be a corps of very reflective people" because they're going to leave before they could ever reach that level of effectiveness as a teacher. So it's such a structure of efficiency and really thinking that the only capital is that they're a body in a room. And if you just follow what we tell you to do, you can't mess it up.

Because corps members were not expected to make a career out of teaching, many believed that they were taught to approach teaching mechanistically and required to follow a set of prescribed steps to reduce the possibility of failure. Teaching, thus, was consistently portrayed as a low-skilled occupation that required little creativity, imagination, or critical thinking. As Au (2011) notes:

> The metaphor of Taylorism can be mapped on to US schools in a very simple and neat way. Students are the "raw materials" to be produced like commodities according to specified standards and objectives. Teachers are the workers who employ the most efficient methods to get students to meet the pre-determined standards and objectives. Administrators are the managers who determine and dictate to teachers the most efficient methods in the production process. The school is the factory assembly line where this process takes place. (p. 27)

According to this model, teachers have little control over the materials and methods that they use, relying instead on outsiders to guide their choices and decisions, an approach to instruction that ultimately has a dehumanizing effect on both teachers and students. Because of the relentless focus on efficiency and production, teachers began to describe their classroom in ways that echoed the "New Taylorism":

> I think of routines in my own classroom as ways that we cut down on time, very quick things that we do every day, most of it I direct, they do it and they are praised for doing it quickly and silently. . . . I am placed in a charter system that emphasizes rote recall, traditional bookwork, and high levels of student compliance. Because we are a "turn around school" and working with students who are significantly behind academically there is a culture of "no time to waste" and a strong emphasis on test prep, even in the younger grades.

Similarly, another corps member described how the quest for efficiency manifested itself in her classroom, noting in particular the ways in which the abbreviated segments of time limit the possibilities for deep engagement and learning:

> And it needs to be simple and it needs to be quick because they need to be able to do this independent practice in the block of 15 minutes you have after going through direct instruction, guided practice, and so it never delves deep. It never

delves into kids internalizing something and kids really working to generate something. Everything is divided into 15 minutes and in that block of 15 minutes, you have to have direct instruction, guided practice, private practice, exit slip.

This piecemeal approach to learning reflects the assembly-line mentality of the factory: as tasks are divided into smaller and smaller pieces, they become increasingly devoid of meaning, leading to an overall sense of alienation both for the student and the teacher.

Urgency and Humanity

As a result, several corps members cited a human cost to the drive for high test scores and academic achievement. Realizing how few opportunities students had in the school day to explore interesting questions, communicate openly in discussion, or share personal information led Cora, a first-year corps member, to frame the encroachment of Taylorism into public education as a tension between "urgency and humanity." At Mastery, in particular, the focus on efficiency is explicitly driven by a sense of urgency, as noted in the instructional guidebook:

> Urgency must be built and maintained: teachers must keep a laser-beam focus on the lesson objective, ensure student clarity around the purpose of lesson portion, and provide explicit reminders of the need to be urgent.

Cora, like other corps members and Mastery teachers who were under extreme pressure to raise test scores, struggled with this tension. In particular, Cora worried about the human cost of an efficiency-driven model:

> They (the students) clearly perceive the sense of urgency that drives our reading instruction, but I have feared that this urgency was taking away the humanity behind the experience of literature.

A number of corps members echoed Cora's concerns, believing that the overemphasis on efficiency had created a dehumanizing classroom environment in which students and teachers were objectified—or, as Joey notes below, treated like "cogs in a machine":

> I find this to be particularly true with the amount of urgency that is created in our classrooms. Teachers are pressed to get students to pass exams and meet benchmark results and, in turn, students feel pressured to do well and are merely cogs in the machine.

The limitations of the prescribed curriculum in reflecting the lived experiences of students was mentioned most frequently by African American and Latino corps members, who repeatedly commented on the ways in which their cultural histories were marginalized throughout their own K–12 education. Driven by a desire to make their teaching and lessons culturally relevant (Ladson-Billings, 1995), many of these teachers were similarly confounded by the limitations of prescribed curricula. Even with rich autobiographical histories to draw upon, these teachers found themselves torn between a personal belief that culturally relevant teaching could transform the educational experiences of minority youth, and the pressures exerted by their schools to conform to a more mechanistic instructional approach. Kayla, for example, shared the following anecdote in a written assignment:

> When I joined the ranks of Teach for America, it was my honest intention to engage my students in manners that would truly invite them into the classroom. However as a first year teacher I have found it grueling to do so. . . . However as I consider my students, I see similar sentiments of frustration with schooling that does not include their experience. Their experience mirrors many of the sentiments of disengagement and disenchantment with an educational system that alienates a minority existence that I felt in my own educational experience.

Although Kayla entered Teach for America with the intention of incorporating her students' cultural experiences into her lessons, she ultimately found it "grueling to do so." Similarly, Raina expressed frustration regarding the ways in which social studies curricula explicitly favored European American ideals at the expense of other perspectives. Despite her strong convictions about the inclusion of minority experiences in the classroom, she remained unsure of how to navigate the rigid curriculum to which her school subscribed:

> We live in a society where European-American ideals are forced upon the students in our educational system. Despite the fact that America is a melting pot of many different ethnicities, curriculum fails to incorporate other cultures. This is something that I could attest to growing up. For example, we learned on the European-American version of slavery; as though no African American left any information about what they experienced during slavery. . . . I always thought I would introduce my students to various cultures when I taught and now as a teacher, I often wonder how I can incorporate culture into my lessons when I have such a rigid curriculum to follow. Students' various cultures are silenced through the curriculum I have to follow and it is important to their educational success that I allow them to explore and express these cultures.

To some degree these teachers were wrestling with whether or not their own ideals or desires were compatible within their respective environments, given the constraints. While Raina and Kayla might have originally imagined themselves as multicultural educators determined to provide an educational experience that addresses the unique needs of their students, they found themselves instead confronted by a different reality, one in which they were forced to adhere to pedagogical and curricular approaches that seldom spoke to the unique and differentiated experiences of their students.

TFA and the Problem of Urban Education

The 2010–2011 Philadelphia corps members entered a challenging and complex political environment with the added burden of having to interpret, adopt, and enact the identity of urban educators. While many viewed teaching as the primary avenue for addressing a range of pressing societal concerns, a conviction which helped them to endure trying circumstances, these teachers found themselves subject to systems that framed them as low-level workers and that consistently extolled efficiency at the expense of humanity. Sadly, these conceptions of teaching and teachers began to infiltrate the consciousness of even the most determined corps members, leading to a sense of powerlessness in the face of unyielding curricular mandates. For example, even those teachers who brought their own autobiographical narratives to bear on teaching and learning and expressed a commensurate desire to incorporate a vast spectrum of cultural experiences into their classrooms struggled to make their visions a reality.

However, this chapter has primarily aimed to illustrate that the lenses through which corps members view their teaching practice offer valuable insights into how they experienced their socialization as urban educators. That a significant number of corps members drew upon "Taylorism" and factory metaphors to theorize their experiences in Philadelphia suggests the extent of their disillusionment and disempowerment. Without opportunities to reconcile their hopes for their students with the pressures to conform to a scripted curriculum, the constant threat of administrative surveillance, and the emphasis on urgency and efficiency, corps members are more likely to feel overwhelmed and hopeless in their respective settings.

By creating spaces in which corps members can both acknowledge and analyze the kinds of frameworks they bring to their classrooms, teacher educators are inviting TFA teachers into a tradition of critical practice. As Morrell (2008) notes, "Becoming critically literate entails coming to understand ourselves separately from the discourses that surround us; becoming critically literate also entails having the skills and sensibilities to ask demanding questions of the ideas, concepts and ideologies that are presented to us as fact" (p. 38). Thus, by making frameworks like "Taylorism" the subject of critical inquiry, we can encourage corps members to consider the economic and political forces that influence the everyday operations of schooling and to contend with a discourse of structural and systemic inequality otherwise elided in their preparation by Teach for America, Mastery, and the school district. Furthermore, by recognizing these frameworks as a starting point for working with corps members in teacher education courses, we can model what it means to make student knowledge a starting point for classroom instruction. As Kincheloe & Hayes (2007) note an emphasis on students' lived realities must be paired with a commitment to exposing the political, social, and economic forces that shape those realities if urban education is to be a transformative enterprise (p. 6). If our goal as teacher educators is to prepare thoughtful and inquiring practitioners, then we must design and teach courses that reflect these ambitions. Thus, teacher education courses must serve as a site from which to challenge and reimagine dominant discourses in an effort to expand what corps members consider "possible" within urban schools and classrooms.

References

Achinstein, B., & Ogawa, R. (2006). (In)fidelity: What the resistance of new teachers reveals about professional principles and prescriptive educational policies. *Harvard Educational Review, 76*(1), 30–63.

Au, W. (2011). Teaching under the new Taylorism: High-stakes testing and the standardization of the 21st century curriculum. *Journal of Curriculum Studies, 43* (1), 25–45.

Callahan, R. (1962). *Education and the cult of efficiency.* Chicago: University of Chicago Press.

Cochran-Smith, M.,& Lytle, S. (2006). Troubling images of teaching in No Child Left Behind. *Harvard Educational Review, 76*(4), 668–697.

Darling-Hammond, L., Holtzman, D.J., Gatlin, S.J., & Heilig, J.V. (2005). Does teacher preparation matter? Evidence about teacher certification, Teach for America, and teacher effectiveness. *Education Policy Analysis Archives, 13*(42), 1–48.

Fairbanks, A. (2011, July 27). Walton Family Foundation gifts Teach for America 49.5 million. *Huffington Post.*

Foucault, M. (1977). *Discipline and punish: The birth of the prison.* New York: Random House.

Hopkins, M. (2008). Training the next teachers for America: A proposal for reconceptualizing Teach for America. *Phi Delta Kappan, 89*(10), 721–25.

Kenway, J. (2001). Remembering and regenerating Gramsci. In K. Weiler (Ed.), *Feminist engagements: Reading, resisting and revisioning male theorists in education and cultural studies* (pp. 47–65). London: Psychology Press.

Kincheloe, J., & Hayes, K. (Eds.). (2007). *Teaching city kids: Understanding and appreciating them.* New York: Peter Lang.

Kliebard, H.M. (1975). Bureaucracy and curriculum theory. In W.F. Pinar (Ed.), *Curriculum theorizing: The reconceptualists* (pp. 51–69). Berkeley, CA: McCutchan Publishing.

Koerner, M., et al. (2008). Why we partner with Teach for America: Changing the conversation. *Phi Delta Kappan, 89* (10), 726–729.

Lack, B. (2009). No excuses: A critique of the Knowledge Is Power Program (KIPP) within charter schools in the USA. *Journal for Critical Education Policy Studies, 7*(2), 126–153.

Laczko-Kerr, I., & Berliner, D.C. (2002, September 6). The effectiveness of "Teach for America" and other under-certified teachers on student academic achievement: A case of harmful public policy. *Education Policy Analysis Archives, 10*(37).

Ladson-Billings, G. (1995). But that's just good teaching! The case for culturally relevant pedagogy. *Theory into Practice, 34*(3),159–165.

Mastery Charter Network. (2010). *Instructional guidebook.* Philadelphia, PA: Author. On page 39, there are no page numbers listed for this article- it's part of a digital archive.

Morrell, E. (2008). *Critical literacy and urban youth.* New York: Routledge.

Oakes, J., et al. (2002). Research for high-quality urban teaching: Defining it, developing it, assessing it. *Journal of Teacher Education, 53*(3), 228–234.

Popkewitz, T. (1998). *Struggling for the soul: The politics of schooling and the social construction of the teacher.* New York: Teachers College Press.

4

Becoming a Teacher in an Era of Curricular Standardization and Reductionist Learning Outcomes:
A Poetic Interpretation

LISA WILLIAM-WHITE

California State University Sacramento

On the Political Context and Method

Here, Spoken Word poetic discourse (William-White, 2011a, 2011b; William-White & White, 2011; William-White, Muccular & Muccular, 2012) brings to life a teacher/teacher-educator's interpretative and reflective view of what it means to be a teacher in a local community in 21st-century America, an era shaped by curricular standardization and reductionist learning outcomes. Clearly, the macro- and micro-level forces that shape praxis should be made visible within schools. We need to ask: what is behind the federal focus on global competition, social efficiency policies, and increased intensification on standardized curriculum? For critical educators, all of these forces prove antithetical to a critical pedagogy that embraces differentiated learning experiences for students from low socioeconomic backgrounds and those from culturally and linguistically diverse communities. In contrast to this stark reality, this piece beckons teachers to examine their own curricular and professional journeys, while providing a space for their learners to engage in the same process of self-knowledge and inquiry, called the currere (Pinar, 1974,

1975; Pinar & Grumet, 1976; Pinar, Reynolds, Slattery & Taubman, 1995; Pinar, 2012), disrupting the traditional norms that undermine schools as sites of democratic learning.

These issues are centralized in the speaker's philosophy for training pre-service and practicing teachers in a "social justice" department that offers both elementary and secondary teaching credentials as well as a Master's degree in Education. The department's mission and goals have an explicit focus on preparing candidates to: (1) advocate a social justice perspective across school, community, and political contexts; (2) use and further develop students' cultural funds of knowledge, bilingualism, bi-dialectalism, and biliteracy; (3) lead students to achieve at academically high standards across the core curriculum; (4) guide students to explore issues of prejudice toward people of different races, socioeconomic classes, language and language varieties, abilities and disabilities, and sexual orientation; and (5) promote school transformation toward equity and social justice on multiple levels. Yet the speaker's department has recently been eliminated because of the economic crisis in the State of California and a sentiment within the college that the teacher performance expectations espoused by this department are being met in all teacher preparation pathways college-wide. Thus, the speaker maintains that the elimination of this department aligns with the greater national assault on providing quality education for CLD populations (William-White, forthcoming). It is these tensions that shape the speaker's poetic discourse offered at the commencement ceremony for the final cohort of emergent teacher candidates.

These candidates will now exit their program to seek careers within schools that are steeped in the standards and accountability milieu, and they will enter a broader professional climate that does not embrace critical multicultural education studies and critical pedagogy within K–12 public education. In addition, many of these candidates will now enter the local job market seeking employment in a community where they will also compete with recruits from Teach for America and The New Teacher Project for a limited number of jobs in the region. Recently, both organizations were heralded by the Obama administration as innovative alternatives to meeting the needs of America's diverse students. And Kevin Johnson, the mayor of the city, has established partnerships with these organizations, seeking coalition building to transform the local school system. To date, few attempts have been made by Mayor Johnson to establish partnerships with the College of Education, though the mayor did invite members from the college to a special screening of "Waiting for Superman" in an effort to promote his schools-of-choice position (KCRA 3). Interestingly, Johnson, recently touted as the "education mayor" when presented at a CommonWealth Club of California meeting, co-chairs the U.S Department of Education Mayor's Advisory Council (California Competes), where he advocates for mayor-controlled educational policies. Johnson also played a key role in passing California's Race to the Top (RTTT) Common Core Standards.

In addition, Johnson recently married Michelle Rhee, founder of the New Teacher Project and former chancellor of D.C. Public Schools; she is also founder of Sacramento-based StudentsFirst, an organization touted as "a national movement to transform education" (StudentsFirst). Thus, the ties between the U.S. Department of Education, the mayor, local educational entrepreneurs, local school boards, and non-profit/for-profit organizations are vast, wide, and enmeshed—all of which shape the professional and curricular landscape of emergent teachers locally.

Finally, this piece, through its style and content, raises the questions: *What does it mean to be/become a teacher in the current educational landscape? What should be taught and for whose benefit? And who profits?* Designed as a performance narrative (William-White, 2011a, 2011b; William-White & White, 2011; William-White et al., 2012), it probes these questions while capturing the speaker's personal philosophy on teaching. It also challenges emergent teaching candidates to reflect deeply about their backgrounds and agency while considering the curriculum landscape ahead as a site for liberatory praxis. Finally, this piece illustrates how spoken-word discourse is an artistic and emancipatory pedagogical, political, and research-embedded aesthetic that allows for critical inquiry related to national and local educational discourses.

Framing the Poetic

Canadian curriculum theorist and teacher Ted Aoki once said:

> [T]o become a teacher one undergoes a ritual that allows one entry into a culturally shaped and culturally legitimated world in which are prescriptions of years of training, certification, automatic membership in a teacher's association, apprenticeship, scrutiny and evaluation by legitimated seniors, and so on. Once allowed into this culturally shaped world one is governed by rules of conduct and socially accepted behavior, which are presumed to be "becoming" of people called teachers, and by codified ethical prescriptions of personal and interpersonal interaction. It is a domain of conduct governed socially by a codified School Act, provincially legislated, which sets out the bounds within which typical teachers are expected to act out their typical roles. Those who learn the roles well are typified by being labeled "teachers." (Pinar& Irwin, 2005, p. 337)

The National Council for Accreditation of Teacher Education (NCATE) adds:

> [T]o help the nation compete in the global economy, today's teachers will have to educate all students. . .to the same high learning outcomes. They must ensure that all children master rigorous course content, be able to apply what they learn to think critically and solve problems, and complete high school "college- and work force ready." (http://www.ncate.org/LinkClick.aspx?fileticket=zzeiB1Oo qPk%3D&tabid=715, p. 1)

Yet I contend that our greatest challenge in our vocation is to dance the dialectic—the ongoing tension to fight for moral purpose as a beacon for emancipatory praxis. This pedagogy must also enable critical consciousness and agency—the bedrock for participant-democracy. It is this act of teaching and the struggle to embrace a moral purpose that aligns with McLaren's (2003) views:

> For teachers. . .we must begin candidly and critically to face our society's complicity in the roots and structures of inequality and injustice. It means . . . that . . . we must face our own culpability in the reproduction of inequality in our teaching, and that we must strive to develop a pedagogy equipped to provide both intellectual and moral resistance to oppression, one that extends the concept of pedagogy beyond mere transmission of knowledge and skills and the concept of morality beyond interpersonal liberation. Pedagogy in this instance must be linked to class struggle and the politics of liberation. (p. 43)

To Be/come a Teacher: A Poetic Interpretation

Curricular decision making is philosophical
And pedagogical
It's shaped by the virulent winds that blow
It's political
Many times, acultural . . .
And a powerful,
symbolic artifact
. . . Revealing views
on cultural capital!

It's embroiled in federal discourses
Policies
And *mandates!*
It's shackled to federal bureaucracy

And ideologies
Dictated by the feds
And the State
It trickles down through CCTC[1], NTA[2]
And organizations like NCATE[3]
All of this, in the historic moment, reflects and shapes
The teaching landscape![4]

Curriculum is both a product and
A symbolic *concept,*
Though we thought that
Tyler's principles and Schwab's structures[5]
were ancient precepts
Cuz the developmental phase of curriculum
Gave way to reconceptualization
then internationalization

But, we've come back to *must-have-skills*
In the learning situation
Check out how the Common Core dialogues
have swept over this nation!
Ed Hirsch's views of knowledge
still shape the conversation!

You see organized Bodies dictate
other bodies
and lives
Yet the ends and means discourse
Like learning outcomes
Serve well to disguise
Curriculum from these frames
Allow learning that is commodified!
A form of economic capital
ETS,[6] for example, has monopolized

It's all quite interesting, you see:
"We have entered the age of the corporatization
And businessification of education"[7]
The US "lead[s] the charge toward"
Public school privatization
The Reading First Initiative, as an example,

Mostly helps for-profit organizations[8]
Bush bedded with McGraw-Hill is
a prime point for consideration![9]
And the critique of Voyager[10]
In tandem with their profit ledger
Is worth more interrogation
On these facts, we must mobilize
To change the situation

How does 2012 affect your career choice?
Your philosophy?
Your efficacy?
Question what shapes your pedagogical trajectory?
Hopefully not merely NCLB[11]—
Or standardized accountability!

These ideas extolled as well
by "our pal"[12] Arne
US Department of Education
Secretary
Speaking about the needs of the nation
Publically
Blogging vociferously
Emphasizes that education is the civil rights issue[13]
Of the 21st century
shows the disparate outcomes related to
Illiteracy
Suspensions and expulsions
mostly of Black males
actually
says that we have much *work to do*
to eliminate the inequities
And he used his federal authority
Recently
to waive portions of the law called NCLB
Supported by a White House Domestic Council Member on Policy[14]

Yet,
He also engages in an educational doublespeak
Teacher evaluation

still the target in his reach[15]
As well as testing accountability
Rid the system of educators whose students don't reach proficiency
Leads to corruption and adulteration
Just ask Atlanta[16]
And Michelle Rhee![17]

Though Arne elevates states' rights
Giving them greater authority
Under NCLB
There is a caveat, however, to this flexibility
As long as the State's goals
Reflects "Race to the Top's"[18]
Veracity
Then, and only then, will the learning systems be deemed
as holding credibility
The standards discourse *still* at the helm
envisioning
what's
good for the country.

So, ask yourself
"Are my students well prepared for futures that they seek?"
Will they continue to pursue learning
Throughout their life's trajectory?
Can they analyze, reason
and communicate
effectively?
These questions. for ten years, is what PISA[19] says it seeks
reading, math and scientific literacy
their foci for competency
Compare the performance outcomes
of 15-year-olds
in major world economies;
ascertain kid's readiness
for participating in their societies

Cogs in the machine
another view of this ideology!

[Hook]
How 'bout a pedagogy
That repels
Tech rationality,
or the nationalist scheme of world domination
and social efficiency[20]
an ideology conceived by the BRT[21]
and birthed through NCLB!
Can we embrace a pedagogy that is truly free?
An embodiment of this historic moment
Where our present,
unites our past
To interrogate this democracy?
Inquiry which harkens to Giroux, Kincheloe
and Steinberg's legacy!
Analysis and Synthesis reflecting the currere—
curriculum as autobiography.
A method first advocated by Pinar
In the 1970s

One where we interrogate and examine the "best practices"
Utilized for "Other People's Children"[22]
We can question the methods and strategies
That we use to mold
and school 'em
Unveil the value-added perspectives
Embedded in textbooks and curriculum,
Testing companies' goals,
and
politicians' jargon
Understand the relationship between these entities
And their profit margins

Question the delivery mechanisms
in Common Core's prescription
And of course let's not forget looking at those
Making the decisions
In the system
Teachers!!! Dialogue is the key to educate and disarm them!
Reveal the isms,
schisms

And, class divisions
magnify them!
To liberate them.

See I'm a product of segregated schooling in the 1970s
The Build Academy, I attended
in elementary
Legacy published in the *Journal of New York Life and History*
To Build
Unity, Independence,
Liberty, and
Dignity
That acronym, today, still speaks volumes
to me
The school was grounded and mobilized
By community advocacy
Black liberation
And economic mobility
Under the guidance of, yes, Saul Alinsky[23]
A community activist who focused on
Radical tactics of militancy
From the Industrial Area Foundation
He founded in the 1950s
This foundation,
And these teachers at Build
Would forever shape my childhood school memories
Positively
Soul-nourishing curricula,
progressive views
Like Dewey

We need more educational activism
Which informs
sound pedagogy!
I'll be the first to admit that all *this* would look suspect
To those who live far, *far* from the political *Left*
On this, I can and must attest
Yet, McLaren says "we're on a fetish quest"
To be the best
Thus, arts, music
and social studies

Is a "step-child" in the schooling process
We've communicated clearly "screw the rest!"
and so we test!
YES, WE TEST!
And negate a focus on civic responsibility
Or modeling community activism
and agency
Prescriptive teaching and automation
trumps critical consciousness
and literacy
This is what educational policy, over the years, has taught me
Reductionist pedagogy is all I can see
Thusly.
it all begins from Pre-K
moves Up and Through
the university!

But, there is an alternative paradigm to this process
Imagine this scenario for a moment—
Let's?:
"Teacher!
What, today, are we planning to study?"
We must and *should* have an answer to such innocent queries!
"You mean, Teacher, *my* learning can actually begin with *me*?"
Yes, examining the life lived
The intent of the methodology!
The currere . . .
A drastic departure from API[24]
And AYP[25]

See, the life world enables us to look back
On the self as data
To concept map our path
In a manner,
That matters,
Not standards!

The regressive and progressive comes together
In this stage
How one is formed by family?

One's culture?
This age?
Look at all this in tandem
with what's presented on a page!
Then comes the analysis—the process of sorting
Of sorting it all out
To consider the life world
And what's it about
To think more intently,
Intrapersonally
Even psychically
On the path,
Yet laid out

Remove the gimmicks
And strip down to a poor curriculum[26]
Not because we teach the poor
Or minority children
Rather remove the crutches and devices
Which are impediments to learnin'
Which offer teachers diversions
Abdicating critical thinking
And intensified learnin'
Begin with students' own stories
Most *imperative*
to serve them!

You see, we're constructed and produced by our environment
On this truth we must be aware
Yet, never tolerant
Question all of it!
The agency to shape one's reality
Is called subjectivity
A form of empowerment
Born of consciousness
Not merely common sense

The synthesis of all this . . .
This is where the process ends
But the truth of the matter the journey begins here
Once again

The storied life of study
Only death can suspend.

Remember,
In this teaching landscape
Ask what forces shapes one's destiny?
Is our time any different than the
critical theorists in Frankfurt, Germany?
The Civil Rights workers in Mississippi?
Or the folk school educators
in rural Tennessee?

What you teach today should *mean something* to the CHILDREN,
Their families,
The larger community,
And globally?
Through the currere,
we promote deep inquiry
Biliteracy
And by God, let's not forget
To affirm culture
and linguistic diversity!

To know thyself,
Is the most important learning opportunity
Remember,
pedagogical relevance, here, is certainly the key!

On the local stage, Mayor Johnson heralds
getting back to academic quality
Espouses schools of choice,
Parent involvement
human capital
and teacher accountability

The NEA[27] calls for a systemic,
collaborative approach to ensuring quality
collaborating with effective teachers CAN connect
communities,
they believe

Yet, Johnson's efforts belie this thinking
He displays a different form of agency
Use the rhetoric of community mobilization
And organizing
To promote *HIS* legacy

He holds summits[28] every month
Brings guest speakers on educational equality
Yet, most of them champion competition
charters
options
and such views as Joel Klein
and Michelle Rhee,
Remember, again, what happened to those teachers in DC?
He challenges all to STAND UP[29]
That's the name of the local organization
And it focuses on results-oriented outcomes
In local public education

Embraces varied innovations
For high school completion

And
college graduation

And it partners
with educational leaders
Those who espouse
entrepreneurial education?

And you might ask yourself: "How might these goals relate to me?"
Well, let's see . . .
TFA, NLNS, and TNTP[30]
are all partners
related to his vision
his philosophy
What implications does this pose
for educational equality?!?
Are they, or *are you,*
Ready

to imbue a critical pedagogy?
Or examine what's happenin'
Through a Marxist ideology?

Remember
Teachers and students, alike, must Conceptualize,
Analyze
Criticize
Reflect on how schooling helps them
To understand their own lives!
Praxis means action
Lived reflectively
The teacher is the center
Of learnin'
And
deep intellectual inquiry
Students, too, are the authors
Of their own life stories
and destinies!

[Hook]
How 'bout a pedagogy
That repels
Tech rationality,
or the nationalist scheme of world domination
and social efficiency
an ideology conceived by the BRT
and birthed through NCLB!
Can we embrace a pedagogy that is truly free?
An embodiment of this historic moment
Where our present,
unites our past
To interrogate this democracy?
Inquiry which harkens to McLaren, Pinar,
and Freire's legacy!
Analysis and Synthesis reflecting the currere—
curriculum as autobiography.
*We desperately need a curriculum
Offered in a new key!* [31]
One that upholds the tenets of social justice
And democracy

References

Berta-Avila, M., & William-White, L. (2010, October). A conscious agenda for cultivating future teachers' equity and social justice paradigms. *Teacher Education and Practice, 23*(4):1–37.

California Competes: Higher education for a strong economy. (2011, June 22). Business Executives and Mayors to Focus on California's Economy and Lack of Skilled Grads.Retrieved March 30, 2011 from http://californiacompetes.org/wp-content/uploads/2011/06/PR_California_Competes.pdf.

Common Wealth Club of California. (2011, April 20). Michelle Rhee and Kevin Johnson: How to Transform American Education. Retrieved March 30,2012 from http://www.youtube.com/watch?v=OCcNzh7C_Tk,

Delpit, L. (1995). *Other people's children: Cultural conflict in the classroom.* New York: The New Press.

Giroux, H.A. (1997). *Pedagogy and the politics of hope: Theory, culture, and schooling.* Boulder, CO: Westview Press.

Hirsch, E.D. (1987). *Cultural literacy: What every American needs to know.* New York: Houghton Mifflin Company.

KCRA 3. (2010, September 30). Mayor Touts 'Waiting for Superman'. Retrieved April 22, 2012 from http://www.kcra.com/video/25224071/detail.html.

Kincheloe, J.L. (2009). No short cuts in urban education: Metropedagogy and diversity. In Steinberg, S.R. (Ed.). *Diversity and multiculturalism: A reader.* New York: Peter Lang.

McLaren, P. (2003). *Life in schools: An introduction to critical pedagogy in the foundations of education* (4th ed.). Boston: Pearson Education, Inc.

The New Teacher Project (TNTP). Retrieved March 30, 2012, from www.tntp.org

Pinar, W.F. (1974). *Currere:* Toward reconceptualization. In J. Jelinek (Ed.), *Basic problems in modern education* (pp.147–171). Tempe: Arizona State University, College of Education.

Pinar, W.F. (1975). *Currere:* Toward reconceptualization. In W.F. Pinar (Ed.), *Curriculum theorizing: The reconceptualists* (pp. 396–414). Berkeley, CA: McCutchan.

Pinar, W.F. (2012). *What is curriculum theory?.* (2nd ed.). New York: Routledge.

Pinar, W.F., & Grumet, M. (1976). *Toward a poor curriculum.* Dubuque, IA: Kendall/Hunt.

Pinar, W.F., & Irvin, R.L. (Eds.). (2005). *Curriculum in a new key: The collected works of Ted Aoki.* Mahwah, NJ: Lawrence Erlbaum Associates.

Pinar, W.F., Reynolds, W.M., Slattery, P., & Taubman, P.M. (1995). *Understanding curriculum.* New York: Peter Lang.

Schiro, M.S. (2008). *Curriculum theory: Conflicting visions and enduring concerns.* Thousand Oaks, CA: Sage.

Schubert, W.H. (1986). *Curriculum: Perspective, paradigm, and possibility.* New York: Macmillan.

Siskar, J.F. (1997, January). The B.U.I.L.D. Academy: A historical study of community action and education in Buffalo, New York. *Afro-Americans in New York Life and History,21*(1), 19–39.

Steinberg, S.R. (2009). *Diversity and multiculturalism: A reader.* New York: Peter Lang.

StudentsFirst. Retrieved March 30, 2012, from www.studentsfirst.org

Teach for America (TFA). Retrieved March 30, 2012, from www.teachforamerica.org.

Transforming teaching: Connecting professional responsibility with student learning. (2011).*Commission on Effective Teachers and Teaching.* Retrieved March 30, 2012, from http://www.nea.org/assets/docs/Transforming_Teaching%282%29.pdf

William-White, L. (2011, May). Dare I speak of oppression on *sacred* ground [emphasis added].*Cultural Studies <=> Critical Methodologies, 11*(3), 236–242.

William-White, L. (2011b, June). Scholarship revolution. *Qualitative Inquiry, 17*(6), 534–542.

William-White, L. (2012). Advocating for Multicultural Education and Social Justice in the Age of Economic Uncertainty, *International Review of Qualitative Research.* 5(2), 175–204.

William-White, L., Muccular, D., & Muccular, G. (2012). Reading, writing, and revolution: Spoken word as radical "literocratic" praxis in the community college classroom. In B. Porfilio & M. Viola (Eds.), *Hip-hop(e): The cultural practice and critical pedagogy of international hip-hop* (pp. 197–219). New York: Peter Lang.

William-White, L., Muccular, D., Muccular, G., & Brown, A. (Forthcoming). *Home, school, and third space: Research in the fight for curriculum transformation for critical consciousness.* New York: Peter Lang.

William-White, L., Sagir, A., Flores, N., Jung, G., Ramirez, A., Osalbo, J., & Doan, H. (2012, March). Arugula, pine nuts, and hegemony: Seven women's choreopoetic reflection on the absence of cultural relevance in educational discourse. *International Journal of Qualitative Research, 25*(2), 135–149.

William-White, L., & White, J. (2011, October). Color marks the site/sight of social difference: Dysconscious racism in the "Age of Obama."*Qualitative Inquiry,17*(9), 837–853.

Notes

1. California Commission of Teacher Credentialing.
2. National Teachers Association.
3. The National Council for Accreditation of Teacher Education (NCATE) is the profession's mechanism to help establish a performance-based system of accreditation with P-12 schools playing a more significant role in designing preparation programs, selecting candidates, assessing candidate performance and progress, and placing them in clinical experiences which are a major focus of the reform efforts taking place within

NCATE. To date, eight states have signed on for reform of teacher education, including California. See http://www.ncate.org/LinkClick.aspx?fileticket=zzeiB1OoqPk %3D&tabid=715 for the blueprint, which asserts the following: "The education of teachers in the United States needs to be turned upside down . . . teacher education must shift away from a norm which emphasizes academic preparation and course work loosely linked to school-based experiences. Rather, it must move to programs that are fully grounded in clinical practice and interwoven with academic content and professional courses" (p. ii).

4. See the forthcoming text by William-White, Muccular, Muccular, and Brown (2013) for exploration of research focused on the historic moment and its relationship to curriculum.
5. See Schiro (2008) for discussion of Tyler; and Shubert (1986) for discussion of Schwab and Tyler.
6. See http://www.ets.org/s/outage.html as the leader in assessment test services for education.
7. See McLaren (2003), p. 43.
8. See Policy Brief: No Child Left Behind: Where Does the Money Go? athttp://epsl.asu.edu/epru/documents/EPSL-0506-114-EPRU.pdf
9. See McLaren (2003), p. 43.
10. See criticisms of the Voyager Curriculum at http://publicadvocategotbaum.com/new_n ews/releases_5_6_03.html.As governor of Texas, George W. Bush pushed a proposal giving $25 million in state money to after-school programs that would aid Voyager, which had contributed more than $45,000 to Bush and over $20,000 to Bush's lieutenant governor running mate.
11. The federal No Child Left Behind (NCLB) Act specifically states that only curricula and teaching methods that are scientifically proven to work [raise achievement] will be funded.
12. See http://blogs.ajc.com/get-schooled-blog/2011/05/04/dear-teachers-i-want-to-work-with-you-and-not-against-you-your-pal-arne-duncan/
13. See the official blog of the US Department of Education http://www.ed.gov/blog/2012/03/answering-questions-of-fundamental-fairness/
14. See story at http://www.nytimes.com/2011/08/08/education/08educ.html?pagewanted=all
15. See Arne Duncan's Open Letter to Teachers at http://www.ed.gov/blog/2011/05/in-honor-of-teacher-appreciation-week-an-open-letter-from-arne-duncan-to-americas-teachers/
16. See the coverage of the Atlanta test score scandal at http://www.huffingtonpost.com/2011/07/12/six-atlanta-officials-rep_n_895604.html
17. See the coverage of Michelle Rhee's test score scandal at http://www.huffingtonpost.com/2011/08/22/michelle-rhee-eager-for-s_n_932965.html

18. See http://www2.ed.gov/programs/racetothetop/index.html. The Race to the Top program is built on the framework of comprehensive reform that requires that reform occur as part of a comprehensive plan to meet goals for student outcomes, including closing achievement gaps.

19. See http://www.pisa.oecd.org/pages/0,3417,en_32252351_32235907_1_1_1_1_1,00.html

20. "Social Efficiency advocates believe that the purpose of schooling is to efficiently meet the needs of society by training youth to function as future mature contributing members of society" (Schiro, 2008, p. 4). Schiro further states that "Educators must . . . find the most efficient way of producing a product—the educated person—who meets the terminal objectives of the curriculum and thus fulfills the needs of society (or client) . . . the most efficient achievement of a curriculum's terminal objectives results from applying the routines of scientific procedure to curriculum making" (p. 5).

21. See http://susanohanian.org/show_research.php?id=85 for an overview of the curriculum embroil of the Reading First initiative, its relationship to corporate entities and profits, and Bush's NCLB law. Ohanian mentions the Business Roundtable, an organization serving 200 of America's largest corporations, and the conflict of interest that exists between these corporations and curriculum suppliers.

22. See the work of Delpit (1995).

23. See http://politicalticker.blogs.cnn.com/2012/01/22/who-is-saul-alinsky-a-gingrich-line-explained/ where we see the media and GOP candidates speaking about the radical views of Saul Alinsky, linking him to Obama.

24. Academic Performance Index.

25. Adequate Yearly Progress.

26. See the philosophy behind the currere in Pinar & Grumet (1976).

27. See http://www.nea.org/assets/docs/Transforming_Teaching%282%29.pdf

28. Education that Works: Ideas for Sacramento, was a summit hosted by Mayor Kevin Johnson and held on March 9, 2009, at the California Museum in Sacramento, CA. Panel members focused on three topics: Educational Options; Accountability for Results; and Human Capital. Featured speakers were: Reverend Al Sharpton; Cory Booker, mayor of Newark; Joel Klein, chancellor, New York City Department of Education; and Michelle Rhee, chancellor, D.C. Public Schools. The latter two panelists are noteworthy for several reasons. First, in April 2003, Chancellor Joel I. Klein's decision to supplement Phonics Curriculum with the New York City Passport program, developed by Voyager Expanded Learning of Dallas, is a point of public scrutiny based on adoption of a costly program that had not been researched or tested for results. This same curriculum series is linked to allegations of cronyism and profiteering through corporate ties with the Bush Administration. Michelle Rhee, former chancellor of D.C. schools, is a controversial figure whose record as a teacher and as a chancellor had been highly criticized. Rhee's boasting of student achievement on test scores in her classroom

has been questioned based on accuracy of results. She was also responsible for undertaking radical changes in school reform as chancellor, backed by the mayor and the chancellor of New York Public Schools, Joel Klein. Allegations were made about the accuracy of standardized test scores due to erasure and correction of answers. Rhee recently founded StudentsFirst.org, an organization focused on educational reform in several areas, including merit pay and teacher assessment; she is also married to Sacramento Mayor Kevin Johnson. Confirmed panelists also included: Larry Berger, CEO and co-founder, Wireless Generation; Tim Daly, president, New Teacher Project; Josh Edelman, executive officer, Chicago Public Schools Office of New Schools; Mike Feinberg, founder, Knowledge Is Power Program (KIPP); Howard Fuller, board chairman, Black Alliance for Educational Options (BAEO); Larry Rosenstock, CEO, High Tech High; and Don Shalvey, founder, Aspire Public Schools. I, along with my 2009 student teacher candidates, attended this summit. See http://www.cityofsacramento.org /mayor/documents/educationThatWorks_ideasForSacramento.pdf for the working White Paper that was created to begin local education reform.

29. See http://www.standup.org/.STAND UP's goal is to identify and address the city's education challenges in order to create an environment that is results oriented and embraces innovation. STAND UP will focus on increasing academic achievement as well as improving school graduation and college completion rates by undertaking research projects and identifying, supporting, and partnering with the nation's leading entrepreneurial education organizations. The five main pillars at the heart of the organization's vision include: accountability, school choice, human capital, parental involvement, and effective policy. The organization strives to partner with the following organizations: Teach for America, The New Teacher Project, New Leaders for New Schools, Healthcorps, Any Given Child, Revolution Foods, City Year, and Parent Revolution. See http://cee-trust.org/members/profiles.aspx?id=21

30. Acronyms stand for Teach for America, New Leaders for New Schools, and The New Teacher Project.

31. See Pinar & Irwin (2005).

5

Learning to Teach:
Values in Action

ANTHONY CODY

Pathways into the classroom have been shifting over the past decade, as traditional credential programs are challenged by alternative routes to certification such as Teach for America (TFA). The formal ways in which these approaches go about preparing teachers embody distinct values. Neither of these pathways, however, provides teachers who have actually begun teaching with the reflective, critical environment necessary to make sense of the conflicting mandates teachers face in today's classrooms. In this chapter I will look at the values embedded in the ways I learned to teach in the 1980s and 1990s, and contrast that to reports and first-hand experiences with teachers who have come to the classroom via TFA.

Our values are not always consciously articulated or stated, but all of our significant actions and decisions draw on them. So when we seek to understand different approaches to something like learning to teach, it is useful to do some digging, to uncover the values at work.

The Credential Program: Theory and Practice

I began to learn to teach in 1986 when I entered the Educational Research and Applications (ERA) program at UC Berkeley's School of Education. This program was led by Dr. Lawrence Lowery, whose focus was on child development from a

Piagetian perspective (Oswalt, 2012). Our classes in pedagogy emphasized the ways in which the development of the mind affected the cognitive challenges students could master, and we learned about the various challenges that were appropriate for each developmental stage. The program included about 75 student-teachers, the majority of whom were at the elementary level. There was a cohort of about eight of us who were learning to teach science, and we met weekly with a retired science teacher who guided us and helped us think about the challenges we were facing in our student teaching assignments. The program required us to teach two semesters of science, one at the middle school level, and one at the high school level.

I came to teaching with a strong social justice framework. I was raised in Berkeley, and I experienced school integration firsthand in 1968, when, as a fifth grader, I changed schools as the result of a citywide integration project. I began my credential program in my late twenties and had been a student activist for much of the preceding decade, participating in the movements to defend affirmative action and to fight apartheid in South Africa. My core values focused on equity, compassion, and social justice. These values were not, however, fully reflected in the ERA program. In fact, in the spring of 1987, I authored a petition raising the concern that the challenges of teaching in urban, economically and culturally diverse classrooms were not adequately addressed by the courses we were taking. Almost every student in the program signed it, and it apparently provoked some discussion among program leaders. But it was a one-year program, so if there were changes made as a result, I wasn't there to see them.

There were several key values embedded in this credential program. There was a respect for the child as an individual thinker, which was manifested in an academic interest in how children develop, and attention to the ways in which we craft instruction to build their abilities. This meant attending to research in child development and viewing the struggles children had in learning through that lens.

Respect for Experience

There was also respect for experience. In addition to the formal coursework, we had a cohort group of about eight that met weekly to discuss what was happening in our classrooms, under the guidance of a retired science teacher. Since we all faced similar challenges and shared ideas and resources with one another, this class functioned in some ways as a support group. This respect for experience also came out in the emphasis on learning by working with skilled teacher practitioners in whose classrooms we served as apprentices. These master teachers were carefully selected and were highly attentive to our teaching. I was observed for every lesson I taught that year and received formal and informal feedback from these teachers frequently. I also observed at least one period of their teaching every day. They had both taught for at least 20 years and had very different approaches.

The high school teacher with whom I worked, Lois Peterson, was fairly traditional and taught structured, teacher-centered classes. She organized lab activities for the biology students of the sort familiar to us all. My other mentor, Warner Freeman, was a bit different. He was using a self-paced science curriculum called the Intermediate Science Curriculum Study (ISCS) from the 1970s that allowed the students to progress through a series of investigations working in small groups. It was exciting to see how he worked to guide and motivate the students, and how he mixed occasional front-and-center presentations with autonomous student work. This curriculum was part of the post-*Sputnik* wave of curricular reforms that reshaped science instruction in the 1960s and 1970s. The central philosophy was one of constructivism, using inquiry as the process to engage students in making discoveries about the natural world themselves, with significant teacher guidance (Lorsbach & Tobin, 1997).

The values I learned from these two mentors stayed with me. From Lois Peterson, I learned the importance of a strong grasp of the science content and determined ways to share it with students through lab activities, readings, and presentations. Warner Freeman was a bit more creative, and he inspired in me a lifelong interest in the inquiry process in science. He modeled confidence in students' ability to work independently and always pushed them to the limits of what they could do on their own. He also had a great heart, and I recall one day when he commented on our interactions with students. He told me: "The subject your students are studying is *you*. They watch everything you do." He helped me understand that when I taught my students, I was showing them the way a man could behave in the world, the way he respected women, the way he dealt with conflict.

But the process of "credentialing" as a certification that one is prepared to teach is problematic, in that it suggests a beginning and end to the process. Traditional credential programs such as the one I experienced are more extensive than the cursory training TFA corps members receive, but when the year-long program is finished, the work is done. You are a teacher. However, when I started teaching in Oakland, I had so much yet to learn!

As a Teacher Have I Joined "the System"?

Growing up in Berkeley I was made aware that there are class, race, and gender sub-texts to all of our social interactions, and the relationships between teachers and students are especially laden, as the teacher cannot help but embody authority and serve as a representative of the *system* to students. My experience as a student-teacher brought all this home to me, as I experienced these dynamics firsthand. This was not, however, discussed much in my credential program. Certification was a some-what technical process, housed in the university, where issues like race and class were academic constructs. In the classroom, they are vivid realities, embodied in con-frontations with defiant or apathetic students.

Fortunately, a year after I began teaching in Oakland, I was invited to join a collaborative research group called the Learning to Teach Collaborative. This group was led by a UC professor named Sandra Hollingsworth, and some gradu-ate students who were especially interested in how teachers learned to teach literacy.

The group placed a high value on reflection, and the value of different perspec-tives. We operated from what might be termed a social constructivist view of learning, in which we placed ourselves firmly in the roles of both teacher and learn-er. One member, now a principal in Vallejo, recently described these as our guid-ing values: "Collaboration. Reflection. Public practice. Teacher as professional. Courage to challenge one's own biases and the innate prejudices of the education-al system" (email communication, April 28, 2012).

We were all dealing with cross-cultural experiences in our diverse classrooms, so it was especially valuable to have the perspective of an African American in the group. We met regularly for the next decade and authored a book together, *Teacher Research and Urban Literacy Education, Lessons and Conversations in a Feminist Key* (Hollingsworth, 1994). Although the group began with an explicit focus on learn-ing to teach literacy, it wasn't long before the emphasis shifted to the issues that were bubbling up from within our teaching practice. As the book explained:

> The combination of the compelling need to learn about the contexts in which they
> were teaching, the safety of the collaborative conversation, and the strength of their
> own personal convictions about relational learning gave (group members) a moti-
> vation, a context, and a means to come to learn what they needed to begin to
> develop more-successful-than-not literacy lessons for urban students.
> (Hollingsworth, 1994, p. 57)

A middle school science teacher, I was a bit out of place, but I was hungry for an opportunity to discuss the challenges I was facing. We met monthly, and, over potluck dinners, lively discussions would unfold over how to reach the quiet ones, the angry ones, or the parents of our students. I was the only man in the group, and the others were mostly elementary teachers. One African American teacher, Jennifer Smallwood, had a great way of challenging us to think about things from a different cultural perspective.

Sandra Hollingsworth (1994) explained:

> The teachers in our group initially questioned their personal power to teach and learn from their own beliefs and experiences in a political climate that support-ed authoritative standards. Adopting a critical perspective about the social norms of that climate—and receiving the support to move through the emotional stress that accompanies such a perspective—was crucial to claiming their own profes-sional voices within their schools—and attaining the personal and political free-dom to reconstruct classrooms that supported the diverse values and ways of being instead of restricting them. . . .(p. 30)

As we were getting our credentials, our classes and weekly cohort meetings were places where issues of practice could be discussed and reflected on.

After graduation, similar conversation spaces were hard to find. Faculty meet-ings covered the procedural business of running a school. School-based in-service conversations were planned around academic and/or administratively determined concerns, and rarely allowed much room for discussion of the broader issues sur-rounding teaching and learning in schools, or, for that matter, day-to-day teacher concerns. It was as if these issues were to have been dealt with in preservice teacher education. If a teacher were to acknowledge that she had concerns or problems about which she didn't know what to do, she was considered ineffective. Thus teach-ers' voices that might have brought common concerns forward for public consid-eration were silenced. So they took away from school meetings new certainties or knowledges that an external "expert" or "authority" had given, tried to put that knowledge into practice in their classrooms, and felt like failures if the new knowl-edge didn't resolve their (unspoken) concerns.

Thus we "discovered" and noted the importance of having places for conver-sation about our specific teaching concerns situated in the larger world of educa-tion, without receiving feedback that would either negate our experiences or disempower our need to construct new ways of knowing. (Hollingsworth, 1994, pp. 30, 37-38)

The fact that this group continued for more than a decade, long after we had all passed the stage where we would normally be considered to be learning to teach, is a testament to the rich challenges we all faced, and the value we placed in having a critical circle of colleagues for support and dialogue.

Giving Novice Teachers Veteran Mentors

I became involved in teacher education from the other side of the equation in 2008, when I initiated a project in the Oakland schools to provide mentoring to novice science teachers. Turnover among our science teachers was very high, and this meant that at many schools there were few veteran teachers available to support newcomers as they entered the profession. All of our new teachers were coming through alternative credential programs such as Teach for America and The New Teacher Project's Oakland Teacher Fellows. I organized a project called TeamScience that provided each novice teacher with an experienced teacher who would meet with them weekly to help them with curriculum and class management. The goals were to make these beginning teachers more effective and encourage them to stay beyond their two-year commitment. This program is described in a report I shared on my blog:

> In the first year, we were focused on learning basic mentoring skills. How do we talk to our teachers about the issues they are facing? How do we use these mentoring tools? We had to learn to be good mentors first. Now that we are in our third year, we are learning what we can do as science mentors. Many of our beginning teachers have been trained to "cover" large amounts of material, because that is what is on the test. Sometimes they do not understand how to teach or assess their students' deeper understanding. So we have spent time this year probing how much our students are really grasping, and developing strategies to deepen this. (Cody, 2011)

I served as a mentor myself to about twenty of these teachers over a period of several years. As a result, I got a clear picture of how they were learning to teach, and the values that were guiding their induction. I am going to focus on Teach for America for this discussion and draw on my own experiences as well as those of some other TFA corps members.

The work that TeamScience did with the novice teachers drew on training and materials developed by the New Teacher Center (NTC) in Santa Cruz. Our project was a partnership with NTC, and we used tools they developed for use in the state's Beginning Teacher Support and Assessment (BTSA) process (Moir, 2008).

These tools placed a high value on reflection and inquiry into student learning. A typical session might involve reviewing student work to see where students were struggling and trying to identify next steps to take with students at different levels. We also explicitly sought to honor the expertise of the veteran teachers, and the weekly conversations between mentor and novice were designed to create a space in which all sorts of challenges could be discussed.

The Teach for America Path into (and out of) the Classroom

The TFA corps members we were working with were explicitly recruited for a two-year commitment. Research has shown that 57% of TFA corps members have no intention of making teaching their career, and this was one of the main reasons we were losing just over 50% of them after year two, and 75% after year three (Donaldson & Johnson, 2011). The program placed a high value on service, but this is seen as something one did for a relatively short time, with missionary zeal.

They were prepared for the classrooms by attending a six-week summer institute that combined instruction from current teachers, most of whom had 3 or 4 years' experience, with team-teaching summer school classes. This institute emphasized the basics of classroom management and procedures—sort of a crash course—so that they could hit the ground running in the fall. Once they begin teaching, corps members also attend courses related to teaching. But this means they are burdened with all the pressures of being a beginning teacher, plus the need to attend classes and do coursework.

TFA places a very high value on equitable access to college for all students. The view came through that children in poverty have not been appropriately challenged to perform academically and providing them with teachers who had succeeded in that arena could reshape them and provide them with the academic skills needed for college.

I spoke with Jameson Brewer, a TFA corps member who teaches in Atlanta. He is unusual in that he went through a traditional teacher-preparation program but was unable to get a job—until he committed to TFA and went through their training. Here is how he describes his preparation to be a teacher:

> I attended Valdosta State University from 2003–2007. I studied to become a high school history teacher. My studies were divided between history classes so that I could master the content while the other time was spent in education classes (e.g., pedagogy, methods, special education, reading in the content area, etc.). I was

required to amass 80 hours of observation in both middle and high schools and teach a few small lessons prior to student teaching. I did my student teaching at Valdosta High School. I taught 12th grade economics. In all, I amassed 1216 hours of class and lead teaching time.

I recall my undergraduate training had a heavy focus on the value of ethics. From the official Georgia Professional Standards Commission's code to a system of personal ethics. It was my professors and truly my mentor teacher who helped me establish those personal ethics. For example, while we prepared our students to do well on the end of course test in economics, our main focus was ensuring they experienced a democratic educative experience when in our classroom. Call it rogue, but the values we operated under put more emphasis on the human than on the state-mandated standard. The values instilled in me during my traditional training can be summarized by the following statement that I begin every class year with and what I say to parents on open house night. "Is it important for you to know who Hammurabi was for my class? Yes. Is it important for you to know it for the state test? Yes. But, in reality, NO ONE will care if you know who he was five or ten years from now, unless you are on *Jeopardy*. BUT, what people will care about is do you understand how to relate to others, do you understand the real meaning of democracy, justice, oppression, human relations, and your place and role in the world. If you are good at taking tests and getting A's in class but make no real impact in your own life, your communities, and the world, then no one will remember you just like most don't remember Hammurabi unless they have to."

He then described his training with TFA:

The TFA training was the exact opposite. The focus is SOLELY on student assessment, raising test scores, and the standards. All to pass along the "value" to students that their best option in life is to ace a series of tests so that they can go to college and get a "good" job that is starkly different than their present lives. The values celebrated during TFA's Institute are those corps members who have "perfected" good classroom management, good instructional delivery, and content knowledge (among other similar things). And while I do believe that all students should have the option to go to college, I do not believe that everyone should. Nor do I believe that teachers, like TFA teachers, should advocate for what is essentially a brain drain of the communities that they serve. If the value message is "do good so you can get out of here," how then are these communities' issues/problems ever going to be solved if the best are leaving?

Part of my work with the TeamScience program was to serve as a mentor to novice teachers, including a number of TFA corps members. I observed some of the same things mentioned by Jameson Brewer. The drive for equity was pursued with the belief that success on tests is a key vehicle. I sat in on a meeting with a mentee and his TFA coach, who made it very clear that the focus of their monthly meetings would be student data and that they would focus "relentlessly" on improving student scores. Corps members were directed to set a "big goal," which was 80% mastery on tests. Many also put up charts tracking student test performance. One of my mentees was a first-year high school biology teacher. Her students were doing poorly on her weekly tests, so her TFA advisor suggested that she make her daily assignments more like her tests. So her instruction shifted to worksheets with multiple choice and short answer questions. As her mentor I felt in a bind. Clearly she was under intense pressure from her TFA advisor to more effectively prepare her students for tests. The students' test scores improved, but to her credit, this teacher was not satisfied. Although students were, for a while, happy to be doing better, they soon became bored with the worksheets. The next year this teacher joined a Project Based Learning group I was helping to lead and shifted her instruction to more engaging, meaningful projects.

Learning to Teach: Beyond the Credential

In contrast to the traditional credential programs that value tradition and respect expertise, embodied in the apprenticeship alongside an experienced mentor, the TFA model rejects any formal relationship to experienced teachers, who are sometimes even portrayed as the reason students have failed in the past. The corps member advisors are usually TFA "veterans" who have taught for 2 or 3 years and moved into these staff positions.

The ERA credential program at UC Berkeley was far from perfect, but the combination of coursework and extensive experience as a sort of apprentice to an experienced teacher has a lot to recommend it. This combination is rooted in a respect for tradition and expertise. The attention to child development was also helpful, though lacking the deeper social context that greatly affected interactions with students.

The Learning to Teach collaborative group to which I belonged is a useful model to consider. The open-ended format meant that discussions often focused on the most urgent issues that faced us as we learned to teach. The sort of "critical friends" atmosphere that we created allowed us to explore and deepen our own perspective and be challenged by others. And the way this group operated over more than a decade underscores the fact that learning to teach is not completed in one's first year, but is a process, enriched by challenging dialogue with others.

Leslie Minarik, one of the Learning to Teach collaborative group members, said that our group has stayed a working community because we are committed to a common belief: that we must discover how to be better teachers for the sake of the children we were all deeply committed to. In the beginning, I thought of leaving several times because it was hard to find the extra time and because it was often emotionally unsettling and wrenching to deal with the issues we talked about and to have to face what I was doing. It was hard sometimes to take a leap of faith and trust that the time would be worthwhile because it did not look like a traditional place where we could find answers to our classroom problems. Our group supported our roles as intelligent identifiers of problems and of knowledgeable professionals able to find solutions. (Hollingsworth, 1994, p. 171)

Learning to teach is an extended process. For reflective practitioners this is a process that never ends, as we are continually thinking about what is going on, and engaging in dialogue with others to better understand and improve our work. Teach for America turns teacher preparation into a collection of techniques to be learned, with a relentless focus on getting students to "invest" (or believe) in the importance of test scores. TFA corps members are not given space to engage in the kind of reflective discussions that allow us to explore the social dynamics we encounter as teachers. Within a comprehensive credential program, there are often places for these discussions to occur, but the dialogue ends when we leave the credential program and begin our teaching careers. As we reconsider learning to teach as an extended, reflective process, collaborative groups such as the one to which I belonged ought to be explored and supported.

References

Cody, A. (2011, January 30). TeamScience tames teacher turnover in Oakland. Living in Dialogue [Web log]. *Education Week*. Retrieved from http://blogs.edweek.org/teachers-/living-in-dialogue/2011/01/teamscience_tames_teacher_turn.html

Donaldson, M.L., & Johnson, S.M. (2011, October 4). TFA teachers, how long do they teach, why do they leave? *Education Week*. Retrieved April 30, 2012, from http://www.edweek.org/ew/articles/2011/10/04/kappan_donaldson.html

Hollingsworth, S. (1994). *Teacher research and urban literacy education: Lessons and conversations in a feminist key*. New York: Teachers College Press.

Lorsbach, A., & Tobin, K. (1997). Constructivism as a referent for science teaching. Exploratorium Institute for Inquiry. Retrieved April 29, 2012, from http://www.exploratorium.edu/IFI/resources/research/constructivism.html

Moir, E. (2008). Building a quality teaching force: Lessons learned from alternate routes. In C.E. Feistritzer (Ed.), *Building a quality teacher force* (pp. 36–59). Retrieved April 30, 2012, from http://ptgmedia.pearsoncmg.com/images/9780132382120/samplechapter/FeistritzerCh3.pdf

Oswalt, A. (2012). Jean Piaget's theory of cognitive development. Seven Counties Services, Inc. Retrieved April 29, 2012, from http://www.sevencounties.org/poc/view_doc.php?type=doc&id=41157&cn=1310

Part II. Becoming a Teacher: Teacher Education in an Age of Austerity

6

The Corporate Takeover of Teacher Education:
Exposing and Challenging NCTQ's Neoliberal Agenda

BRAD J. PORFILIO AND LAUREN HOFFMAN

Over the past decade, U.S. political leaders, Western CEOs, educators, psychologists, think tank organizations, and the public at large have collectively called for a radical overhaul of teacher education. These groups' reactionary call is supported by the false idea that *dysfunctional teacher educators*, rather than unjust policies, systemic inequalities, and historical forces are perpetuating a bleak social reality in the United States. At today's historical moment, the United States is grappling with strained racial relations, youth alienation, a grossly inequitable distribution of wealth and resources, as well as heightened unemployment (Taubman, 2009, p. 3). The push to overhaul teacher education is rooted in the corporate world's desire to profit from every element of social life, including social domains as teacher preparation, that have been considered social goods designed to ameliorate rather than to commodify humanity (Cochran-Smith, 2009; Hinchey & Cadiero-Kaplan, 2005; Porfilio & Yu, 2006; Sleeter, 2008).

One of the most recent attempts to commercialize teacher education comes from the research and policy group the National Council on Teacher Quality (NCTQ). This organization consists mainly of business leaders, scholars, and administrators who support the elimination of traditional teacher education programs[i] as well as promote the corporate takeover of U.S. K–12 schools. NCTQ has recently joined with *U.S. News and World Report* to determine not only what standards the 1,400 schools of education in the United States must employ to evaluate whether their students will be *effective* in K–12 classrooms but also to collect data such as "course syllabi, textbooks and reading packets, student-teaching placement information, admissions standards, course requirements, and graduate and employer surveys," with or without the cooperation of schools of education, in order to "review and rate teacher education in the nation's 1,400 schools of education" (Sawchuk, 2011).

The purpose of this chapter is twofold: We will critically expose NCTQ's agenda for teacher education as well as highlight an alternative model of assessment to counter the technical, commercial agenda being promoted by neoliberal corporate entities such as NCTQ and *U.S. News and World Report.* First, we illuminate the various initiatives these groups have supported for schools of education, examine several of the criteria the groups use to gauge whether a teacher education program is preparing students to become effective teachers, and suggest how the groups' educational vision is inextricably linked to ensuring that our next generation of teachers become docile individuals who unwittingly keep in place the structures and policies designed to oppress the many and benefit the few. Second, we argue that schools of education must develop a vision of teacher preparation that is socially generative rather than commercial and technical in nature. They must not only help students recognize the social, political, and economic forces creating injustice in schools and in the wider society but also guide them to develop emancipatory visions of how teachers can generate critical forms of pedagogies and activist initiatives that have the potential to eliminate social inequalities and build institutional structures based on democracy, equity, and fairness. To aid us in the process of making teacher education a space for educating teachers to challenge injustice, to embrace diversity, and to advocate for minoritzed social groups, we outline an intelligent form of evaluation that is different from the technical model of assessment dominating life in schools of education.

NCTQ and the Neoliberal Hijacking of Teacher Education: An Overview

In 2000, NCTQ was created from "the Teacher Quality Initiative, a joint project of the Education Leaders Council and the Thomas B. Fordham Foundation" (Sue & Fore, 2002). Educational Leaders Council and the Thomas B. Fordham Foundation's purpose for creating NCTQ was to promulgate their corporate vision for higher education, as the groups were already key players during the Bush presidency for promoting the school voucher movement and tuition-tax credits as corporate solutions to eradicating the achievement gaps plaguing K–12 schools. To achieve their aim, the groups first used their political clout with the Bush regime to garner $5 million in unsolicited grants from the U.S. Department of Education in 2001–2002. The funds aided them in supporting their campaign to privatize teacher education through "alternative teacher certification and credentials" (Neas, 2003). Next, in 2003, NCTQ joined with the Educational Leaders Council to forge the American Board for Certification of Teacher Excellence (ABCTE). The ABCTE demonstrated that it defined promoting teacher excellence purely in neoliberal terms as it secured a "multiyear grant worth $35 million from Secretary of Education Rod Paige to develop a fast-tracked route (standardized test) for alternative teacher certification" (Neas, 2003).

Like the two major political parties in the United States, NCTQ has continued to wield its influence to promote the corporate takeover of teacher education and K–12 schools. For instance, in 2005, the organization started to evaluate teacher education programs by standards they deem necessary to equip "new teachers with the knowledge and skills they need to succeed" (NCTQ, n.d.). However, we did not become intimately familiar with NCTQ's plans to prepare future teachers and school administrators as mere technicians in K–12 classrooms and eliminate traditional forms of teacher education until the group focused its interest on teacher education programs in Illinois—the state in which we teach and conduct research. In 2009, NCTQ joined Advance Illinois to study the "performance of Illinois' 53 undergraduate and graduate teacher preparation programs, along with three independent recruitment and training programs, against a set of 30 common standards" (NCTQ, 2010, p. 1). NCTQ found a suitable partner in Advance Illinois because the organization consisted mainly of business and political leaders who supported whole cloth the Obama administration's educational agenda. For instance, Advance Illinois supports several corporate initiatives backed by the Obama administration and numerous political pundits in the United States, such as "lengthening the school day or year, attracting teachers in high-need fields, incenting high-performing teachers to teach in low-performing schools, rewarding outstanding performance (e.g., teachers preparing students to become obedient test-takers), or coaching new or struggling teachers" (Advance Illinois, n.d.) as the panacea for eliminating educational disparities in the United States, instead of recognizing that educational and social inequalities can only be eradicated if educational leaders and citizens confront and subvert the "societal inequities that overwhelm both students and the schools they attend" (Thomas, 2011, p. 75). Additionally, Advance Illinois supports other initiatives designed to control edu-

cators' and school administrators' labor and alienate students, including basing decisions on teachers' tenure and reduction-of-force decisions on performance (which
is based in part on students' performance on high-stakes tests) rather than on seniority, basing teacher education programs' accreditation on their graduates' ability to
have K–12 students perform well on high-stakes examinations, and revising principal preparation programs to ensure that future educational leaders develop the
"essential skills" to "use data to inform instruction" (Advance Illinois, n.d.).

When looking specifically at the set of standards NCTQ has designed to
gauge whether teacher education programs are "preparing their future teachers for
tomorrow's classrooms" (NCTQ, n.d.), it becomes even more apparent that the
organization supports neoliberal educational reform efforts predicated on position-
ing current and future teachers to function as dutiful workers in K–12 classrooms.
According to NCTQ, several of the nuts and bolts of what teachers ought to be
able to do in classrooms are to "learn and practice specific techniques for managing the classroom," to "practice teaching the content of their intended subject areas,"
and to use "scientific" reading methods that are *a priori* said to have the power to
foster literacy in K–12 classrooms (NCTQ, n.d.). Not coincidentally, the organization fails to generate any standards that are designed to determine whether teacher
education programs are guiding students to become stewards of social transformation inside and outside of K–12 classrooms. Clearly, it does not serve the interest
of those political and economic leaders who support technical and commercial
forms of teacher preparation to embrace any transformative aims for teacher preparation, such as educating students to understand how educational institutions are
set up to serve the interests of the power elite, to understand the relationship
between knowledge and power, or to recognize the "complexities of educational
practice and an understanding of and commitment to a socially just, democratic
notion of schooling" (Kincheloe, 2004, p. 24). It also does not serve the interest
of the elite to support teacher preparation programs that infuse coursework and
related activities designed to help in-service and pre-service teachers implement
social justice initiatives and pedagogies inside and outside their learning communities. Unlike technical knowledge, which is easily measured and quantified by commercial and political interests on teacher credential examinations, social justice
education is designed to generate emancipatory knowledge predicated on aiding
future and current teachers to "understand how social relationships are distorted
and manipulated by relations of power and privilege" and how educators and students can overcome oppression "through deliberative collective action" (McLaren,
2003, p. 72).

NCTQ's Findings and the Deans' Technical Response: Failing Teacher Education

In just over a 12-month period, NCTQ conducted its research and released its findings to establish which "education schools are truly producing *the best possible teachers*" (emphasis in original) in Illinois (NCTQ, n.d.). Many of the academic deans in Illinois were not pleased by NCTQ's major finding—that many of the institutions of higher learning were not doing enough to train teachers to be purely compliant technicians in K–12 schools. In fact, only one of 111 programs housed within 53 academic institutions received a grade of A-. Nine other programs received a grade of B (NCTQ, 2010, p. 2). This spurred the deans to write a collective response to NCTQ's new ratings report. Rather than vocalizing their concern with NCTQ's technical view of what it means to be an effective teacher, its failure to support social justice coursework and other pro-social initiatives in schools of education, and its commercial and mechanistic view of education, the higher education institutions' response centered on the process of the study. The major complaint they have with NCTQ's report is that it is too "narrow in focus and emphasizes static inputs rather than outcomes of actual candidate performance."

One dean's response to the NCTQ report also illustrates that the deans have little concern that NCTQ and other corporate groups may be attempting to implement a jaundiced vision of teacher education. She explains:

> We are confident that NCTQ and Advance Illinois will join us in our quest to ensure that each and every P–12 student in Illinois gets a world-class education in a classroom staffed by an excellent teacher. We wish that the analysis of our elementary education and special education programs that NCTQ conducted was more helpful in this endeavor. Because the research methodology utilized in this process does not meet the rigorous standards that are accepted in our field, those set forth by the American Educational Research Association, the value of the feedback that has been provided to us is minimal. (Lukasik & Schultz, in press).

The dean's response focuses on NCTQ's inadequate research methodology instead of on its failure to embrace a vision of teacher education predicated on preparing students to be transformative intellectuals, cultural workers, and social advocates inside and outside of their classrooms, and indicates that administrators across Illinois lack the courage or critical insight necessary to interrogate the corporate world's mission to commercialize teacher education as well as produce compliant school teachers.

The academic deans apparently got their wish that NCTQ be more scientific in attempting to accurately discern whether the 56 Illinois educator preparation programs are preparing teachers to become agents of the neoliberal status quo. After reading the academic deans' response, NCTQ decided to abandon its evaluation of teacher education programs based upon reviews of syllabi and materials culled from the institutions' websites. Instead, NCTQ joined a new neoliberal partner, *U.S. News and World Report*, to broaden the scope of input to judge whether schools of education are producing effective technicians in K–12 schools. These groups are now evaluating "course syllabi, textbooks and reading packets, student-teaching placement information, admissions standards, course requirements, and graduate and employer surveys to review and rate teacher education in the nation's 1,400 schools of education."

After several conversations among the academic deans in Illinois, it was decided to follow suit with the chancellors of the California State and University of Maryland systems, who did not comply with NCTQ's and *U.S. News and World Report*'s request for assistance in reviewing their teacher education programs. However, the deans' response to the corporate world's latest attempt to exert control over teacher preparation in the United States is similar to their initial response in 2010. They chided the organizations for not using proper research methods that would adequately assess whether schools of education are preparing schoolteachers effectively, rather than critiquing the organizations' vision and agenda for the education of current and future teachers.

On a micro-level, however, we witnessed administrators surreptitiously aligning their programs with the organizations' standards for evaluation. For instance, faculty members were told that NCTQ's technical standards must be "crystal clear in all syllabi." This is despite the fact that NCTQ's vision for teacher education is in direct opposition to our college of education's transformative educational vision, which the administration outwardly embraces. The administrators took steps to align with NCTQ and *U.S. News and World Report*'s standards because they apparently wanted to avoid an unfavorable evaluation of their programs, as this might cause administrators, potential students, and educational leaders situated in K–12 schools near campus to view the college of education in a negative light. In turn, the college of education and the larger institution may have been compelled to grapple with several deleterious effects, such as a decrease in student enrollment, in alumni donations, and in K–12 schools' support for student-teaching placements and observations.

Based upon the Illinois experience with NCTQ and *U.S. News and World Report*, it is quite possible that academic deans across the United States, particularly administrators who are trying to make their programs more attractive than those of their competitors to teacher candidates, will be complicit in supporting the corporate takeover of teacher education. Most academic deans' vision for educating future teachers differs little from that of the CEOs who are attempting to eliminate their very programs. Academic administrators in schools of education and corporate reformers of teacher education believe educating current and future teachers to become compliant workers is something to be lauded rather than to be problematized. Even if some academic administrators have a more generative vision for teacher education, they are compelled to determine whether supporting this vision is worth facing reprisals—losing their jobs or respect of their peers within their institution, losing student tuition dollars, losing respect from other educational leaders, or failing to win a golden prize from *U.S. News and World Report* and NCTQ, that is, being ranked the best neoliberal school of education in the nation.

Critique of Technical and Instrumental Form of Evaluation by NCTQ

Fundamental to the work of NCTQ is its technical and instrumental form of evaluation, which assumes its members are the experts who possess a special set of tools and competencies that enable them to deliver assessments and judgments about the effectiveness and quality of state education, teacher preparation programs, school districts, and teacher unions. Unfortunately, NCTQ staff believe they can render these judgments in a disengaged and distanced manner while not interacting with the individuals or groups from the particular context or entity. They establish their own pre-determined narrow and technical criteria for what they believe is quality, and they thereby eliminate the ambiguity and particularity of the context they are judging and avoid the complexity of issues and moral dilemmas intrinsic to the specific setting. The evidence they use to make their judgments and the way in which they use it is highly questionable as well. They use such things as course syllabi, program descriptions, and test score data as evidence for their decisions—without considering that any evidence should be considered provisional, revisable, emergent, constrained, and located in specific contexts (Upshur, 2000). The purpose of the NCTQ approach to evaluation is to solve concrete problems by reducing complexity and difference by establishing its own criteria and goals for what it believes should be valued in education and society. Unfortunately, NCTQ staff discern the quality of programs and policies in terms of measurement by thinking criterially with explicit comparison of the object in question to a set of standards. They do not conceptualize quality as *experience* that would draw on both the subjective and intersubjective meanings we attach to events and practices and the narrative accounts that inform our understandings and interpretations. They merely set their own criteria, analyze documents they deem meaningful, and make judgments, based on minimal evidence, that influence public opinion in ways that are harmful to many students, especially those from minoritized populations.

Schwandt (2008) suggests there are several reasons why this way of conceptualizing and implementing evaluation should be a concern for those of us who care about the well being of a good society and educating individuals for citizenship. One reason is that it communicates a belief that the public can be easily influenced by superficial claims that reflect bombast over argument, spin over substance, and image over reality. It assumes there is no need to think carefully about an issue or come to a reasoned position through rational public debate. NCTQ publishes its results in the mainstream media without ever engaging in any dialogue with the individuals involved in the program, policy, or entity being evaluated, and do not consider the specifics of different contexts. Another concern about this type of evaluation is its growing threat of technical professionalism. The neoliberal work of NCTQ strips away the moral discourse that is so desperately needed regarding the social, political, economic, and moral issues in education and society. Unfortunately, NCTQ reduces the work of education to one of supplying technical expert services void of critical analysis and knowledge and ignores the cultural and social dimensions of education. Another reason for concern is that this type of evaluation tends to value all-or-nothing solutions, represents a lack of tolerance for ambiguity, and discounts the capacity of citizens to produce multiple perspectives and solutions. NCTQ's reports have actually included grades for states and programs, which is an example of how they oversimplify the complexity of making judgments about quality. Finally, this type of evaluation demonstrates managerialism, which emphasizes efficiency, problem solving, and procedures for determining outcome achievement, when it should be about critical analysis, questioning, experimenting, and generating multiple visions of what is good and right. NCTQ has blatantly ignored the importance of engaging in any type of meaningful dialogue, critical analysis, or belief in multiple perspectives and the interpretive nature of making judgments about quality.

Evaluation in an Intellectual Society

Schwandt (2008) argues that evaluation should be understood as a moral, practical, intellectual disposition and outlook on social and political life, not merely a process by which methods are employed to judge *effectiveness* or *results* for some predetermined criteria. He states that individuals who engage in evaluation have a responsibility to address complex issues in society, and this cannot be accomplished when evaluators merely focus on methods, limited evidence, and simple solutions. Evaluation should probe moral understanding of what makes life and work worthwhile and just, not merely focus on solving technical problems. Schwandt discusses the following dimensions of evaluation that should be considered when evaluating any type of program, policy, or institution. It should be obvious how NCTQ misses the mark on all of these components.

One major aspect of intelligent evaluation is understanding the nature of evidence in evaluation. This entails "knowing what evidence is and what one can and cannot do with it in evaluation as well as being able to competently communicate those understandings to the public" (Schwandt, 2008, p. 145). Pellegrino (1999) suggests there is an ethics of evidence that must be considered when doing any type of evaluation, including (1) using evidence that is not misleading, (2) revealing the limitations and weaknesses in data or methodology, (3) assuming a moral responsibility for the quality of evidence used, and (4) understanding the policy implications regarding how evidence is created and interpreted. What NCTQ does is use course syllabi, course descriptions, employer surveys, admissions procedures, policy statements, decontextualized documents, and test scores as evidence of quality and then makes judgments on entire programs and policies. NCTQ evaluators have failed to recognize that there is not one standard of evidence that can ever determine quality, effectiveness, or outstanding performance. They make bold and harsh judgments based on evidence that is limited, narrow, and self-serving.

Another important dimension of intelligent evaluation is understanding evaluation as argument in which evaluators share a clear chain of reasoning to their conclusions and judgments (Schwandt, 2008). It is far too common for evaluators to assume that findings are justified just because they specify their methods as opposed to establishing the credibility and validity of an argument. NCTQ evaluation reports do not make reasoned arguments for their judgments and are instead satisfied with proving their case using their narrow, decontextualized data and criteria. When their results are questioned, they defend their methods as opposed to engaging in the messy questions and scrutiny of stakeholders.

Finally, an intelligent belief in evaluation involves recognizing the complexity of social systems and the limitations we face in predicting, planning, and controlling (Schwandt, 2008). This means we need evaluators who are committed to innovation and self-criticism, and to making wise judgments in relation to a range of political, moral, and ethical concerns. There is a need to recognize the modesty in evaluative claims while continually questioning the understanding and reasoning behind them. This is not evident in NCTQ evaluations because they do not demonstrate open-mindedness or tolerance to opposing views and do not critically consider the complexity and difference of contexts.

Contemporary Evaluation Illustrations

Many deans of colleges and schools of education around the country have expressed concern about NCTQ's purpose and lack of transparency, methodology, and procedures for ratings, and have stopped sending NCTQ requested documents. Benner (2012) specifically indicated the NCTQ evaluations are flawed conceptually as well as in the development and interpretation of standards, sampling, method, and data analysis. The deans have not indicated that all is perfect with teacher education, but many have called for more systematic and collegial ways to include the teacher education community in the evaluation process. There are several contemporary examples of how evaluation can be conceptualized in response to this request and ultimately be seen as a meaningful and moral-political-critical practice.

For example, evaluation can be framed with a commitment to democratic social justice, equality, or empowerment (Greene, 2006). Deliberative democratic evaluation (House & Howe, 1999) advocates for democracy and the public interest and promotes and demonstrates these ideals in the evaluative work. This requires evaluators to have more than the ability to work with methods and scientific knowledge, but they must also have an ability to engage in deliberation of values, interests, and facts to reach judgments. Evaluation can also be conceptualized as Responsive Evaluation, in which participants craft their own accounts of experience in narratives without avoiding the ambiguity of meaning (Abma & Stake, 2001). In this case, the evaluator not only values the context and experience, but also uses it with the participants in judging the merit and worth of what is being evaluated. A related notion of evaluation is understanding it as a reflexive process in which the lived experience is the context, and there is a focus on human issues, social action, and the voices of participants who are typically marginalized (Kushner,

2000). Evaluation as advocacy is another way to conceptualize evaluation, which represents a value to commitment to democratic pluralism and thereby commitment to advocacy (Greene, 1997). Finally, critical evaluation fully situates the program or policy to be evaluated in it contested socio-cultural practice, and judgments of merit or worth occur through critical reflection and theorizing about power, opportunity, and privilege (Everitt, 1996).

These notions of evaluation allow for individuals not only to be involved in the process but also to assume responsibility for asking meaningful questions and learning what it takes to make critical judgments about difficult topics. The voices and insights from the insiders can support the much-needed moral discourse about social, cultural, and political issues impacting education while also demonstrating the value of their local knowledge and expertise. NCTQ was criticized for not considering these ideas when it rendered its judgments about the effectiveness and quality of state education, teacher preparation programs, school districts, and teacher unions. It certainly can stand to learn a great deal about evaluation as a moral-political rather than technical undertaking if it takes the critique seriously and reexamines the meaning, purpose, and practice of program evaluation.

Acts of Resistance to NCTQ

As we have demonstrated in this chapter, NCTQ's and *U.S. News and World Report's* desire to evaluate teacher education programs and provide a technical vision for preparing current and future teachers is a systemic reflection of corporate impulses dominating most elements of social life at today's historical juncture in North America. One important step in confronting corporate control over education is to get beyond the procedural forms of evaluation embraced by NCTQ, other educational conglomerates, and numerous academic deans and teacher educators and consider the concepts of evaluation discussed above. We need to uncover the emphasis on corporate education in these standardized evaluations and fully explore democracy, social justice, equity, and critical pedagogy in education. This requires learning about evaluation in a new way and educating the public about its meaning and purpose. We need to provide counter narratives for the spin provided by NCTQ and promote public discourse about what should matter in education.

Moreover, we must engage in more generative acts of resistance—rather than merely critiquing a corporate organization for not using sound research methodology—and confront the corporate takeover of education in particular and the social world in general. For instance, we have found several alternative forms of youth culture ripe for providing emancipatory guideposts for recognizing the constitutive forces, policies, and social actors responsible for breeding human suffering and social inequality in schools and in society. To take one example, several youth-led organizations across North America share their research projects and personal experiences to articulate how the neoliberal agenda is impacting K–12 schools. One is the Ya-Ya network of New York City, which is not only committed to exposing how the U.S. government uses urban high schools to cajole disaffected urban youth to join the military but also has brought together city-wide anti-racist, anti-sexist youth and "allies with the LGBTQ community" to foster critical awareness of institutional oppression and promote social and economic justice in schools and in society (Ya-Ya network, 2012). If these public acts of resistance continue, we have the potential to remake schools and society according to the ideals of justice, equity, love, and freedom, rather than perpetuating the unjust power structures and values undergirding life in an age of corporate domination.

References

Abma, T.A., & Stake, R.E. (2001). Stake's responsive evaluation: Core ideas and evolution. In J.C. Greene & T.A. Abma (Eds.), *Responsive evaluation, new directions for evaluation* (pp. 7–21). San Francisco, CA: Jossey-Bass.

Advance Illinois. (n.d.). Retrieved from http://www.advanceillinois.org/

Benner, S. (2012). Flawed research leads to unsound recommendations. *Reviews by Others*. Retrieved May 7, 2012, from http://nepc.colorado.edu/files/Students%20teaching.pdf

Cochran-Smith, M. (2009). "Re-culturing" teacher education: Inquiry, evidence and action. *Journal of Teacher Education, 60*(5), 458–468.

Everitt, A. (1996). Developing critical evaluation. *Evaluation, 2*(2), 173–188.

Greene, J. (1997). Participatory evaluation. In L. Mabry (Ed.), *Evaluation and the postmodern dilemma: Advances in program evaluation* (Vol. 3, pp. 171–190). Greenwich, CT: JAI Press.

Greene, J. (2006). Evaluation, democracy, and social change. In I. Shaw, J. Greene, & M. Mark (Eds.), *The Sage handbook of evaluation* (pp. 118–140). Thousand Oaks, CA: Sage.

Hinchey, P.H., & Cadiero-Kaplan, K. (2005). The future of teacher education and teaching: Another piece of the privatization puzzle. *The Journal for Critical Educational Policy Studies, 3*(2). Retrieved from http://www.jceps.com/index.php?pageID=article&articleID=48

House, E.R., & Howe, K.R. (1999). *Values in evaluation and social research.* Thousand Oaks, CA: Sage.

Kincheloe, J.L. (2004). The bizarre, complex, and misunderstood world of teacher education. In J.L. Kincheloe, A. Burszty, S. Steinberg (Eds), *Teaching teachers: Building a quality school of urban education*. New York: Peter Lang.

Kushner, S. (2000). *Personalizing evaluation*. London: Sage.

Lukasai, J., & Schultz, B. (in press). Reflecting on insider/outsider critiques of teacher education, or "don't talk about my momma." In E. Daniels & B.J. Porfilio (Eds.), *Dangerous counterstories in the corporate academy*. Charlotte, NC: Information Age Publishing.

McLaren, P.L. (2003). Critical pedagogy: A look at the major concepts. In A. Darder, M. Baltodano, & R.D. Torres (Eds.), *The critical pedagogy reader* (pp. 69–96). New York: Routledge.

National Council on Teacher Quality. (n.d.). Retrieved from http://www.nctq.org/p/

National Council on Teacher Quality. (2010). *Ed school essentials: A review of Illinois teacher preparation*. Retrieved from http://www.nctq.org/edschoolreports/illinois/illinoisReport.jsp

Neas, R.G. (2003, November 18). Funding a movement: U.S. Department of Education pours millions into groups advocating school vouchers and education privatization. Retrieved from http://www.scribd.com/doc/36148707/EPRU-0311–49-OWI-1

Pellegrino, E.D. (1999). The ethical use of evidence to biomedicine. *Evaluation and the Health Professions, 22*(1), 439–446.

Porfilio, B.J., & Yu, T. (2006). "Student as consumer": A critical narrative of the commercialization of teacher education. *The Journal for Critical Educational Policy Studies, 4*(1). Retrieved from http://www.jceps.com/index.php?pageID=article&articleID=56

Sawchuk, S. (2011, January 26). NCTQ, *U.S. News* launch teacher education review. *Education Week, 30*(18), 4.

Schwandt, T. (2002). *Evaluation practice reconsidered*. New York: Peter Lang.

Schwandt, T. (2008). Educating for intelligent belief in evaluation. *American Journal of Evaluation, 29*(2) 139–150.

Schwandt, T. (2009). Toward a practical theory of evidence for evaluation. In S. Donaldson, C. Christi, & M. Mark (Eds.), *What counts as credible evidence in applied research and evaluation practice?* (pp. 197–212). Los Angeles: Sage.

Sleeter, C.M. (2008). Teaching for democracy in an age of corporatocracy. *Teachers College Record, 110*(1), 139–159.

Sue, T., & Fore, R. (2002). The national council on teacher quality: Expanding the teacher quality discussion. Retrieved from ERIC database, ED477730

Taubman, P.M. (2009). *Teaching by numbers: Deconstructing the discourse of standards and accountability in education*. New York: Routledge.

Thomas, P.L. (2011). Orwellian educational change under Obama: Crisis discourse, utopian expectations, and accountability failures. *Journal of Inquiry & Action in Education, 4*(1), 68–92.

Upshur, R.E.G. (2000). Seven characteristics of medical evidence. *Journal of Evaluation in Clinical Practice, 6*(2), 93–97.

Yaya network. (2012). Get ready to graduate. Retrieved from http://yayanetwork.org/GetReadytoGraduate

Note

1. For example, some of most ardent supporters of free-market reform in K–12 schools and in teacher education are members of the National Council on Teacher Quality Advisory Board, including Wendy Kopp, CEO and founder of Teach for America; Fredrick F. Hess, American Enterprise Institute; Michelle Fienberg, founder of the KIPP foundation; Eric A. Hanushek, senior fellow of The Hoover Institution; and Michelle Rhee, founder and CEO of Students First and former Chancellor of D.C. Public Schools.

7

Right-Thinking People:
Becoming a Teacher Educator in the Age of Austerity

JOHN L. HOBEN

How is it that life so often seems to get in the way of education? While positivistic and neoliberal models of education may denigrate learning rooted in everyday life, becoming a critical educator requires learning the situated, narrative, and historical nature of human knowledge. Yet as a beginning teacher-educator I often struggle to find my voice amid the rapidly intensifying demands of a neoliberal academy which marginalizes knowledge rooted in critical narratives of the local and the everyday (Apple & Buras, 2005; Aronowitz, 2000). In saying this, I am reminded how, writing over 30 years ago, the great psychoanalyst and critical theorist Erich Fromm (1976) cautioned us against forms of education that separated having from being, or that, more specifically, encouraged the former at the expense of the latter. For Fromm, "the character traits engendered by our socioeconomic system, by our way of living, are pathogenic and eventually produce a sick person, and thus, a sick society" (p. 7). The extent of this sickness is a profound and often unacknowledged part of our social condition (Durkheim, 2006), as, within the modern world, abjection and anomie become closely allied to a lost sense of self and place, "the older melancholy of the poor, the expropriated, the oppressed and the abjected" (Gilroy, 2005, p. 91).

In contrast, by writing one's self into history and place, narrative can help us to create new forms of critical consciousness that at once challenge and redefine neoliberal and positivistic forms of "right thinking." In the part of Canada where

I live and teach, Newfoundland, "the general tendency of many young people to leave, especially those with post-secondary education, combined with declining birth rates and the devastating effects of the collapse of the groundfish fisheries, with no recovery in sight, has depopulated many rural areas of almost their entire younger generations" (Royal Commission Report, 2003, p. 39). As a new form of colonialism, globalism creates profound social disorganization and isolation that leads to the individual becoming "an outsider within a social system . . . [where] the outcomes of egoism and anomie . . . carry with them the predicament of lone-liness and a profound break with humanity" (Travis, 1990, p. 226). In similar fash-ion, a curriculum which imposes meta-narratives of progress and competitive individualism helps to perpetuate modernism's self-destructive attachments (Durkheim, 2006; Pope, 1975; Travis, 1990). In contrast, the therapeutic and com-memorative aspects of critical narrative, by building shared meaning and bridging connections between individuals and communities, help us to open new "horizons of possibility" (Simon, 1992) and thereby to counter deep, destructive feelings of despair, which is the destructive legacy of contemporary commodity capitalism.

Becoming a teacher for me is about finding one's voice, about acknowledging vulnerability and pain, but coming to see such a confession as an opportunity for broadening critical consciousness and coming to terms with the historical and inter-pretative nature of personal identity and community. In a world where blind obe-dience to capitalism is a form of suicide, critical narratives of place and self allow us to create "geographical mythologies that mark the new paths of destiny . . . move-ments [which] often cause terrible suffering, but there is also in them a desire of liberation that is not satiated except by re-appropriating new spaces, around which are constructed new freedoms" (Hardt & Negri, 2001, p. 397). Rather than edu-cating for hierarchy and capital, I contend that resuscitating a pedagogy of hope requires a form of teaching and learning premised on the simple idea that teach-ers "affect the lives of students not just in what we teach them by way of subject matter but in how we relate to them as persons" (Noddings, 2003, p. 249). How, I ask, can we as educators and teacher-educators, examine the strategies and tac-tics of a politics of austerity capital by mapping the way academic education forms—and is continually informed by—the currents of the past and the practices of daily life?

Empire and Small Towns: Global Capital on the Margins

One response to oppression and injustice is storytelling, our way of insisting that we are not disposable, but that our lives have meaning (Giroux, 2009). My story begins in Newfoundland and Labrador, Canada, a place known on a somewhat superficial level as the setting for films such as *The Shipping News* (2001), or the site of the sinking of the *Andrea Gail* in the Hollywood blockbuster *The Perfect Storm* (2000). Newfoundland and Labrador is a region of great natural beauty and vibrant rural communities, a part of the world where tensions between past and future are remarkably evident as words and phrases such as "sustainability" and "ecological responsibility" become a part of the fabric of everyday culture. But Newfoundland and Labrador, like much of Atlantic Canada, is also a region where large oil and gas and mining resources attract investment from global multinational corporations, and traditional ways of life are threatened by the collapse of fishing stocks in large part due to the failure to responsibly regulate industrial fishing techniques.

In the wake of this collapse, education in Atlantic Canada has been through a period of unprecedented change. Standardized testing, and a centralized curriculum top-heavy with learning objectives emphasizing positivistic knowledge, reflects the inroads of global capital and the growing influence of international oil and gas conglomerates. In a 2006 report, the Atlantic Canada-based peer review team for the Organization for Economic Co-operation and Development's Directorate for Education examined the contributions of post-secondary educational institutions to regional development. While democratic education was not given much emphasis, the report did note "difficulties of attaining a level of human capital needed to make the region globally competitive . . . [with] both supply and demand side issues at work" (Locke, Garlick, Beale, & Greenwood, 2006, p. 65). Indeed, according to the authors, answers to many of the challenges facing the region can be found in increasing the rigor of public and higher education, a concept defined in relation to the amount of consolidation, measurement, and standardization exhibited by educational institutions (Locke et al., 2006, p. 64).

Although it is understandable that building wealth to create prosperous and viable communities would be a focus in a region which has a long history of poverty and outmigration, healthy communities also require a sense of the importance of a critical citizenry aware of the need for robust democratic values. In our search for sustainability, educators must resist—both individually and collectively—the temptation to allow the subordination of social justice to corporate capital. Thus, instead of seeing education as a means of building democratic communities, "[t]he relation of ownership, having become for more and more men the critically important relation determining their actual freedom and actual prospect of realizing their full potentialities, [is] read back into the nature of the individual" (Macpherson, 2011, p. 3). The word "democracy" does not occur once in the entire report, underscoring the growing loss of the traditional association of higher education and the humanities, which identifies learning as a necessary public good (Nussbaum, 2010). While the report does briefly discuss the importance of preserving the heritage of local communities, "hyperspecialization" (Macedo, 2006, p. 19) and technical skills training supersede the demands of locality, public memory, and commemorative space.

No longer the vehicle of a shared public good, schooling in the age of austerity has neglected the core values of social justice and democracy by creating the hierarchical, centralized educational system demanded by free market radicals (Giroux, 2009; Kelly, 2009). This is a dehumanizing educational system that has failed to maintain the priority of human relationships and voices over a kind of instrumental rationality that aims to minimize any opportunity for individual autonomy and social praxis (Simon, 1992; Tite, 2008). Living in the shadow of the state of exception (Agamben, 2005), teachers and teacher educators alike appeared to be positioned somewhere between two poles: what Fraser (1989) calls "leading publics capable of setting the terms of political debate . . . [and] enslaved publics [which] must oscillate between marginalization and co-optation" (p. 301).

Although organizations such as the Atlantic Institute for Market Studies may applaud the demand for more efficient and rigorous forms of skills-based learning, the single-minded quest for such market and standards-driven policies also obscures a more disconcerting absence of any distinct conception of education as a democratic public good. While the report's authors may be well meaning, in the absence of any expression of countervailing values, such free-market-based policies can become both exclusive and debilitating. In many ways it must be seen as part of a larger trend whereby "the modern period is increasingly dominated by instrumentally orientated market and bureaucratic practices that treat wealth and efficiency as goals that properly dominate all other concerns" (Baker, 1989, p. 95). Such an educational vision must be understood in relation to the social changes brought about by globalization, which create the sense of placelessness so essential to capital's need to create standing reserves of cheap mobile labor. A commentary on the Institute's website on AIMS submissions to the Standing Committee on International Trade (CITT) of the House of Commons demonstrates a similar propensity to place free market principles over democratic values and social justice, regarding a proposed free trade agreement between Canada and the European Union (McIver, 2011).

Despite the commentary's use of seemingly innocuous terms such as "facilitating labour mobility," "dismantling supply management," and "revising our government procurement practices," critical teachers and learners must continue to challenge the way in which trade and technical forms of education increasingly seem to be branded—and sold—in tandem. As an influential Provincial report commented nearly a decade ago, "there is a growing appreciation that, with higher levels of education, come greater employment opportunities and income levels" (Royal Commission Report, 2003, p. 132). But what types of education and to whose benefit? Unfortunately, the AIMS submission to the Standing Committee says little about the massive disruption caused to rural communities by the closure of fish-processing plants, often the only source of income accessible to local communities. It also neglects to highlight the growing amount of natural resources which are processed in huge factory freezer trawlers offshore or fish which is caught and shipped out of the region to be processed overseas. This occurs despite the role played by overfishing and a shortsighted emphasis on the economic bottom line resulting from the collapse of the northern ground fish stocks—an ecological catastrophe to a decimated resource which has not yet recovered despite a 20-year fishing ban.

In a sense, this neoliberal educational vision is a form of romance in which all deprivation and hardship eventually work out for the best. Although educational plans and strategic reports tend to relate globalization in abstract terms, its destructive effects are most readily seen on the personal level. What the neoliberal stance on education fails to convey is the importance of critical narratives of self and place as ways of responding to the precariousness of lives lived on the margins of global capital. In my own case, such market ideals are always encountered in relation to a sense of place and self which is rooted in personal history, more specifically in my memories of the traditional way of life lived by my grandparents and their generation.

Autobiography, Romance, and Suicide

"Autobiography," claims Janet Miller (2005), "whether in the form of teachers stories or teachers' and researchers' examinations of the filters through which we perceive our work, must move through and beyond traditional framings of educational situations and issues in order to 'take us somewhere we otherwise couldn't get to' (Behar, 1996, p. 14)" (p. 54). My maternal grandfather was a lighthouse keeper. Although he died before I was born, I listened in earnest to the stories my grandmother told me about shipwrecks, sailors adrift on wreckage, fierce winter storms, and bodies being salted and kept over winter for proper burial. In the early years of the past century, he worked on the northeastern coast of Newfoundland on a small rocky island, near the area's summer fishing grounds and directly in the path of schooner traffic up and down the shore. The second part of this romance was his love of books, often the schoolbooks of my two uncles whose mother had died when they were young boys and who had been taken in by my maternal grandmother.

Another prominent part of my family history was my grandmother's indomitable spirit. She was the one who, every evening, lit the warning light at the end of the point; she was as strong and as big as my grandfather and never shied away from manual labour. I knew her as a storyteller and a woman who loved life. Surviving a radical hysterectomy in her thirties due to ovarian cancer, my grandmother raised two of my father's brothers who were ten and six when their own mother died. She regaled us with stories of mischief and wonder: of how while a servant she once attended church in the finest clothes of the lady of the house (a doctor's wife), of getting her father's Sunday clothes (and a white rabbit they had caught) full of soot while a girl, and surviving a fall through the harbor ice during a late night crossing, coming home from church. She labored in the woods with axe and bucksaw and later traveled all across North America with one of the surrogate sons she had taken in and raised.

What my grandmother did not tell me, and what I did suture together, were the ways in which their lives were vulnerable and marginalized. Living through the Depression in a merchant economy where provisions and fishing supplies were obtained from one of few storeowners in the area, work was often hard, and circumstances left little for conspicuous consumption. Schooling in such a context was often seen as superfluous, since the fishery did not require literacy skills but merely a strong back and a willingness to resign oneself to a life of hardship with few material comforts. Education, for those lucky few who could afford it, often meant leaving the community—a pattern which continues to this day (Corbett, 2007; Kelly, 2009). Many of the women in the communities married young or obtained work as domestic servants. This was the fate of my grandmother's sister, Alva, a beautiful girl who settled in St John's as a servant for a relatively well off-family. Although my grandmother pleaded with her mother not to let her sister go (she herself had been a domestic), she was nonetheless sent away and, as fate would have it, was found dead several months later from an apparent suicide. Strangely enough, my grandmother insisted that her sister had in fact been murdered, perhaps to cover up a rape or unwanted pregnancy.

Although the social forms that confronted my great aunt and my grandmother were both structural and cultural, they were also learned. Most young women, my grandmother included, received very little formal education past their early teenage years. Learning was instrumental, and the only political content of the curriculum was related to Newfoundland's status as a colony of the British Empire. Later, when confederation came, allegiances shifted to the new union with Canada, though illiteracy rates remained high. Education was, however, related to a Province-wide push for industrialization in the 1960s. In large part this was related to a drive for modernization and the resettlement of innumerable fishing villages perched precariously along the island's rocky coastline. That education was organized and financed by churches meant that small communities often had three or four schools, each belonging to a separate Christian denomination. This meant work for my father and my mother, who were both teachers. My parents married and lived in the garden above the house where my mother had been raised, living in the small fishing community all of their lives.

I left my community at the time of a Province-wide shutdown of a 500-year-old ground fish fishery, a catastrophe that was of profound economic, ecological, and cultural scope. Education, then, became synonymous with leaving personal attachments and breaking ties with local, rural cultures (Corbett, 2007; Kelly, 2009) in search of upwardly mobile cultural capital and *right-thinking* ways of being and doing. After completing two undergraduate degrees in the Province's only university, I returned to my hometown to teach, only to find little work. I soon enrolled in law school in central Canada, a conservative, elite setting in which I began to feel isolated and disconnected. After 5 years outside of the Province, I decided to return home to pursue graduate studies in education, and later a doctorate on the issue of teacher censorship. In this setting, I started to reflect on my past and to begin to see my home community as more than a dysfunctional casualty of progress or as lacking in those qualities which were deemed to be essential by a corporate-authoritarian educational system. In short, I began to feel as though I was part of a story that mattered even as I realized that I could not escape the "touch of the past" (Simon, 2006) that conditioned both the historical reality I inhabited and the new personal identity that I gradually created by reimagining my own existence.

The "colony," says Gilroy (2005), "can once again be identified as a special kind of place which [demonstrates a] necessary reliance on divisions within humankind" (p. 49). Many of my friends and relatives have left the Province, never to return. Indeed, leaving is a home for us in many ways. These include a childhood friend who left home to fight in Afghanistan, a sister who works seasonally in central Canada so she can live her winters at home, countless friends and neighbors who are migratory workers in the construction or oil and gas industries and live in low-income areas or even in recreational campsites, and a cousin who moved from St. John's to British Columbia with an MBA, only to take his own life in his early forties. All of them, I realize, feel caught by economic necessity but so desperately want to return home; contrary to the dominant narratives of globalization and corporate capital, for them the stubborn attachments to place degraded by formal education and economics alike could be seen as worthwhile and meaningful. What I forgot, however, were the subtle ways in which resistance surfaces. Indeed, "given discourses suggesting [rural people] are lazy and draining government coffers, and a political climate that supports withdrawing support from rural communities at a time when [they are also threatened by] environmental degradation . . . the very fact that they still live and work in their communities is an indicator of resistance" (MacDonald, Neis, & Grzetic, 2006, p. 207).

Suicide and Agency: Writing as Loss

In becoming a teacher I have come to see teaching as being about agency, about finding hope and solace in the ever-present possibility of imaginative transformation. As a central part of this process, writing can be a way of defining what right thinking means for one's self, rather than having it imposed by corporate capital or an authoritarian education system. Rather than seeing loss as escapable, critical teaching and learning views loss as a learning experience and an opportunity for social praxis (Kelly, 2009). Indeed, all writing, because it is a form of commitment, entails loss—loss of the account that, because another has been spoken, remains unsaid. But this act of commitment is a form of being that is rooted in agency instead of having (Fromm,1976) as we "remain hopeful, [and] demand that we see the present as incomplete, and, thus, open to the challenge of what is not yet present" (Simon, 2006, p. 111). In contrast, the type of writing and learning emphasized by neoliberal educational organizations emphasizes the importance of the individual's ability to adapt to a society which simply "consists of relations of exchange between proprietors" (Macpherson, 2011, p. 3). Here, learning becomes "instrumentalist," as educational reformers emphasize "the mechanical learning of reading skills while sacrificing the critical analysis of the social and political order that generates the need for reading in the first place" (Macedo, 2006, p. 17).

Yet in many of modernism's marginal spaces, quite often the changes individuals face seem so radical that they find themselves confronting "loneliness as a way of life" (Dumm, 2008) or what Felman (2002) once termed "the abyss of trauma" (p. 90). Indeed, my mother once told me that my grandmother would sit up at night by herself with a lantern just after her sister died, waiting for her to tell her who took her life. I remember hearing how my grandmother begged her mother not to send Alva into the city instead of letting her come live with her. What secret knowledge led her to such fears, I wondered. Was it her own experience as a domestic or her knowledge of the disdain for "bay people" held by those who lived in the capital city? This idea of keeping watch—of being watchful even when one is not able to intervene—led me to try to express this feeling of dread in a poem about my great aunt. Strangely enough, this was a piece that I first shared in a class on autobiographical teaching and learning, a class I would later teach:

Pendulum

My grandmother said you
were beautiful
and your voice was like
the sound of the first birds of spring
and your long black tresses
fell like the shadow of the moon
on the face of the unmoving sea.

You left your young love
for the city of crowded storefronts
and muddy streets,
a servant girl from Carmanville,
far from your home in the little cove,
where rocky cliffs and rolling
meadows leapfrogged
in the face of the blue
and boundless deep.

But in the end they say
this was the way the thing went:
frantic whispers as creaking steps
approached the wooden door;
his hand across your open mouth
and the long descent
into perfect blackness
you and the child dangling above
the feet you saw so firmly planted
upon the attic floor.

Although "the relationship between history and trauma is speechless" (Felman, 2002, p. 33), it is not inaccessible, beyond imagination or feeling. While I am unsure whether this was an act of agency or of victimization, I do believe that in some way both schooling and the law failed my great aunt—the former, perhaps, by leaving her without a literacy of resistance-in-place, the other by failing to provide her with any semblance of justice or equality. Yet I remain hopeful that writing can honor her memory by conveying some sense of the pain and displacement she once felt. "While narrated memories are a sign of civic life," says Roger Simon (2006), "the motivated, authorized character of that civitas is very much an issue of how such memories might construct the substance and terms of one's connection to those who have gone before us" (p. 133). This is an act that, like the social condition itself, suggests no easy answers and is complicated by our own stakes in different interpretative stances. In many ways it reminds me of the importance of learning to "name the constant need to catch up with the hidden reality of history that always remains a debt to the oppressed, a debt to the dead of history, a claim that the past has on the present" (Felman, 2002, p. 32).

As Richard Kearney (2002) claims, "it is this curious conflation of empathy and detachment which produces in us. . .the double vision necessary for a journey beyond the closed ego towards other possibilities of being" (p. 13). Similarly, I see the imaginative capacity as a means of accessing "desiring production" (Deleuze & Guattari, 1987)—of my own desire to understand the radical isolation of subalternity and the freedom that takes this historical event as its point of departure. "Spectating permits a gaping distance between self and other," maintains Boler (1999, p. 184). "Who," she asks, "is permitted the luxury of spectating; and what is the cost to others when we choose the comfortable safety of distance?" (p. 184). This poem is very dark. I am not sure what is true or what is hinted at in either my representation or the event as it is constructed in my own family history. Perhaps, given the event's enigmatic nature, I am expressing in some way "the fear . . . that unnatural silences will envelop me, either lulling me into comforting quiet of supposed completeness or muffling the sound of my questions" (Miller, 2005, p. 62).

While we can never recover lost time, in commemorative narrative "selves evolve in the time frame of a single telling as well as in the course of the many tellings that eventually compose a life" (Ochs & Capps, 1996, p. 23). Although it is impossible for the teacher to exist independently of place, community, and history, neoliberal ideals in education as well as in broader society make the assumption that "right-thinking people" (Herman & Chomsky, 1988, p. xii) prioritize market principles over all other aspects of life and all other public goods which can be found in human communities. As Thomas Dumm (2008) points out, "in our culture—a civilization of consumers if ever there has been one—the lonely self seeks to possess something to call its own, and ends up confusing that something with itself" (p. 53).

Creating critical counter-narratives that change, alter, or challenge public memory is one way of educating for social justice (Yeoman, 2004). In similar fashion, displacement and this calling into question of cultural and personal identities are part of the process of unlearning so necessary to critical transformation (Kumashiro, 2000). What Jean Francois Lyotard (1984) calls the "little narratives" of everyday life are important junctures in which we can see the tensions and contradictions of the grand narratives of globalism and colonialism that deny the importance of local community and personal identity. Colonialism, patriarchy, and a merchant economy required that many young rural women move to a city which was a site of monetary security and upward social mobility and placed them in situations in which they were vulnerable and often exploited. Within contemporary society we risk having this pattern reproduced as rural economies are threatened by outmigration, the death of conventional resource-driven economies, and the demise of local forms of knowledge.

"Body and community," says Bauman (2000), "are the last defensive outposts on the increasingly deserted battlefield on which the way for certainty, security and safety is waged daily with little, if any, respite" (p. 184). Counteracting our tendency for self-violence (that is, leaving the body and leaving the community) requires educating for critical citizenship and reminds us of the need to cultivate a sense of the dangers of empire. As poet Anne Compton (2005) wonders: "Why do the good words build houses/in air? . . . Why is back the most beautiful direction?" (p. 28). Perhaps it is because memory is a type of shared public space, one where imagination and desire are not ruled by the strict boundaries of logic and practicality but become emblematic of the need to rediscover compassion as the forgotten sixth sense. In memory at least we can recall our power to make an end to suffering, to make longing a type of reprieve that at least hints at the possibility of deliverance.

Barbarians at the Schoolhouse Gates

In *Waiting for the Barbarians* (1982), Coetzee's protagonist, a magistrate who is working on the outer regions of the Empire, is complicit in a system that brutalizes and denigrates the barbarians who live beyond its borders. The magistrate has little empathy toward these outsiders until, out of pity, he decides to hide a fugitive barbarian girl in his home. This transgression pits the law against empathy and his own desire: it makes him, as an insider, identify with the outside and thereby lose his status as an agent of the Empire's law. From its citizens the Empire simply requires obedience to law as a minimum basis of its sovereign power. But on its margins it is violent, ruthless, and without any semblance of human compassion—a lesson the magistrate learns as he is subsequently tortured for the unfounded suspicion that he has knowledge about an impending barbarian invasion. Of course, the real knowledge that the magistrate holds is the knowledge that civilization founded upon law alone is merely a pretence, or that the boundary between legal reason and feeling, like the boundary between self and other, cannot be so easily drawn. This is the threat that violence needs to neutralize by obtaining a confession from the magistrate, a confession that he is complicit with the Other and hence can be safely branded and exiled as a traitor. This confusion of categories, then, is the real threat to the Empire's own internal order. Poignantly, perhaps, it is a confession that never comes.

As Coetzee's novel suggests, the struggle to reconstruct social forms is intimately connected with the struggle to radically redefine and recreate one's own way of life—a lesson that is also intimately connected to the struggle to become a transformative teacher in the modern world. In contrast, positivism and neoliberalism insist that agency resides in the ability to transform oneself to meet the demands of market forces. Against this crisis logic that provides much of the persuasive force of austerity capital, schooling needs to take up the search for new forms of social relationships as a means of conceptualizing living otherwise. Such disruptive daydreaming recognizes the dangers of exploitative servitude and a form of necessity that is dangerous—or as in my great aunt's case—catastrophic. As part of this process, it is by recognizing the inevitability of loss as necessitating both commemoration and social agency that both individual narrative and critical teaching and learning find their place in a praxis of the present (Kelly, 2009).

Right-thinking people are not those who place technical and positivistic knowledge in the service of market ideologies ahead of the search for social justice and democratic ideals. "The specialist," says Ortega y Gasset, "knows very well his own tiny corner of the universe; he is radically ignorant of all the rest" (cited in Macedo, 2006, p. 19). Yet it is this very model of technical specialization that free market ideology privileges over and above any educational vision which links identity, ecology, and sustainability to narrative and place. Indeed, learning to find solace and solidarity in the local is central to an understanding of how identity and public memory shape democratic possibility. Democracy is, in large part, about learning to claim and connect public space in a world where there seems to be little reprieve from the demands of global capital, which insinuates itself into all aspects of daily life.

Teaching is not simply about appropriating knowledge or making oneself a marketable commodity. As Milan Kundera argues, "the struggle of [wo]man against power is the struggle of memory against forgetting" (cited in Ochs & Capps,

1996, p. 21). This insistence upon the importance of reclaiming the past, coupled with a need to make the familiar strange, lies at the heart of democratic teaching and praxis. But this is a difficult process that requires a hopeful patience as well as a willingness to destroy old selves. Indeed, according to Megan Boler (1999), "Witnessing . . . cannot capture meaning as conclusion . . . rather than falling into easy identification, as a witness we undertake our historical responsibilities" (p. 186). Standing in the place of others, while a difficult and sometimes impossible process, teaches us to explore the relationship between freedom and social responsibility by linking the search for social justice to imaginative speech and critical interpretative acts.

Teaching for me, then, is the art of making poetry out of tragedy and the past's mute suffering. It is about creating meaning and beauty in an often harsh and unforgiving world (Doyle & Hoben, 2011). In many respects the dark forces that confronted my great aunt and my grandmother—the hidden exiles of sexual exploitation, poverty, and diaspora—are still at work in present-day society (Mehta & Singh, 2008). Moments of critical realization are a part of the construction of identity that lies at the heart of the struggle to create more hopeful and meaningful lives. Working through loss requires re-appropriating memory from oppression and writing oneself into history even in the presence of uncertainty and self-doubt. In some sense, my poem represents the tragic nature of those secrets we keep from ourselves about our own complicity and the true measure of human suffering. Yet I also remember that despite the hardships she had suffered, my grandmother never lost her sense of compassion. For the rest of her life, she went out of her way to give love to those who most needed it, as she did for my two uncles who lost their own mother at an early age. This idea of surrogacy and of moving forward in some ways is at least a partial anecdote for the harshness of the world and the inability of our education system to address such forms of human failing and such terrible, sometimes overwhelming forms of loss. Quite simply, as a teacher, sometimes you just have to sit at the window and watch. Hope is like that: she sails in all weather, always making time against unforgiving winds and tides.

References

Agamben, G. (2005). *State of exception.* Chicago: University of Chicago Press.

Apple, M.W., & Buras, K.L. (2005). *The subaltern speak: Curriculum, power, and educational struggles.* New York: Routledge.

Aronowitz, S. (2000). *The knowledge factory.* Boston: Beacon Press.

Baker, C.E. (1989). *Human liberty and freedom of speech.* New York: Oxford University Press.

Baker, J. A., Terry, T., Bridger, R., & Winsor, A. (1997). Schools as caring communities: A relational approach to school reform. *School Psychology Review,* 26(4), 586–602.

Bauman, Z. (2000). *Liquid modernity.* Cambridge, UK: Polity Press.

Boler, M. (1999). *Feeling power.* New York: Routledge.

Coetzee, J.M. (1982). *Waiting for the barbarians.* Harmondsworth: Penguin Books.

Compton, A. (2005). *Processional.* Markham: Fitzhenry and Whiteside.

Corbett, M.J. (2007). *Learning to leave: The irony of schooling in a coastal community.* Halifax: Fernwood Pub.

Deleuze, G., & Guattari, F. (1987). *A thousand plateaus: Capitalism and schizophrenia.* Minneapolis: University of Minnesota Press.

Doyle, C., & Hoben, J. (2011). No room for wonder. In J. Kincheloe & R. Hewitt (Eds.), *Whatever happened to soul? A manifesto of revival* (pp. 115–127). New York: Peter Lang.

Dumm, T. (2008). *Loneliness as a way of life.* Cambridge: Harvard University Press.

Durkheim, E. (2006). *Suicide: A study in sociology.* London: Penguin.

Felman, S. (2002). *The juridical unconscious.* Cambridge: Harvard University Press.

Fraser, N. (1989). Talking about needs: Interpretive contests as political conflicts in welfare-state societies. *Ethics,* 99(2), 291–313.

Fromm, E. (1976). *To have or to be?* New York: Harper & Row.

Gilroy, P. (2005). *Postcolonial melancholia.* New York: Columbia University Press.

Giroux, H. A. (2009). *Youth in a suspect society.* New York: Palgrave Macmillan.

Hardt, M., & Negri, A. (2001). *Empire.* Cambridge, MA: Harvard University Press.

Herman, E.S., & Chomsky, N. (1988). *Manufacturing consent.* New York: Pantheon.

Kearney, R. (2002). *On stories.* London: Routledge.

Kelly, U. (2009). *Migration and education in a multicultural world: Culture, loss, and identity.* New York: Palgrave Macmillan.

Kristeva, J. (1987). *Black sun: Depression and melancholy.* New York: Columbia University Press.

Kumashiro, K.K. (2000). Teaching and learning through desire, crisis, and difference. *Radical Teacher,* 58, 6–11.

Locke, W., Garlick, S., Beale, E.J., & Greenwood, R. (2006). *Supporting the contribution of higher education institutions to regional development: Peer review report.* OECD, Directorate for Education, Programme on Institutional Management in Higher Education. Retrieved from http://www.oecd.org/dataoecd/35/59/38455547.pdf

Lyotard, J.F. (1984). *The postmodern condition.* Minneapolis: University of Minnesota Press.

MacDonald, M., Neis, B., & Grzetic, B. (2006). Making a living: The struggle to stay. In P.R. Sinclair & R.E. Ommer (Eds.), *Power and restructuring* (pp. 187–209). St. John's: ISER Books.

Macedo, D. (2006). *Literacies of power.* Boulder: Westview Press.

Macpherson, C.B. (2011). *The political theory of possessive individualism: Hobbes to Locke.* Oxford: Oxford University Press.

McIver, D. (2011, December 1). AIMS submission to the House of Commons respecting CETA negotiations on a Canada-European Union trade agreement. Retrieved from http://www.aims.ca/en/home/library/details.aspx/3266

Mehta, K., & Singh, A. (Eds.). (2008). *Indian diaspora: Voices of the diasporic elders in five countries.* Rotterdam: Sense Publishers.

Miller, J. (2005). *Sounds of silence breaking: Women, autobiography and curriculum.* New York: Peter Lang.

Noddings, N. (2003). Is teaching a practice? *The Journal of the Philosophy of Education Society of Great Britain, 37*(2), 241–251.

Nussbaum, M.C. (2010). *Not for profit.* Princeton, NJ: Princeton University Press.

Ochs, E., & Capps, L.L. (1996). Narrating the self. *Annual Review of Anthropology, 25,* 19–43.

Pope, W. (1975). Concepts and explanatory structure in Durkheim's theory of suicide. *The British Journal of Sociology, 26*(4), 417–434.

Royal Commission on Renewing and Strengthening Our Place in Canada (2003). *Our place in Canada: Main report.* St. John's: The Royal Commission. Retrieved from: http://www.exec.gov.nl.ca/royalcomm/finalreport/ default.html

Simon, R.I. (1992). *Teaching against the grain.* New York: Bergin & Garvey.

Simon, R.I. (2006). *The touch of the past.* New York: Palgrave Macmillan.

Spivak, G.C. (1988). Can the subaltern speak? In C. Nelson & L. Grossberg (Eds.), *Marxism and the interpretation of culture* (pp. 271–313). Chicago: University of Illinois Press.

Tite, R. (2008). All stars and discards: Schooling and the rest of our lives. In M. Gardner & U. Kelly (Eds.), *Narrating transformative learning in education* (pp. 75–95). New York: Palgrave Macmillan.

Travis, R. (1990). Halbwachs and Durkheim: A test of two theories of suicide. *British Journal of Sociology, 41*(2), 225–243.

Yeoman, E. (2004). Je me souviens: About the St. Armand slave cemetery, memory, counter-memory and historic trauma. *Topia, 12,* 9–24.

8

Neoliberalism and Teacher Preparation:
Systematic Barriers to Critical Democratic Education

JOHN M. ELMORE

In the last quarter century, many critical pedagogues have pinned much of their hope for grass-roots reform in our nation's schools on teacher education programs that are committed to fostering the development of teacher-intellectuals who will appreciate and carry forward an agenda of social justice via libratory education in their respective classrooms (Apple, 1993; Giroux, 1988; McLaren, 2006; Zeichner, 2006). Certainly a fundamental inspiration for this cause can be found in the work of the late Paulo Freire (1970), who made clear the critical role that teachers play in true libratory education, pointing out that we can educate and liberate or we can mis-educate and oppress. However, true education, Freire contended, must always lead to liberation. Greatly influenced by the work of Freire, Henry Giroux (2003) has focused much of his writing on the somewhat obvious (yet mostly ignored) connection between the enlightened teacher-intellectual, or what he termed the "transformative intellectual," and the institutional programs that inspire and empower such "agents of hope" (McLaren, 2006). Even a casual inspection of the multi-faceted circumstances now surrounding teacher preparation programs and the brand of teacher they are currently seeking to generate, raises many concerns in regard to the potential for critical-democratic education in the United States. In short, as American education continues to be moved in a direction characterized by neoliberal terms such as "standardization," "productivity," "accountability," and the popular yet elusive term "excellence," *teacher education* programs have generally capitulated to the pressure of power and transformed themselves into *teacher training* programs.

To be clear, this is not a mere matter of semantics; *to train* is very different than *to educate.* Not only do such efforts change the nature of teacher preparation, they also fundamentally change the outcomes, fostering the development of teachers who willingly embrace their submissive roles as mere voice boxes for self-defined philosopher kings, such as state boards of education, and the imperialistic agenda set forth in No Child Left Behind and, more recently, Race to the Top. Put directly, the typical purpose of the contemporary teacher *training* program is the development of teachers who can seamlessly and efficiently adapt to the current circumstances of American schooling—learning to cope with, but not challenge, all of its well-documented inequality and anti-democratic practices. Sadly, the realization of educating and inspiring "transformative intellectuals," "agents of hope," and "integrated citizens" via true critical democratic teacher education has never been further from grasp.

Upon investigation into the roots of this transformation, three elements seem worthy of deeper inspection: (1) the nature of neoliberalism and its assault on democratic education, (2) the proletarianization of teachers and teacher work, and (3) the co-opting and capitulation of teacher education programs and teacher preparation faculty. All three of these elements are intertwined and play separate but powerful roles in a process that can only be described as a movement away from the principles of social democracy and preparation for participation in public time and toward a culture conducive only to authoritarianism and privatization, the central tenets of neoliberalism.

A Brief Introduction to the Logic of Neoliberalism and Its Educational Agenda

Neoliberalism is a socio-political perspective that is defined solely within the logic of capital and offers as key evidence for its claims the leaps in human progress that have been fueled by individual desire for profit and power, leading inexplicably to what Adam Smith (1776/1937) termed the "vile maxim." David Harvey (2005) describes it well:

> Neoliberalism is in the first instance a theory of political economic practices that proposes that human well-being can best be advanced by liberating individual entrepreneurial freedoms and skills within an institutional framework character-

ized by strong property rights, free markets, and free trade . . . there has every-where been an emphatic turn towards neoliberalism in political-economic prac-tices and thinking since the 1970s. (pp. 18–19)

Arguing that an unfettered freemarket is the best, if not only, path to progress, equality and a merit-based version of social justice, public institutions are viewed through the lens of neoliberalism as, at best, social distractions and, at worst, anti-quated seeds of Bolshevism. For the advocate of neoliberalism, anything that oper-ates outside the free-market model, whether a public school, a library, or a post office, is actually counterproductive to human progress. Robertson (2007) argues that the mobilisation of neo-liberal ideas for reorganising societies and social rela-tions, including the key institutions involved in social reproduction, is a class pro-ject with three key aims: the (i) redistribution of wealth upward to the ruling elites through new structures of governance; (ii) transformation of education systems so that the production of workers for the economy is the primary mandate; and (iii) breaking down of education as a public sector monopoly, opening it up to strate-gic investment by for-profit firms. To be realised, all three aims must break down the institutionalised interests of teachers, teacher unions, and factions of civil soci-ety who have supported the idea of education as a public good and public sector, and as an intrinsic element of the state-civil society social contract. (p. 2)

The neoliberal agenda, therefore, defines all things public as bloated, ineffec-tive, and wasteful; privatization is offered as the only path to efficiency, effective-ness, and fairness. All things public, therefore, must be privatized, and profit must become the motivating factor driving not only citizens but all societal institutions. This is the "capitalization of social life"—the changing of all social activities into commodity status with some market value (Rikowski, 2002). Of course, the impact of capitalism on social life was also aptly described by Marx and Engels (1906); "It has resolved personal worth into exchange value, and in place of the numberless indefensible chartered freedoms, has set up that single unconscionable freedom—Free Trade" (p. 44).

Of particular interest here in the United States is the compatibility of neolib-eralism and participatory democracy. As citizens are trained to embrace a neolib-eral view of society, the need for a collective democratic voice is diminished as citizens come to define themselves along neoliberal lines—solely as customers and consumers. The result of such training can even bring citizens to the point of view-ing both themselves and their fellow citizens as "products" to be sold on a market, judging the quality of all social institutions solely in terms of their prospective mar-ket value. Rikowski (2002) describes it well:

. . . it is value (not *values*) that becomes crucial. Old traditional modes of working, professional values, notions of public service and putting community needs before the drive for profit—all become liabilities for capital accumulation as educational institutions shift from becoming public goods to private commodities. Community needs are placed within the context of the *market* and profit making potential. They are reconfigured. (p. 117)

Citizens do retain a voice within neoliberalism, but only as that of a consumer; the only vote cast is by purchasing a particular product versus its competitor. Predictably, any sense of a collective voice or drive to advance a common good is seen as misguided; it is suggested that the natural selection of the free market will separate the billionaire from the defective individual living under a bridge. To tinker with that process through social welfare programs, argues the neoliberal, is to upset the natural balance of the free market. The result is a system of pure Social Darwinism in which any collective social responsibility to care for the less capable or less fortunate among us is deemed a waste of time and resources—Smith's "vile maxim." For a participatory democracy, such a retreat from all things public means, in effect, a retreat from democracy itself. As traditional schooling has been systematically reconstituted over the past quarter century to centralize these goals of capital accumulation, consumerism, and work-force preparation (what Neil Postman [1995] referred to as the "gods of economic utility and consumerism" [p. 12]), we have seen a steady increase in the rate of de-politicization among citizens, especially among young people.

The specific role of education from the neoliberal perspective is to privatize the mind, to move the citizen away from any sense of collective social responsibility that was celebrated by previous generations and toward an epistemology that blindly embraces the logic of capital and the vile maxim. From the neoliberal perspective, this is argued as being for the good of the individual student, that is to say, accommodating students to the current social and economic reality of the United States *should* be the sole purpose of education. To do anything other than this is to "cheat" poor students out of their chance to live the American Dream. Put more directly, students are to be trained to accept the current conditions as being "as good as it gets" and focus their attention to absorbing the dominant culture at a level that will allow them not to rid our society of homelessness but to avoid being homeless themselves. Hursh (2001) describes the impact of neoliberalism on education well:

The neo-liberal state, through the use of standards, assessments, and accountability, aims to restrict educators to particular kinds of thinking, thinking that conceptualizes education in terms of producing individuals who are economically productive. Education is no longer valued for its role in developing political, ethical, and aesthetic citizens. Instead, the goal has become promoting knowledge that contributes to economic productivity and producing students who are compliant and productive. (p. 7)

Certainly teachers' efforts to encourage students to question the validity of economic policies such as those espoused by neoliberalism are not just counterproductive but are dangerous to those in power.

To this end, neoliberalism views both schools and teachers solely as instruments of cultural transmission and reproduction. Therefore, as instruments of the powerful, teachers, schools, and the curriculum must be controlled so that they do not stray from the neoliberal script. The result is that our country spends hundreds of millions of dollars creating, proctoring, grading, and analyzing standardized tests for the sole purpose of maintaining an undemocratic despotism over teachers and their classrooms. Also worth noting is that this process effectively serves the neoliberal purpose of transferring public monies into the hands of private corporations. The testing industry alone reaps millions of dollars annually as a result of high-stakes testing, not to mention the myriad test-prep and tutorial companies that have sprung up across the country over the past few decades (Miner, 2005). One of the clear and immediate impacts of the neoliberal agenda of education is the domination and control of teachers, or what Giroux (1988) referred to as the "proletarianization" of the teaching profession.

Proletarianization of the Teacher and Teacher's Work

A central goal for democratic education was articulated quite well by Bertrand Russell, who argued that the key purpose of school is to give a sense of the value of things other than domination, to help create wise citizens of a free community, to encourage a combination of citizenship with liberty, individual creativeness, which means that we regard a child as a gardener regards a young tree, as something with an intrinsic nature which will develop into an admirable form given proper soil and air and light. (Chomsky, 2003, p. 12)

In direct contrast to Russell's view, Anton Makarenko (cited in Spring, 2007), who was the architect of the Soviet education system under Joseph Stalin, stated: "I believe personality can be stamped out in mass; however much attention must be paid to the quality of the dies" (p. 52). Makarenko argued that children should "not be educated as wild flowers, but as fruit trees," pruned and shaped for maximum social output. The difference in regard to the role of the teacher that is necessitated by these two perspectives on education is immense. For Russell, the teacher was to be the model of engaged citizenship for her or his pupils, and the classroom was to be a sanctuary of freedom and a laboratory of democracy. For Makarenko, the teacher was a rogue entity that must be harnessed and controlled so as to assure that they and their respective classrooms could act as finely crafted tools of the state. It does not require a well-trained eye to recognize that education in the United States has come to represent the sentiments of Makarenko much more than those of Russell, and that the draconian measures taken to de-professionalize teachers over the past few decades have been detrimental to the potential of critical democratic education in the United States.

The de-evolution of the classroom teacher into what Giroux (1988) so aptly referred to as the "information clerk" has been a steadily accelerating process since the publication of *A Nation at Risk* by the Reagan Administration in the early 1980s (p. 64). It was this document, in conjunction with its unholy sister publication, *Action for Excellence*, that spelled out the neoliberal agenda for public education in the United States. In short, schooling in the United States was to be focused solely on filling the needs of an anticipated global workforce while simultaneously generating a political apathy within the mass citizenry so as to better control what Alexander Hamilton termed the "great beast" (Chomsky, 2000). Pragmatically, this has meant applying the logic of capital to schooling via the application of the corporate model in managing educational institutions at all levels, while philosophically it has meant a trivializing of teaching and learning so as to perpetuate and maintain a political environment in which participatory democracy might best fade from the collective social memory.

Obviously, such objectives fly in the face of critical educators and, in many ways, even the self-image of the more traditional teacher. It should be seen as no coincidence that much of the blame in the troubling thesis of *A Nation at Risk* was laid at the doorsteps of our nation's teachers: they were undoubtedly "enemy number one" from the neoliberal perspective, with its aristocratic view of social control. In short, teachers were defined as academically flabby, lazy, and rogue entities desperately in need of control. The narrative was carefully crafted; teachers were ruining our children, and any path to excellence would have to be established in spite of them, not with them. More to the point, the teacher problem would need to be dealt with if so-called excellence in education were to be achieved. Enter standardized testing and the term "teacher-proof curricula" that is now used to describe the state-mandated educational standards found across the country. The plan established in the early 1980s by the Reagan administration called for an increase in accountability, which, as Alfie Kohn (2000) has defined it, was code for "more control over what goes on in classrooms by people who are not in classrooms" (p. 34).

Strangely, the hypocrisy of the Reagan administration went virtually unnoticed, as the same political platform that had shrilly demanded smaller government and, to this same end, promised the demise of the recently erected federal department of education, systematically charted a path for public education that moved the unequivocal power to legitimize cultural knowledge into the hands of an increasingly powerful elite. Barry, Osborne, and Rose (1996) describe how the purveyors of neoliberalism neutralize any potential hypocritical scent:

> Paradoxically, neo-liberalism, alongside its critique of the deadening consequences of the "intrusion" of the state into the life of the individual, has none the less provoked the invention and/or deployment of a whole array of organizational forms and technical methods in order to extend the field in which a certain kind of economic freedom might be practiced in the form of personal autonomy, enterprise, and choice. (p. 10)

This movement from local control to national control over schools, which has been a key steppingstone of the neoliberal agenda for education and the resulting proletarianization of teaching, has churned forward at a steady pace for the last 25 years. The results were most obvious when in 2001 President George W. Bush signed an education bill that established mandatory federal testing in our nation's schools—one of the most authoritarian acts in regard to education a democratic government has imposed since the Old Deluder Satan Act. This from a president who proudly termed himself a Reagan Republican. . .the same Reagan who argued that even establishing a federal department of education was an example of federal government sticking its nose into state business at an unconstitutional level.

Whether the architects of *A Nation at Risk* really understood the nature of the snowball they had pushed down the hill is arguable, but the end results have been an avalanche of authoritarian measures designed to control every aspect of teacher work and to de-professionalize teachers to a point where they can be easily managed, coerced, and controlled. This, incidentally, has always been the goal of authoritarian education systems: control every element of the mass dissemination of information and the resulting validation of official knowledge so as to maintain the power structure of a given society. From the view of the authoritarian, teachers are also necessary evils. They are mere mouthpieces for the true voices of power, and therefore they must be strictly monitored and controlled. The proletarianization of the teacher is a key component in advancing the neoliberal agenda of education, and the accomplishment of this agenda requires an adjustment in teacher preparation programs in order to produce teachers with characteristics useful to management. Hursh (2001) states:

> Governmental and quasi-governmental organizations seek to govern without specifying exactly what must be done, but by presenting the requirements or standards as rational and non-controversial, and providing a limited range in which it must be implemented. This makes it possible for social actors, such as teachers, to have a false sense of choice and freedom. (pp. 6–7)

Teacher Education and Teacher Education Faculty: "The Bought Priesthood"

There was a time not so long ago when higher education and the academics that reside within its ivory tower walls overtly set the education agenda for our democratic society. Our nation's schools looked to universities and university faculty to define what K–12 schooling needed to include and how it needed to function in order to best prepare their students to not only be successful at the next level but to be prepared for the responsibilities of democratic citizenship. A very obvious example of this influence can be seen in the efforts of James Conant who, through the establishment of the SAT, had a massive impact (for better or worse) on the curricula of high schools all over the country for decades. Undoubtedly, teacher education programs were central to this influence by educating future teachers and preparing them to carry specific perspectives, values, and missions into the classrooms of our nation's schools. Academics have historically embraced this role of democratic gatekeeper and, heeding the proclamations of individuals like John Dewey (1916), saw their work as a critical line of defense for the maintenance and continued improvement of democratic life. The thought of ceding such critical responsibilities to centralized powers and authoritative accreditation agencies would have been seen as democratic heresy to academics of the past, yet the evidence that such submission has taken place is overwhelming. The complete resignation on the part of teacher preparation faculty across the country to imperialistic entities such as the National Council for the Accreditation of Teacher Education (NCATE) and state boards of education is evidence of the current circumstance. While it is true that the ceding of power over teacher preparation has not been an agenda of teacher education faculty, it is also true that teacher education faculty have done little to prevent the loss.

The resigned capitulation of teacher preparation faculty has made the neoliberal agenda in education possible. Stated clearly, academics across this country have both wittingly and unwittingly been key enablers to the neoliberal agenda, and the collective resignation to powerlessness is palpable on university campuses across the United States. Curricula have been re-aligned according to pressures from corporations and authoritarian agencies, and safeguards of tenure and intellectual freedom have been slowly and systematically relinquished—bartered away in exchange for salary increases and healthcare premiums. Democratic pedagogy has been driven from classrooms to accommodate mandated quantitative assessments, and intellectual freedom has been replaced with authoritative matrices and professor-proof rubrics. Entire courses have been deleted to accommodate a value system that we have had no part in defining. Our students are now defined as customers, our classrooms have become delivery mechanisms, and the quality of our work is now judged in terms of productivity and efficiency.

The development of critically conscious, democratic educators is hard to imagine within the walls of teacher preparation programs where, in the name of profit (University of Phoenix) or in the name of efficiency, teacher education has been reduced to teacher training. If education is to be true—that it is to liberate—within the United States, teacher educators will need to take a look in the mirror, re-evaluate their mission, and recommit themselves to the cause of fostering the development of teachers who will enter our nations' schools prepared to fight on behalf of democracy against the onslaught of neoliberalism.

Defending Education in the Age of Neoliberalism

In a democracy, according to John Dewey (1916), "the ultimate aim of production is not production of goods, but the production of free human beings associated with one another on terms of equality" (p. 36). However, in the United States, rather than being a potentially subversive activity that could lead students to question and challenge the power structure of the status quo, education has been reduced to the communication of mechanical, suppressed, benign information that endorses the perspective and agenda of the dominant culture of society. Rather than making visible the realities faced by the voiceless and oppressed members of society, students are being taught that the only impact they can possibly have on the disenfranchised and destitute is to avoid becoming one of them. The path that is offered to this end is training—specifically, career training. In fact, learning for any other reason has come to be viewed as a waste of time for many students, especially working-class university students who now must struggle to pay dramatically increasing tuition and fee rates at public universities. The universities have responded to this devaluation not by encouraging students to embrace more socially profound reasons to learn but by realigning curriculums to better serve the desires of their customers (once known as *students*). For example, the liberal arts, once considered an invaluable core to democratic education and fertile ground for the development of critical consciousness, has been realigned and branded as *career-oriented* liberal arts. Freire (1973) stated, "By excessively narrowing a man's specialization, it constricts his horizons, making of him a passive, fearful naïve being," and while career training "may amplify man's sphere of participation [economically speaking], it simultaneously distorts this amplification by reducing man's critical capacity through exaggerated specialization" (p. 31). This career-focused "specialization" is code for the removal of student choice in course selection and the continual prioritization of close-ended training over open-ended learning. Perhaps the most damaging effect of this realignment is that the path to success offered to students requires nothing more than mere absorption of predefined facts, which are to then be regurgitated on standardized examinations. It is important to keep in mind that aside from the damage this type of education does to the potential for social democracy, ultimately it is the students and their education that suffer the most and, in the end, have the most to lose. McLaren (2006) asks this question:

> Do we want to accommodate students to the existing social order by making them merely functional within it or do we want to make students uncomfortable in a society that exploits workers, that demonizes people of color, that privileges the rich, that commits acts of imperialistic aggression against other countries, that colonizes the spirit and wrings the national soul clean of a collective social conscience? Or do we want to create spaces of freedom in our classrooms and invite students to become agents of transformation and hope? (p. 86)

Certainly the authoritarian-type neoliberalism that has burrowed its way into U.S. education proclaims that this evolution in American education is about effectiveness and assuring the highest output in student performance—performance that is gauged solely in terms of the efficiency in delivering and receiving a dominant version of truth. The reality is that it is this relentless pursuit of the perfect system that is being used to justify the manipulation of democratic institutions of education into creating products—the students—who will be defenders of the status quo, and who will fuel the engine of capital by taking their place as mindless consumers and compliant workers in the wheels of our society's corporate machinery.

While awareness of this threat is critical for every member of the academy, teacher education programs,with which we quite literally have an opportunity to change the landscape of American education via the transformative intellectuals we prepare to impact our communities, must rise to meet the anti-democratic challenge of neoliberalism.

References

Apple, M.W. (1993). *Official knowledge: Democratic education in a conservative age.* New York: Routledge.

Barry, A, Osborne, T., & Rose, N. (1996). *Foucault and Political Reason: Liberalism, Neo-Liberalism, and Rationalities of Government.* Chicago: University of Chicago Press.

Chomsky, N. (2000). *Chomsky on miseducation* (D. Macedo, Ed.). Lanham, MD: Rowman & Littlefield.

Dewey, J. (1916). *Democracy and education: An introduction to the philosophy of education.* New York: The Macmillan Co.

Freire, P. (1970). *Pedagogy of the oppressed.* New York: Herder and Herder.

Freire, P. (1973). *Education for critical consciousness.* New York: Seabury Press.

Giroux, H. (1988). *Teachers as intellectuals: Toward a critical pedagogy of learning.* Westport, CT: Bergin and Garvey.

Giroux, H. (2003). *The abandoned generation: Democracy beyond the culture of fear.* New York: Palgrave Macmillan.

Harvey, D. (2005). *A brief history of neoliberalism.* New York: Oxford University Press.

Hursh, D. (2001). Neoliberalism and the control of teachers, students, and learning: The rise of standards, standardization, and accountability. *Cultural Logic,* (3).

Kohn, A. (2000). *The case against standardized testing: Raising the scores, ruining the schools.* Portsmouth, NH: Heinemann Publishing.

Marx, K., & Engels, F. (1906). *Manifesto of the Communist Party.* Chicago: Charles H. Kerr and Co.

McLaren, P. (2006). *Life in schools: An introduction to critical pedagogy in the foundations of education* (5th ed.). Boston: Allyn and Bacon.

Miner, B. (2005). Keeping public schools public: Testing companies mine for gold. *Rethinking Schools.* Winter 2004/2005.

Postman, N. (1971). *Teaching as a subversive activity.* New York: Knopf.

Postman, N. (1995). *The end of education: Redefining the value of school.* New York: Knopf.

Rikowski, G. (2002).Education, capital and the transhuman. In D. Hill, P. McLaren, M. Cole, & G. Rikowski (Eds.), *Marxism against postmodernism in educational theory* (pp. 111–144). Lanham, MD: Lexington Books.

Robertson, S. (2007). "Remaking the world"': Neo-liberalism and the transformation of education and teachers' labour. In L. Weis & M. Compton (Eds.), *The global assault on teachers, teaching and their unions* (pp. 11–30). New York: Palgrave.

Smith, A. (1937). *The wealth of nations.* New York: P.F. Collier & Son. (Original work published 1776)

Spring, J. (2007). *Wheels in the head: Educational philosophies of authority, freedom, and culture from Confucianism to human rights.* New York: Routledge.

Zeichner, K.M. (2006). Reflections of a university-based teacher educator on the future of college and university-based teacher education. *Journal of Teacher Education, 57*(3), 326–340.

9

Too Late for Public Education?
Becoming a Teacher in a Neoliberal Era

JULIE A. GORLEWSKI AND DAVID A. GORLEWSKI

First they came for the Communists, but I was not a Communist so I did not speak out.
Then they came for the Socialists and the Trade Unionists, but I was neither, so I did not speak out.
Then they came for the Jews, but I was not a Jew so I did not speak out.
And when they came for me, there was no one left to speak out for me.
—German anti-fascist Martin Niemoller

Education, like many public aspects of society today, is engulfed in the ideologies of neoliberalism. As educators with a combined half-century in the field, we (the authors) have experienced and participated in many initiatives intended to improve teaching and learning. Some have been worthwhile; others, a waste of time and resources. The current movement, however, resembles nothing less than an assault on public education—perhaps even on the notion of "public" as an entity of value.

Although we spent many years in K–12 schools, we currently serve as teacher educators. This perspective provides us with unique insights into the effects of contemporary reform initiatives on the experiences of being and becoming teachers.

Overview

Very few educators—including teachers, administrators, and even teacher educators—are familiar with the term "neoliberalism." Clearly, then, educators are unlikely to be aware of or understand the effects of neoliberal policies on public education. In this chapter, we will explore neoliberalism and consider how it affects students, teachers, and teacher educators. Relevant experiences will be discussed through a brief historical overview revealing common threads that run from *A Nation at Risk* to *Race to the Top* as manifestations of ongoing neoliberal reform initiatives. Individual experiences will be linked to assumptions that produce what we call the *hidden curriculum* of school reform. Examples of the hidden curriculum are embedded in policies connected to preservice observation hours, student teaching, and the practices related to the evaluation of New York State high-stakes testing. Ultimately, we suggest that the neoliberal policies have alienated teachers from their labor and worked to silence the next generation of educators.

Neoliberalism and Education

Neoliberalism should not be confused with the concept of social liberalism or progressivism. Rather, it represents a post-Depression resurgence of *economic* liberalism in which the workings of the so-called "invisible hand" of the free market are seen as the answer to all problems—social and economic.

Harvey (2005) provides a useful definition of neoliberalism in its broadest and most pervasive sense. Neoliberalism, he writes:

> is in the first instance a theory of political economic practices that proposes that human well-being can best be advanced by liberating individual entrepreneurial freedom and skills within an institutional framework characterized by strong private property rights, free markets, and free trade. The role of the state is to create and preserve an institutional framework appropriate to such practices. . . . Furthermore, if markets do not exist (in areas such as land, water, education, health care, social security, or environmental pollution), then they must be created by state action, if necessary. (p. 2)

According to Martinez and Garcia (2000), the key principles of neoliberalism include:

1. *The Rule of the Market*, which liberates "free" enterprise from any bonds (regulations) imposed by the government no matter how much social damage this causes.
2. *Cutting Public Expenditures* for social services such as education and health care.
3. *Deregulation* of any policies, practices, or laws that could diminish profits, including environmental protection and worker safety.
4. *Privatization* of state-owned enterprises, goods, and services through sales to private investors.
5. *Eliminating the Concept of "The Public Good" or "Community"* and replacing it with "individual responsibility." This puts pressure on the poorest and most vulnerable members of society to find their own solutions to their lack of health care, education, and overall social security; then blaming them—if they fail—for being "lazy."

Given the definition of neoliberalism and a review of its key principles, it is easy to see the direction that current reform initiatives at the federal level (*Race to the Top*) are taking.

Lipman (2011) links these tenets directly to the restructuring of public education as it is currently being accomplished:

When President Obama appointed Arne Duncan, former CEO of Chicago Public Schools, to head the U.S. Department of Education in 2008, he signaled an intention to accelerate a neoliberal education program that has been unfolding over the past two decades. This agenda calls for expanding education markets and employing market principles across school systems. It features mayoral control of school districts, closing "failing" public schools or handing them over to corporate-style "turnaround" organizations, expanding school "choice" and privately run but publicly funded charter schools, weakening teacher unions, and enforcing top-down accountability and incentivized performance targets on schools, classrooms, and teachers (e.g., merit pay based on students' standardized test scores). To spur this agenda, the Obama administration offered cash-strapped states $4.35 billion in federal stimulus dollars to "reform" their school systems. Competition for these "Race to the Top" funds favored states that passed legislation to enable education markets. (para. 8)

Lipman notes that *Race to the Top* is actually part of a global neoliberal movement toward the commodification of all forms of existence. This is manifested in education by the marketing of schooling from primary school through higher education. She points out that the global education market now includes education management organizations, tutoring services, teacher training, testing services, online classes, and franchises of branded universities; and she draws a direct line between the public sector and the accumulation of capital:

> Education markets are one facet of the neoliberal strategy to manage the structural crisis of capitalism by opening the public sector to capital accumulation. The roughly $2.5 trillion global market in education is a rich new arena for capital investment. (para. 9)

The Hidden Curriculum of School Reform

Unintended consequences are a critical aspect of teaching and learning. In educating aspiring teachers, we seek to uncover the multifaceted dimensions of teaching-learning processes so all (or, at least, as many as possible) of the consequences of our actions are intended. That is, we hope that our classrooms are places that foster self-actualization, social justice, and a great deal of meaningful, productive learning. To ensure that future teachers are aware of the potential occurrence of unintended consequences, one of the things to which we introduce them is the concept of the *hidden curriculum* that English (2000) defines as follows:

> This curriculum is the one rarely discussed in schools. It is not even recognized by many educators who work in them. The hidden curriculum is the one that is taught without formal recognition. For example, American children are taught to be "neat and clean," "on time," and "respectful" to teachers. These "lessons" are rarely contained within formal curricula. But they are powerful conventions and norms that are at work in schools nonetheless.
>
> The hidden curriculum contains "structured silences"(Aronowitz & Giroux, 1985) that embody expectations and presuppositions about social conduct that often place disadvantaged students "at risk" in schools and work against them by being ignorant of the inherent cultural biases that are embedded in school rules. (p. 16)

Hidden = Invisible

In his explanation of the hidden curriculum, English (2000) makes two points: First, the hidden curriculum *exists*; its effects are powerful and ubiquitous. And second, without explicit attention, that is, a critical approach to the assumptions that produce the hidden curriculum, it is invisible and, thus, unexamined. It is, in fact, the unexamined (and therefore veiled) nature of the hidden curriculum that makes it potentially problematic for students. If, in fact, our education system values behaviors that exemplify neatness and respect, then we should not hesitate to teach it openly and assess related behaviors.

Cultural norms, however, seem natural and normal to those who are cultural natives, so problems arise when what the school culture defines as "respectful" behavior differs from that of a student's home culture. For example, teachers in the United States tend to expect students to make eye contact in order to show respect and indicate that they are paying attention. Not all cultures would perceive student-teacher eye contact as respectful; in fact, it might even be identified as defiant. It is easy to imagine how such a cultural dissonance might arise in schools, as well as how a lack of familiarity with the hidden curriculum of schooling might disadvantage certain students.Fortunately, the potential negative effects can be remedied. Educators who are intentionally reflective about their pedagogies and the cultural norms of schooling can help students learn to navigate cultural differences by revealing and explicating the hidden curriculum.

How does this relate to school reform? Like any social endeavor, school reform is grounded in cultural assumptions. These assumptions are the beliefs that underlie the reform initiatives, the understandings that are so "obvious" that they need not be stated. However, because they tend to be unstated (and therefore unexamined), they are hidden.

Thus, we believe that the hidden curriculum of school reform is analogous to the hidden curriculum that exists in schools. And, if the assumptions that undergird current reform initiatives are allowed to remain concealed, then the unintended consequences could be devastating for public schools, especially those serving our most vulnerable students. Since the cure for concealment is exposure, this piece seeks to reveal two key assumptions that establish, at least in part, the hidden curriculum of school reform.

To be—or to become—a teacher today, we believe that it is essential for educators to understand the context in which they are operating. That context includes a "manufactured crisis" (Berliner & Biddle, 1995)—perpetuated within the neoliberal environment. That crisis is presented to the public in the form of two overriding assumptions about the state of public education today—assumptions that permeate media discussions about schools and become the de facto reasons for school reform employing neoliberal policies:

- Assumption #1—Schools are failing our children and our nation
- Assumption #2—Schools can be reformed by competition, privatization, and standardization.

Assumption #1—Schools are failing our children and our nation

Despite innumerable indicators of success, this assumption (a myth, really) appears to be immortal. Nicholas Lemann (2010) points out the contradictions inherent in this narrative of systemic failure:

> A hundred years ago, eight and a half percent of American seventeen-year-olds had a high-school degree. . . . Now, on any given weekday morning, you will find something like fifty million Americans, about a sixth of the population, sitting under the roof of a public-school building. . . . Education. . .embodies a faith in the capabilities of ordinary people that the Founders simply didn't have.
>
> It is also, like democracy itself, loose, shaggy, and inefficient, full of redundancies and conflicting goals. It serves many constituencies and interest groups, each of which. . .sees its purpose differently. But, by the fundamental test of attractiveness to students and their families, the system—which is one of the world's most ethnically diverse and decentralized—is, as a whole, succeeding. . . . Measures of how much American students are learning—compared to the past, and compared to students in other countries—are holding steady, for the most part, even as more people are going to school.

Lemann makes several significant points. However, the final line of this excerpt is especially noteworthy: achievement of students in U.S. schools has remained generally stable "even as more people are going to school." This means that, despite serving a greater number of students in greater need of support, student achievement has not declined.

There is another important omission hidden in this assumption. Dialogues (and diatribes) about failing schools rarely seem to address the existence of *successful* public (even non-charter) schools. Thousands of schools in urban, suburban, and rural communities across the country are doing excellent work with students. Graduates of effective public schools fill college and university classrooms, medical schools, law schools, and—yes—even schools of education. To claim that our schools are failing implies that our future is bleak, and that the young people (from the past 5 years? 10 years? 50 years?) are incapable of leading our country.

Interestingly, parents of school-age children rate schools as generally successful, while they rate schools nationally ("other" people's schools) as average or below. A Gallup poll released in August 2010 indicates that Americans continue to believe their local schools are performing well, but that the nation's schools are performing poorly. More than three-quarters of public school parents (77%) give their child's school an "A" or "B," while 18% of all Americans grade the nation's public schools that well.(Lopez, 2010)

It seems that the perception of educational failure is related to the proximity to the school.

Another dubious connection made by promoters of educational reform involves public schools and the health of the nation. This takes the form of blaming public schools for not adequately preparing workers for 21st-century jobs. It is no surprise that, as the American economy tries to recover from the 2008 financial collapse (averted only by the infusion of massive amounts of taxpayer dollars into the economy to prop up Wall Street after its reckless excess), public schools and public school teachers are presented as part of the problem.

While it may seem logical to blame loss of jobs on U.S. soil on the lack of qualified (that is, properly educated) workers, in reality it is cheap labor overseas—not bad schools—that is the main reason for industry outsourcing.

Furthermore, as Fareed Zakaria (2008) points out, the United States is not declining; in this global economy, the rest of the world is catching up—a concept he captures in the phrase "the rise of the rest." Finally, it should be noted that when the American economy was booming during the 1990s, credit was given to technocrats and entrepreneurs, and not to the educational system.

Recently (and with echoes of *A Nation at Risk*), former Secretary of State Condoleezza Rice and former New York City Education Commissioner Joe Klein chaired a commission charged with studying the connection between America's educational system and national security. As *A Nation at Risk* spoke of a "rising tide of mediocrity," the Klein/Rice *U.S. Education Reform and National Security Report* (Council on Foreign Relations, 2012) is a manifestation of nearly 30 years of trying, ostensibly, to stem that "tide."

After years of voucher schemes, the development of state content standards, standardized testing, privatization, and school choice initiatives, what were the commission's recommendations? More of the same. There were three: adopt Common Core State Standards (CCSS), enhance opportunities for school choice, and hold schools and teachers accountable through standardized testing measures.

Note that additional funding, enhanced teacher and administrator training, or innovative programming were *not* included in the commission's recommendations for school reform.

Assumption #2—Schools can be reformed by competition, privatization and standardization

Although there is plenty of evidence that standardization, competition, and privatization benefit the wealthy and powerful, what evidence is there that standardized reform built around competition will benefit students most in need of help? Moreover, should this reform initiative fail, how will reformers be held accountable?

Barkan (2012) posits that the policies of ed reformers are wreaking havoc in public education, but equally destructive is the impact of their strategy on American democracy. From the start, the we-know-best stance, the top-down interventions at every level of schooling, the endless flow of big private money, and the imperviousness to criticism have undermined the "public" in public education. Moreover, the large private foundations that fund the ed reformers are accountable to no one—not to voters, not to parents, not to the children whose lives they affect.

It is ironic that reformers demand data-driven and research-based approaches yet ignore the abundance of research that indicates that competition and standardization are detrimental to the students most in need. To achieve social justice, educators must endeavor to uphold the principles of public education that are undermined by competition, privatization, and standardization. As Lemann (2010) states:

> In education, we would do well to appreciate what our country has built, and to try to fix what is undeniably wrong without declaring the entire system to be broken. We have a moral obligation to be precise about what the problems in American education are—like subpar schools for poor and minority children—and to resist heroic ideas about what would solve them, if those ideas don't demonstrably do that.

And, to bring the discussion to its most personal level, Hursh (2001) explains the effects of neoliberal policies on schools, teachers, administrators and students:

> Over the last decade the state has intruded into the lives of teachers and students to a degree unprecedented in history. Teachers are increasingly directed by district and school administrators to focus on raising test scores rather than teaching for understanding. In the Rochester (NY) City School District, high school teachers

report that they are pressured to teach toward the test. Sixth grade math teachers receive from the central administration lessons with practice problems that are to be used three out of every five school days as preparation for the standardized math test. Elementary teachers report that they devote more than a month to test preparation for the English language arts exam by eliminating all subjects other than language arts. In Massachusetts, the test scores of students are posted in the hallways outside teachers' doors. Nationwide, teachers are being deskilled as they implement curriculum developed by others. (para. 19)

This was written more than a decade ago and, as *No Child Left Behind* and *Race to the Top* initiatives have been implemented, conditions have only intensified.

The notion that standardized testing provides an objective and value-free assessment of our students' knowledge and skills leads to the final aspect related to Assumption #2. Cameron (1963) noted—nearly 50 years ago—that

It would be nice if all of the data which sociologists require could be enumerated because then we could run them through IBM machines and draw charts as the economists do. However, not everything that can be counted counts, and not everything that counts can be counted. (p. 13)

Shelves of books have been published dealing with the complexities of assessment and the deficiencies of standardized tests, but suffice it to say that classifying a school district—much less an entire state—as "failing" on the basis of a questionable measurement instrument is indefensible.

Effective assessment is multimodal, longitudinal, and intended to enhance the teaching-learning process. High-stakes standardized tests that result in annual rankings serve none of these purposes.

Poverty and Student Achievement

So, what is preventing American schools from rising to the top of international rankings? David Berliner (2009) published a policy brief entitled *Poverty and Potential: Out-of-School Factors and School Success*. In this brief, Berliner

details six Out of School Factors (OSFs) common among the poor that significantly affect the health and learning opportunities of children, and accordingly limit what schools can accomplish *on their own*: (1) low birth-weight and non-genetic prenatal influences on children; (2) inadequate medical, dental, and vision care, often a result of inadequate or no medical insurance; (3) food insecurity; (4) environmental pollutants; (5) family relations and family stress; and (6) neighborhood characteristics. (p. 1)

Berliner also notes that

These OSFs are related to a host of poverty-induced physical, sociological, and psychological problems that children often bring to school, ranging from neurological damage and attention disorders to excessive absenteeism, linguistic underdevelopment, and oppositional behavior. (p. 1)

Of course, Berliner does not imply that educators should give up on educating students who live in poverty; instead he suggests that reasonable, potentially effective reform initiatives ought to take into consideration the realities and inequities that our students (and their schools) face. Schools may be able to shape the future, but they are shaped *by* the present. While the inadequate performance of students in many urban public schools is alarming, given Berliner's evidence, it should not be shocking. It is unrealistic to expect schools to ameliorate social inequality—especially when systemic inequities remain part of the hidden curriculum.

It is temptingly simple to link teacher effectiveness to student achievement; however, Berliner's data—as well as a wealth of additional research—demonstrates the fallacy of this approach. No one would argue about whether good and bad teachers exist; however, teacher evaluation must consider *many* variables, not merely test results. There are excellent teachers in failing schools, and weak teachers in excellent schools. Simply stated, systemic deficiencies cannot be traced directly to individual competence.

Neoliberalism Today: Personal Perspectives

This is what neoliberalism does: it decreases funding for public endeavors, reducing the resources (material, intellectual, and social) available to resist. Those left in the system work harder for lower pay. Public institutions, inevitably, become debilitated and destabilized. An October 2011 report from the White House (prepared jointly by the National Economic Council, the Domestic Policy Council, the President's Council of Economic Advisers, and the Department of Education) noted that nearly 300,000 teachers lost their jobs over a three-year period—August 2008 through August 2011—with another 280,000 to be cut in 2012.

And these same institutions—ravaged by political philosophies and fiscal practices that have undermined them—are seen as *failing*. This is the projected cycle intended by neoliberal policies.

Throughout our lives, we have been immersed in the field of education, earning certifications in secondary education, elementary education, and educational administration, and earning doctorates in educational leadership and the sociology of education. When we step back from this trajectory, it is clear that we have been seeking an answer to the question of why some children succeed in school and others do not. The answer, of course, is that *schools* succeed for some students quite well—and for other students the current school system fails miserably. We have always worked on behalf of those students for whom school does *not* work well, seeking solutions to existing flaws in the system.

One aspect of our work investigates the experiences and practices of students and teachers in an inner-ring suburban high school, linking these experiences and practices to the social and political realities facing public schools. Among the findings was the revelation that teachers felt demoralized, de-professionalized, and disempowered.

Teacher Labor and Professional Alienation

The de-professionalization may be most evident when viewed through the prism of standardized testing which, in New York State, has been "high stakes" since 1999 in that high school students are required to pass a battery of five state-developed examinations (referred to as Regents Examinations) in order to graduate. And the stakes are now even higher as the mandates of *Race to the Top* require school districts to evaluate teacher competency based on student achievement on those tests.

In this system of test administration and evaluation, teachers must follow a highly prescriptive set of guidelines before, during, and after the tests are evaluated. Prior to grading the tests, teachers must complete a mandated training session in which a series of "anchor" papers provided by the state are read and discussed. The papers range in quality, and teachers, in preparation for the evaluation of the actual tests, are expected to review them thoroughly and to openly discuss various qualities and characteristics. Because teachers are required to rate papers in teams, this process is designed to assure a high level of inter-rater reliability.

The Myth of "Scientific Exactitude"

All of this, to an outsider, gives the impression of precision—what the *New York Times*'s Michael Winerip (2011) facetiously referred to as "scientific exactitude." The process does yield data for each student which, when placed in a grid provided by the state, result in a single raw score. That raw score is compared to the "cut point" set by the state. Quite simply, if the student's raw score is equal to or above the state's "cut point," the student passes the test. If it is below the "cut point," the student fails the test.

Sounds simple, doesn't it? But here's the problem. As outlined by Winerip (2011), New York State's standardized test system has limped through a decade (December 2002 through November 2011) of *inexactitude*. His investigations reveal a series of inconsistencies in New York State mathematics, physics, and English language-arts scores in which the standardized test results during that period appear inflated and at odds with other older and (arguably) more valid measures of student achievement such as the National Assessment of Educational Progress (NAEP) and the Scholastic Aptitude Tests.

The ten-year battle between and among various New York State officials (everyone from New York City Mayor Michael Bloomberg and various education commissioners to the chancellor of the Board of Regents) regarding the validity of the state tests ends, incredibly, in the current reform movement to connect teacher evaluation directly—and exclusively—*to those flawed state standardized tests*. This led a colleague of ours to describe New York State's standardized tests as based on "a sliding scale on an ever-changing rubric."

In short, public school teachers are increasingly alienated from their labors by the very nature of standardized tests, having no control over the tests' content, format, administration, and evaluation. And now, reform initiatives are being designed to assess a teacher's competency (and determine future employment) based on those very same tests.

Student Alienation

Students echoed these sentiments, feeling anxious and discouraged even as they articulated empathy for their teachers, who, students noted, were simply doing what "the state" required. When asked about the effects of "teaching to test," one student replied, "They [the teachers] tell you what to write and you copy it down exactly. The only difference between your essay and the guy next to you is the name at the top of the paper" (Gorlewski, 2011, p. 189).

To counter these disheartening conclusions, we found glimmers of hope in the whispered critiques of students and teachers who were being divided and alienated from one another by state and federal policies. Collective resistance, it seemed to us, could provide a lever for change. Students and educators, aligned together, offered the possibility of challenging the powerful, neoliberal status quo.

Our research practices led to doctoral degrees that allowed access to the relatively privileged space of academia—a place where, we felt certain, we could expand these ideas, continue this scholarship, and even develop strategies for facilitating the solidarity that might shift the tides that were contributing to the growing social inequities caused by neoliberalism. We were (and remain) thrilled by the opportunity to contribute through teacher education. What more perfect space could there be to spark collective resistance on behalf of public schools?

Unsurprisingly, however, public institutions devoted to higher education are not immune to the effects of neoliberal policies. In this economic crisis, faculty members are being expected to teach additional classes with more students. The potential for student dissatisfaction increases. Time for research and time to consider the effects of—and alternatives to—neoliberal policies are being reduced. We are concerned that, in time, our institutions will be perceived as inadequate (as at the K–12 level), making them prime contenders for the solutions offered by privatization, standardization, and the free market.

No Money for Schools

Neoliberalism has not been weakened by the economic crisis; it has been invigorated and fortified. Today, multimedia giants ensure that everyone *knows* there is no money to support public institutions. To help our economy, so the rhetoric goes, workers in these institutions must forego their apparently substantial salaries and reportedly lavish benefits. And, we are reminded, we must make these sacrifices for the greater good—for the common good. Because, according to neoliberal economists, our society will become more just and less unequal by starving public institutions. Competition is presented as the key to equity, and privatization the key to democracy.

We don't believe this and neither should you. Careers in health care, the airline industry, and manufacturing have been decimated by the neoliberal dedication to unfair application of policies supporting deregulation, privatization, and artificial competition. Labor unions and public workers are under attack. If educators must scramble to maintain their positions, it is impossible to work on behalf of others. Despite our best intentions, the goal of collective resistance is likely to succumb to Maslow's hierarchy of needs. We haven't given up, but it may be too late for us. Don't wait for them to come for you.

Silencing Teacher Candidates

A recent experience revealed a microcosmic version of the dilemma. Like many states, New York requires teacher candidates to spend at least 100 hours in school settings as a prerequisite for certification.Because there are no policies or regulations requiring K–12 participation, school personnel must be coaxed into accepting teacher candidates. The entire process puts the burden of fulfilling the observation requirement on teacher candidates and teacher education programs; schools can choose to allow candidates to visit their schools—or they can choose to avoid the endeavor altogether, especially since benefits to them, their students, and their faculty are neither obvious nor immediate. As accountability pressures increase (who wants to expose a class to a student observer or student teacher when standardized test results are connected to ongoing employment?), more and more schools are reluctant to accommodate preservice teachers: time, energy, and resources are scarce enough without stretching them further.

Naturally, all these factors affect the perspectives of the faculty and staff who arrange field experiences. We are mindful that our students' presence is dependent on the goodwill of the school community; they are invited guests, and the power relations inherent in these conditions influence every aspect of the interactions that occur in these settings. As experienced K–12 educators who have, for many years, orchestrated field experiences for local colleges and universities, we are particularly sensitive to the issues involved. Sometimes, minor breaches in decorum aggravated teachers. Once, a candidate wore flip-flops to a school's orientation session and the teacher to whom she had been assigned perceived her attire as "disrespectful" and withdrew his participation. On another occasion, a teacher had asked to read a candidate's field notes and, upon reading critiques of her performance, had demanded that the principal remove the candidate from the school grounds and end the fieldwork placement immediately.

While extreme, these examples are not uncommon. So, in an attempt to prevent such problems, students are required to sign contracts that remind them to behave in a professional manner. Examples of the items mentioned in the contract include writing thank-you notes to mentor-teachers (as teachers who allow observers in their classrooms are called), avoiding the use of cell phones and electronic devices, and carrying college identification. In addition, prior to fieldwork, students must pass a fingerprint clearance and complete two mandated workshops: *Schools Against Violence in Education (SAVE)* and *Child Abuse Identification and Prevention.*

Before fieldwork placements officially begin, we discuss the contract with our classes, emphasizing the importance of mutual respect as well as the tension between adopting a critical stance while, at the same time, maintaining awareness of the partial context of the field observer. And we caution them about their field notes, informing them that they might well be asked to share their notes with school personnel.

All of this can easily be understood as part of the development of professional identity—the process through which aspiring professionals adopt the norms and values of the group they hope to join. It seems natural that teacher educators would encourage teacher candidates to respect and defer to the educators they observe in the field. And many professions involve field experiences (sometimes called internships or apprenticeships) that are explicitly designed to mold candidates to the standards of the field—and which are not likely to involve critiques of practicing professionals.

To be meaningful, however, field experiences should be linked with contemporary and historical perspectives of education. In today's world, this necessarily involves the social and political pressures of neoliberalism on public education. Therefore, in the course of discussions grounded in this context, when a student explained that his mentor-teacher had read his field notes, my sense of the situation shifted. We began to think about the *hidden curriculum* of field experiences. In progressive teacher education programs, candidates are encouraged to think critically, to question assumptions, and to adopt multicultural perspectives in the quest for social justice. Then they are placed (based on an unsupported state mandate) in schools where the power dynamic is intense and excessive, where their very presence in the school is dependent on compliance, conformity, and—perhaps worst of all—silence.

Aspiring educators are becoming teachers in a world in which being a teacher increasingly means being threatened, undermined, and regulated. Tragically, many are silenced before they have even begun to develop their voices.

References

Aronowitz, S., & Giroux, H. (1985). *Education under seige.* New York: Bergin & Garvey.
Barkan, J. (2012, April 2). Hired guns on astroturf: How to buy and sell school reform. *Dissent Magazine* (pp. 49–57).

Berliner, D.C. (2009, March). *Poverty and potential: Out-of-school factors and school success.* Retrieved June 6, 2009, from Education and the Public Interest Center & Education Policy Research Unit: http://epicpolicy.org/publication/poverty-and-potential

Berliner, D.C., & Biddle, B.J. (1995). *The manufactured crisis: Myths, fraud, and the attack on America's public schools.* New York: Perseus Books.

Cameron, W.B. (1963). *Informal sociology, a casual introduction to sociological thinking.* New York: Random House.

Council on Foreign Relations. (2012, April 12). *U.S. education reform and national security: Report of a CFR-sponsored independent task force.* Retrieved April 6, 2012, from Renewing America: http://www.cfr.org/education/us-education-reform-national-security-report-cfr-sponsored-independent-task-force/p27948

English, F. (2000). *Deciding what to teach and test: Developing, aligning, and auditing the curriculum.* Thousand Oaks, CA: Corwin Press.

Gorlewski, J. (2011). *Power, resistance, and literacy.* Charlotte, NC: Information Age.

Harvey, D. (1990). *The condition of postmodernity: An enquiry into the origins of cultural change.* Cambridge: Blackwell.

Harvey, D. (2005). *A brief history of neoliberalism.* Oxford: Oxford University Press.

Hursh, D. (2001). Neoliberalism and the control of teachers, students, and learning: The rise of standards, standardization, and accountability. *Cultural Logic, 4*(1).Retrieved February 6, 2012, from: http://www.eserver.org/clogic/4–1/hursh.html

Lemann, N. (2010, September 27). Schoolwork: The overblown crisis in American education. *The New Yorker,* n.p.

Lipman, P. (2011). Neoliberal education restructuring: Dangers and opportunities of the present crisis. *Monthly Review, 63*(3) (pp. 114–127).

Lopez, S.J. (2010, August 25). *GALLUP Politics.* Retrieved February 6, 2012, from Americans' Views of Public Schools Still Far Worse Than Parents': http://www.gallup.com/poll/142658/americans-views-public-schools-far-worse-parents.aspx

Martinez, E., & Garcia, A. (2000). *What is neoliberalism? A brief definition for activists.* Retrieved January 6, 2012, from Corpwatch: Holding Corporations Accountable: http://www.corpwatch.org/article.php?id=376

Nichols, S.L. (2006). *Collateral damage: How high-stakes testing undermines education.* Cambridge: Harvard Education Press.

Winerip, M. (2011, December 18). On education: 10 years of assessing students with scientific exactitude. *The New York Times* (p.A24).

Zakaria, F. (2008, May 3). *The daily beast:* In *Newsweek Magazine.* Retrieved December 6, 2011, from The Rise of the Rest: http://www.thedailybeast.com/newsweek/2008/05/03/the-rise-of-the-rest.html

Part III. Being a Teacher: The Mythology
of Corporate Education Reform

Ignorance Is Strength:
Teaching in the Shadow of Big Brother

LAWRENCE BAINES

"Ignorance is strength," a slogan promoted by Big Brother in George Orwell's novel *1984*, serves as an apt description of the philosophy undergirding educational reform in the United States in recent years. In Oceania, the fictional dystopian country of *1984*, citizens belonged to one of three classes: The Inner Party, the Outer Party, or the Proles (proletariat). The most powerful individuals were the Inner Party, and although their power was vast, they only constituted 2% of the population. Below the Inner Party was the Outer Party, whose members served as the administrative staff or "hands" of the Inner Party. The Outer Party comprised just 13% of the population. The "citizens of the lowest class," the proletariat, were the largest segment by far, with 85% of the population.

If 6,000,000 members of the Inner Party constituted 2% of the population (as stated in *1984*), it can be calculated that the total population of Oceania was approximately 300,000,000, or roughly the population of the United States in 2007. The breakdown of social class in Oceania looked something like this:

Inner Party = 6 million citizens who held most of the wealth and power

Outer Party = 39 million citizens who comprised the professional class and implemented the policies of the Inner Party

Proletariat = 255 million, the poor who had almost no wealth. The Proles were kept occupied with television, pornography, gambling, pseudo-events, and alcohol.

The division of wealth in the United States holds an uncanny resemblance to the three-tiered, unbalanced distribution of Oceania in Orwell's novel. In 2007, the members of the Inner party of the United States, the richest 1% of the population, owned 35% of the wealth of the country, while the next 19% of richest Americans, "the outer party," owned an additional 50% of the financial wealth. Thus, while the richest 20% of the population in the United States held 85% of the wealth, the bottom 80% held only 15% of the wealth (Domhoff, 2012; Economic Policy Institute, 2012; U.S. Census Bureau, 2012). Poor and middle-class people in the United States, who comprise this bottom 80%, share their powerlessness with the hapless Proles of brutish, bleak Oceania.

Linguistic Prestidigitation

One of the defining features of Oceaniac society was the extent to which the Inner Party attempted to manipulate the thoughts and actions of the rest of the population. For example, the Ministry of Truth, which was a bureaucracy dedicated to propaganda, revised history to match the state's perceptions of itself. Similarly, when American bombs began exploding in a country halfway around the world, the president of the United States spoke of "liberation" and referred to the citizens of the country being invaded as "insurgents." Officially, the conflict ceased to be called "The War in Afghanistan" or "the Iraq War" and became "Operation Enduring Freedom" and "The War on Terrorism."

Like the Ministry of Truth and the president, the U.S. Department of Education attempts to shape public opinion through propaganda and linguistic manipulation. A reform that has re-segregated students, has purged schools of arts and physical education, and has made standardized tests the *sine qua non* of schooling is called No Child Left Behind (NCLB). Another reform, designed to obliterate teachers' rights, to mandate alternative routes for teacher preparation, to force corporatization of public schools, and to punish struggling schools is called Race to the Top.

Recall that the original intent of No Child Left Behind was to insure a "highly qualified teacher" [HQT] in every classroom. However, because many states could not afford the expense of training and certifying highly qualified teachers, new legislation was introduced to insure that anyone with a bachelor's degree in anything could qualify as HQT. Perhaps the most extreme example of the inverted interpretation of *highly qualified* is ABCTE (American Board for Certification of Teacher Excellence, itself a nice bit of doublespeak), an organization that sells teacher certification over the Internet. Requiring no course work, no contact with children, no grade point average, and no practice prior to certification, ABCTE's program has been ratified as "good enough" to constitute HQT in 11 states (ABCTE, 2011).

Through its extreme lobbying efforts, ABCTE has somehow persuaded legislators to allow its customers to be exempt from all teacher tests. If a student who wants to teach English in the state where I live goes to the university, requirements for the bachelor's degree include: a minimum of 16 courses in English, 3 courses in English Education pedagogy, 3 courses based in local schools, and 15 weeks of teaching from 8 to 5 every day in a local school. The student at the university must maintain a 3.0 grade point average, get accepted to the Graduate College, and pass all three qualifying tests (Baines, 2010).

In contrast, the bachelor's degree-holding ABCTE student does nothing—no courses in English, no courses in pedagogy, no classroom experience, and no internship. The ABCTE student must maintain no grade point average and is exempt from taking all three qualifying tests. Incredibly, it was the federal Department of Education that handed over millions of dollars in taxpayer money so that ABCTE could launch its profitable, quick-and-easy certification business over the Internet in 2001.

In Texas, a for-profit corporation has quickly become the largest producer of certified teachers in the state. The website for Texas Teachers (http://www.texas-teachers.org/) claims that the process toward certification in Texas is "fast, easy, and affordable," and, from the evidence provided, the description is accurate. In Mississippi, anyone with a bachelor's degree who wants to become a certified teacher can get certified even if they repeatedly fail a basic skills test. If someone who cannot pass a basic skills test constitutes "high quality," then is a person who passes a basic skills test considered a savant?

In the meantime, a corporation has claimed the name American Public Education, and shares of its stock are traded on the New York Stock Exchange. In 2011, American Public Education enrolled more than 83,000 students over the Internet and used only 250 full-time employees, yielding a cool student/teacher ratio of 332:1, a ratio that many of today's reformers could learn to love. Because the emphasis is on quality education (please note sarcasm), the CEO of American

Public Education pays himself a modest salary of only $1,700,000, far less than the CEO of the University of Phoenix, Charles Edelstein, who pays himself $11,300,000 (American Public Education, 2011; *Chronicle of Higher Education*, 2010). The salaries of CEOs of for-profit institutions are somewhat higher than the average starting salary for public school teachers in my state—$31,600. Yet it is the public school teacher who has received the most scorn and ridicule from reformers.

Mastering Doublethink

To achieve their goals, today's reformers have relied upon the general public's apparently inexhaustible capacity for ingesting heavy doses of *doublethink*, the ability to hold two contradictory views in the mind simultaneously. For example, if the goal is teacher quality, then the reformer's solution is to lower standards, to proscribe professional development, and to make teacher certification as effortless as possible. Obviously, to solve the crisis in teacher quality, schools need a flood of virtual strangers who have point-and-clicked their ways to certification without ever having to set foot in a real classroom.

If the reformers' goal is the development of real-life skills and cutting-edge thinking for the 21st century, then the solution must involve a single, timed, multiple-choice test involving no human interaction (certainly, no teacher input) and no tools, save a #2 pencil. If the goal is developing individual talent, then class sizes need to soar, the role of the teacher must be diminished, and the group mean should be valued above all.

Perhaps reformers' most unforgivable "oversight" has been the total denial of the role of poverty in student achievement. According to Reardon (in press), "A given difference in family incomes now corresponds to a 30 to 60 percent larger difference in achievement than it did for children born in the 1970s" (p. 2). Kornrich and Furstenberg (2010) found that rich parents now outspend poor parents on education by a ratio of 9:1, up from 5:1 in 1972. Twenty-two percent of all children in the United States live in poverty, the highest percentage in almost 50 years (National Poverty Center, 2012). Despite burgeoning numbers of poor children, little has been done to moderate the effects of poverty in the classroom.

To narrow the achievement gap and to address the complex, multifarious needs of American children, reformers have suggested and implemented (in many states) the following initiatives:

- A uniform curriculum
- Frequent standardized testing
- Reduced teacher input on curriculum and assessment
- No tenure for teachers
- Evaluations based on test scores
- Reduced per-pupil expenditures
- Decreased funds directed toward improving the physical structures of schools
- Few electives or extracurricular activities
- Larger class sizes
- Abandonment of poorly performing schools

Although none of these initiatives benefits children, they have made money for investors, testing companies, and corporations while lowering teacher salaries, teacher morale, and teacher autonomy.

Wrestling with Big Brother

For a beginning teacher, it would be useful to know how Big Brother operates, but also how to survive in an educational bureaucracy that has been shaped by years of intensely misanthropic policy decisions. In Orwell's novel, the dissident Emanuel Goldstein is a humanistic outlaw of the state who reveals the truth behind the propaganda.

Offered below are three rules for teaching, replete with notes on what Big Brother expects and how Goldstein might respond. A new teacher who wants to make no waves should understand how to kowtow to Big Brother's expectations in an appropriately subservient way. A new teacher who wants to teach in the best interests of the child might consider the Goldstein response.

Rule one: The curriculum is what the State says it is.

What Big Brother wants: Compliance, coverage, submission

The Goldstein response: Teach how to think, not what to think

In some states, the following edicts have been signed into law:

- Students must be tested on a predetermined body of knowledge
- Teachers must be assessed according to student performance on the test
- Teacher preparation institutions that prepared the teacher who taught the students who took the test must be judged by student performance on the test.

With these three laws, the State has mandated that a test score will determine the future career paths and life choices for a child, the amount of pay to be received by a public servant (the teacher), and the probability of survival for a public institution (the college or university where the teacher received his/her education). Under these conditions of vituperative accountability, child-centered teaching is often viewed as "weak" and "irrelevant." Clearly, what a teacher knows and feels about a child's welfare must be subjugated to the will of the State.

It is difficult to overstate the pressures to teach to the test. Recently I visited a kindergarten classroom where the first-year teacher ripped through a math lesson involving "hands-on learning" with wooden blocks in less than 5 minutes before transitioning into a lesson on phonics. Rather than listening to the teacher explain how to use blocks to count, most of the kindergartners seemed intent on discovering the myriad ways that blocks could be stacked one on top of the other to create towers. Of course, a few children were curious about velocity, so engaged in experiments to see how fast a block might travel if it were thrown or kicked across the room with sufficient force. Not a single kindergartner in the class of 22 paid attention to the math lesson at hand.

After my observation, I met with the teacher and her mentor about the lesson. When I suggested that the first-year teacher might consider slowing down and making sure that the students understood what was being taught before moving on, the mentor jumped in. "I guess you could slow down," she said to the first-year teacher. "But, if you do, you probably need to tell the principal that you are going to be way behind and get approval first."

Way behind in math in kindergarten?

Approval for improving a lesson?

An unfortunate side effect of teaching to the test has been that an enormous amount of material must be "covered" within a limited period of time. Curriculum must remain static so that a battery of assessments can be developed and deployed. As a result, it is the rare secondary social studies class that ever brings up recent events, such as the American wars in Afghanistan and Iraq, though they are the longest (the American invasion began in 2001) and most expensive wars in

American history. It is the rare science class that includes reading and discussion of nanotechnology and genomics, though experts agree that these areas are the future of science (Kurzweil, 2005). It is the rare English class that includes literature written after 1960, although one of the purported aims of literature is to "provide a window on life and the world."

Another problem with the State establishing the curriculum is that sagacity is far from guaranteed. For example, only recently has Texas decreed that theories of evolution can be included in science textbooks, much to the chagrin of that state's governor (Williams, A., 2011). In Florida, where students get fined for taking too many courses in college, a law requires that all public school students declare a major by ninth grade.

For the unaware, the State forbids the following in the sanctioned curriculum:

- Any mention of sex or reproduction
- Any image, event, or description that could be construed as unflattering to the State
- Any suggestion of negative activity by a corporation
- Any topic that could be considered controversial

A teacher who attempts to bring sex, current events, relevance, or controversy to the curriculum may be looked upon with derision by the State, because few of these topics show up on end-of-course exams.

Rule two: Money talks.

What Big Brother wants: More money for Big Brother, less money for teachers and students.

The Goldstein response: Always ask, "What is in the best interests of the child?"

The common vernacular is "money talks and bullshit walks," which was derived from individuals who lived in the city but could not afford bus fare, so had to walk to work. The beginning of the "money talks" era of public education can be marked by the State's decision to open up teacher preparation to big business. Today, for-profit online universities and colleges have the largest enrollments in the world. For example, the University of Phoenix enrolls over a half million students every year (National Center for Education Statistics, 2012), many of whom are intent on becoming teachers.

Unregulated "market-based" strategies, which brought down the banking industry around the world and almost bankrupted the financial system of the United States, are being actively promoted as an essential innovation for public education by the State. For example, a stipulation for applying for funding from the federal government through Race to the Top is that schools must give businesses unfettered access to public schools. Schools in states that refuse to give businesses unfettered access to public schools are automatically disqualified from Race to the Top funds.

From the decision to count ketchup as a vegetable in school meals (Nestle, 2011) to the initiative to sell advertising on school property (buses, hallways, morning announcements), public schools are no longer perceived as providing services for the common good but are seen as potential revenue streams for selective investors.

The latest get-rich-quick scheme involves forcing public school students to take online courses in order to graduate from high school. As universities worldwide (including the Massachusetts Institute of Technology) continue to put courses online and iTunes University and Ted.org continue to bulge with ever-expanding arrays of lectures and online courses, one wonders at the logic of forcing students to pay to take an online class through the local school.

However, by now, it should be no surprise that these new laws have been ratified at the same time that for-profit virtual schools have been approved as providers of educational services throughout the nation. Basically, these new laws give corporations free rein to colonize any public school that is left unguarded in states where they have been adopted (Fang, 2011).

State departments of education, tired of decades of budget cuts, have seized upon virtual schools as a way to generate money for themselves. A few weeks after being elected, the commissioner of education in my state closed all school-based online providers and forced all students who wanted to take online courses to take them exclusively through the state Department of Education. Today, ads for the state's "virtual school" pepper the Internet, and the Department of Education has launched a sales campaign to establish its virtual school "brand" worldwide.

As corporate and "non-profit" virtual schools proliferate, so do charter schools, vouchers, magnet schools, and private schools. This eclectic variety of schools has exacerbated the problem of segregation by class and race (Orfield, Siegel-Hawley, & Kucsera, 2011). Despite research that indicates that most charter schools perform no better and usually worse than the local public school (83% perform worse or "about the same"), federal policy continues to reward the most selective schools (charters) and to punish the most accepting (common schools) (Center for Research on Educational Outcomes, 2009).

Even the most celebrated charter schools, such as Knowledge as Power Program (KIPP), pre-select out more difficult students, such as those with limited English proficiency (LEP) or special needs. The act of requiring an oath of attendance and decorum, signed by parents and children prior to consideration for enrollment, precludes the participation of the neediest families (for example, students who may have a parent in prison). Even with its pre-selection process, recent research has revealed that 40% of African American males are kicked out of KIPP schools between grades 6 and 8 (Miron, Urschel, & Saxton, 2010).

One of the original purposes of the American public school was to welcome students of all classes and races. No more. The public that a public school wishes to serve can be as selective as its corporate sponsor wants it to be. Today, public schools in America actively discriminate on the basis of race, gender, social class, religion, and disposition and are rewarded for it.

Rule three: Obedience is expected. Disagreement is reprehensible.

What Big Brother wants: Consistency, docility, economy

The Goldstein response: Tell the truth.

A teacher who is autotelic teaches for the intrinsic rewards of teaching—helping students develop their intellectual, social, and emotional talents (Csikszentmihalyi, 1997). An autotelic teacher does not decide to "start teaching" because the State offers an extra $100 per month for extraordinary efforts at teaching to the test. An autotelic teacher always teaches in the best interests of the child because that is what a teacher is supposed to do.

Despite the altruism at the heart of teaching, the State continues to use models of evaluation commonly associated with manufacturing industries of the early 20th century. Although research in the social sciences has established that incentivizing quotas with money (hauling more iron in a day = higher pay) is suitable for only unskilled jobs, teacher pay-for-performance (higher test scores = higher pay) has become an urgent, popular reform (Pink, 2009).

An elementary teacher in the Dallas Independent School District had received no support for professional development, no money for supplies for his classes, no time off during the day (he was forced to perform various tasks such as lunch duty, by the school), and no help for the special education students in his overcrowded classroom. So when he was ordered by the district to teach 45 minutes longer every day, he wrote a letter of complaint to the school board. Rather than commend the teacher for his steadfast loyalty amid trying conditions, the school board promptly fired him (American Federation of Teachers, 2012).

A newly certified teacher in my program just landed a job mid-year at an urban school that has been labeled "needs improvement." In one of her classes, a remedial reading class, she has been ordered to teach from a script furnished by America's Choice (a subsidiary of Pearson), which sold the urban district a variety of curricular materials. Part of the America's Choice package is an on-site moderator who checks on teachers to insure that the America's Choice script is being followed to the letter.

My student, insecure about holding onto her job, has been reprimanded numerous times by the America's Choice moderator for not staying "on script." However, because the class consists of a majority of limited English proficiency students, my student has been trying to develop lessons that better meet the students' unique needs. However, the needs of her students do not always align with the America's Choice lesson for the day or the end-of-course assessment (also provided by Pearson). The easy road is to stop teaching and to start reading the prescribed script. The hard road is to stop lying and to start teaching.

Common Schools as an Endangered Species

School districts in America are increasingly identified by the demographics of the children they serve. Successful districts serve the very rich in the safest neighborhoods, while failing districts serve the very poor in the most dangerous neighborhoods. President Obama's children attend the artsy, progressive, expensive Quaker school, Sidwell Friends in Washington, D.C. Parents who live in D.C. and lack the president's income and connections, send their children to the institution that is free and closest to home.

Once upon a time, common schools were seen as the solution to income disparity, a place where Americans of all incomes, races, and religions met on equal footing. Horace Mann characterized common schools as the most important institution in a democracy.

Common schools in America have become an endangered species. The proliferation of "choice" has exacerbated the problem of separation (Baines & Foster, 2009). Where do rich and poor, majority and minority, meet in the 21st century?

Participation in churches, synagogues, sanctuaries, and mosques is restricted to adherents of the faith; social organizations and clubs have been on the decline for years (Putnam, 2000). It was once thought that the Internet would help foster communications across class lines, but few of us use the Internet to meet and greet "the other." Rather, we search the world in hopes of finding individuals who share our values and interests. Today there is no place where America's simmering diversity of rich and poor interact. No place.

America is fragmenting into hermetically sealed fiefdoms. Uniformed security guards and iron gates restrict entry to both the ritzy Macmansions of suburbia and the blighted environs of the downtown high school. Rather than bring classes and races together, current educational policy rewards separation and penalizes equal opportunity. When a child never gets the opportunity to work with someone who is different, perspectives remain narrowed, and understanding and empathy are more difficult. In a society as diverse as the United States, a lack of understanding can lead to intolerance, which, in combination with continuing disparities in income, can foster widespread social unrest. Any perusal of history or examination of recent events around the world attests to the eventual outcome of such inequity.

When a poor child struggles at a low-performing school, the curriculum becomes rigid and demanding; his teachers get publicly humiliated; the neighborhood becomes more toxic; finally, the school shuts down (Williams, C., 2011). This cycle of despair is far from inevitable and is, in fact, purposefully and relentlessly being driven by the policies of the State. Rather than continuing a policy of slash and burn, the State might consider (and I know this is a radical proposition) HELPING struggling schools, teachers, and students rather than punishing them.

In a recent experiment, Norton and Ariely (2011) asked Americans in which society they would prefer to live.

In Society A, the wealth is distributed like this:
The wealthiest 20% hold 36% of the wealth
Second tier, next 20% hold 18% of the wealth
Lowest tier, bottom 60% hold 46% of the wealth

In Society B, the wealth is distributed like this:
The wealthiest 20% hold 84% of the wealth
Second tier, next 20% hold 11% of the wealth
Lowest tier, bottom 60% hold 5% of the wealth.

Society A represents the distribution of wealth in Sweden, and Society B resembles the distribution of wealth in Oceania . . . and the United States. The study found that 92% of Americans said that they would prefer to live in Society A. Despite this impulse for equity, American educational reformers in recent years have pushed the country ever closer to the nightmarish plutocracy of Oceania. If the Proles don't begin fighting against the campaign of "ignorance is strength," then the differences between America and Oceania will become indistinguishable. At that point, everyone will come to love Big Brother, because there will be no other choice.

References

American Board for Certification of Teacher Excellence. (2011). About ABCTE. www.abcte.org

American Federation of Teachers. (2012). Sign the petition! Call on Dallas ISD board to stop bullying teachers and the community. American Federation of Teachers, Texas. http://tx.aft.org/allianceaft/index.cfm?action=article&articleID=2123c4d1–4e1e-4dcd-a9fc-1dafe04b24c5

American Public Education. (2011). *2010 annual report*. Charles Town, WV: APEI.

Baines, L.A. (2010). *The teachers we need, the teachers we have*. Lanham, MD: Rowman & Littlefield.

Baines, L.A., & Foster, H. (2009). A school for the common good. In K. Ryan & J. Cooper (Eds.), *Kaleidoscope: Readings in education* (pp. 232–236). Stoneham, MA: Houghton Mifflin Harcourt Publishing Company.

Center for Research on Educational Outcomes. (2009). Multiple choice: Charter performance in 16 states. Stanford, CA: Stanford University. http://credo.stanford.edu/reports /MULTIPLE_CHOICE_CREDO.pdf

Chronicle of Higher Education. (2010, June 23). CEO compensation at publicly traded higher education companies. http://chronicle.com/article/GraphicCEOCompensation at/66017/

Csikszentmihalyi, M. (1997). *Creativity*. New York: Harper Perennial.

Domhoff, G. (2012). Wealth, income, and power. From Who Rules America? website. http://www2.ucsc.edu/whorulesamerica/power/wealth.html

Economic Policy Institute (2012). The state of working America. Washington, DC: Economic Policy Institute. www.stateofworkingamerica.org

Fang, L. (2011, November 5). How online learning companies bought America's schools. *The Nation*. http://www.thenation.com/article/164651/how-online-learning-companies-bought-americas-schools

Kornrich, S., & Furstenberg, F. (2010). Investing in children: Changes in parental spending on children, 1972 to 2007. United States Studies Center, University of Sydney.

Kurzweil, R. (2005). *The singularity is near.* New York: Viking.

Miron, G., Urschel, J., & Saxton, N. (2010). What makes KIPP work? A study of student characteristics, attrition, and school finance. New York: National Center for the Study of Privatization in Education. http://www.ncspe.org/publications_files/OP195_3.pdf

National Center for Education Statistics. (2012). 12 month university enrollments. Washington, DC: Institute of Education Sciences. http://nces.ed.gov/ipeds/datacenter/

National Poverty Center. (2012). Poverty facts. Ann Arbor: University of Michigan. http://npc.umich.edu/poverty/

Nestle, M. (2011, November 16). Ketchup is a vegetable? Again? *The Atlantic.* http://www.theatlantic.com/health/archive/2011/11/ketchup-is-a-vegetable-again/248538/

Norton, M., & Ariely, D. (2011). Building a better America—one wealth quintile at a time. *Perspectives on Psychological Science, 6*(1), 9–12.

Orfield, G., Siegel-Hawley, G., & Kucsera, J. (2011). Divided we fail: Segregated and unequal schools in the Southland. Los Angeles, CA: Civil Rights Project. http://civil-rightsproject.ucla.edu/research/metro-and-regional-inequalities/lasanti-project-los-angeles-san-diego-tijuana/divided-we-fail-segregated-and-unequal-schools-in-the-south field

Pink, D. (2009). *Drive.* New York: Riverhead Books.

Putnam, R. (2000). *Bowling alone: The collapse and revival of American community.* New York: Simon & Schuster.

Reardon, S.F. (in press). The widening socioeconomic status achievement gap: New evidence and possible explanations. In Richard Murnane & Greg Duncan (Eds.), *Social and inequality and economic disadvantage.* Washington, DC: Brookings Institution. http://cepa.stanford.edu/content/widening-academic-achievement-gap-between-rich-and-poor-new-evidence-and-possible-explanations

Texas Teachers. (2011). Want to teach? When can you start? http://www.texasteachers.org

U.S. Census Bureau. (2012). Wealth and asset ownership. Washington, DC: U.S. Census Bureau. http://www.census.gov/hhes/www/wealth/wealth.html

Williams, A. (2011, August 23). Rick Perry's true ID: Creationism in the classroom. The Guardian. http://www.guardian.co.uk/commentisfree/cifamerica/2011/aug/23/rick-perry-creationism-classroom

Williams, C. (2011, March 20). Robert Bobb struggles to erase Detroit schools' $327 million budget deficit. Huffington Post. http://www.huffingtonpost.com/2011/03/21/detroit-schools-budget-deficit_n_838464.html

11

Beware Reformers Bearing Gifts:
How the Right Uses the Language of Social Justice to Reinforce Inequity

ANN G. WINFIELD AND ALAN S. CANESTRARI

Serpents, voices, divinations—warnings ignored, vanity exposed, a hope that beloved peace is at last at the gate, the Trojans breach their *own* battlements and haul their fate into the city. "Equo no credite!" Don't trust the horse!

Not unlike the warriors of antiquity, modern-day teacher warriors, weary of the fight, demonized, distracted by the promise of a solution to the achievement gap, saddled with the pressure to raise test results, and convinced by a shrewd co-optation of progressive language, have capitulated, accepting a model of school reform dominated by corporate values and designed in the image of the market-place. Warnings of what the belly of this wooden horse holds go unheeded by defeated educators and the public, who have become complicit in their own dis-empowerment and dismissed by the neoliberal and neoconservative elite as non-sense. Sadly, the siege is over and the city has fallen, despite considerable critique by today's soothsayers. Like Cassandra, they have the gift of truthful foreshadow-ing but are cursed with eternal disbelief by all who might listen.

Yet we issue another warning.

Fueled by a new brand of fabricated fear, conservative reformers insist that the United States will lose the battle for global dominance unless the business of edu-cation is taken over and guided by the principles of the marketplace. In order for this transformation to take place, public education must be exposed as a misguid-ed experiment. And, of course, teachers—once the highly regarded standard-bearers of public education—must be objectified as the enemy. They stand accused and convicted (along with parents and children) of failing our public schools. They are sentenced to a life dominated by the hysteria and tyranny of high-stakes testing, disempowered and deskilled in an increasingly technocratic milieu of continuous data collection, ranking, and accusation. This is an era when collective bargaining must be dismantled, unions broken, and schools closed. The voices of dissent silenced.

Even schools of education are criticized for losing touch, failing in the preparation of beginning teachers. But what does the wooden horse represent? And what is in the belly of the trophy? What is the chant of the emerging invaders? It should come as no surprise to anyone paying attention today that the prize and the chant is *privatization*, the panacea for everything wrong with America and the new mantra of progressive educational reform. Is education moving in the right direction? According to the business class, no, investment in public education is wasteful. *Public education does not produce results*, chant the new entrepreneurs.

Privatization is antithetical to the historical purposes of public education and represents an evolutionary step backward. Rather than continuing to move purposefully toward democratization, social justice, consensus, and opportunity, this mission hinges on oligarchy, elitism, division, and stratification. The power that drives the mission is apparent. Just follow the money.

Claiming the Same Territory

Much of the public debate about education has become conflated with economic realities that have served to deflect real examination of the roots of persistent inequity in education. This conflation, scripted by conservatives and fueled by media proliferation, has been purposeful and has served to create a situation wherein each side is making the same claim: that the opposition wants to maintain the current racialized and socioeconomic status quo. Right-wing ideologues claim that those who argue for the preservation of, for example, collective bargaining, or against testing, standards, and accountability, are really working to preserve inequity while they march around using the language of social justice to rationalize policies that achieve the opposite.

Meanwhile, in anticipation of criticism, the right has managed to declare itself and its policies as the most direct route to equity and has successfully (in the eyes of a majority) cast its critics as wedded to the past, stuck in an antiquated paradigm that no longer works in this new historical era. Right-wing policymakers have positioned themselves as the champions of the underrepresented at the same time that they have created policies that entrench inequity. In effect, the right, as it has historically done, is using the liberal lexicon to preserve the status quo. They have managed to effectively craft a message of reform that appeals to unsuspecting and apparently naïve liberal educators, using the very same language that progressive educators have used to advance their agenda for years. In effect, the tables have been turned. Being and becoming a teacher in the current era requires an understanding of the mechanisms by which current reformers in education operationalize historically rooted assumptions about human worth, intelligence, and ability.

An Uninterrupted and Unchallenged Monologue

We are concerned that the debate surrounding public education reform has become an uninterrupted and unchallenged monologue. Becoming and being a teacher in such an environment means that new teachers are positioned as acquiescent before they have had a chance to develop their own identities as professionals. New teachers are pushed to comply, seduced themselves by the language that promises to leave no child behind. Indeed, to question the rhetoric is to reject the public's supposed desire for accountability, or to claim that standards are unimportant. Our fears extend to the proliferation of non-governmental bodies influencing local education agendas nationwide. We are interested in shedding light on the degree to which the power elite is actually in the driver's seat with regard to educational policy and how well-funded and highly subscribed educational organizations act as backseat drivers that approve of every turn. We also fear that these current trends are affecting not only just K–12 education but are engaged in a reevaluation of the very notion of what it means to be educated, as state departments of education call for K–24 compliance with the new narrative.

Teachers who enter the profession with an already-developed sense of criticality where reforms are concerned might be attracted to the seemingly less bureaucratic, more holistic charter school movement, only to find themselves mired in the same battle with language and expectations. Fabricant and Fine (2012) reveal the existence of a "promise-evidence gap" (p. 38) and argue that language has been used to disguise the truth and normalize the offenses inflicted upon public education. Deceptive marketing on the part of charter schools claims to create the advantages of higher student achievement, equity, parent engagement, the retention of experienced educators, and curricular and pedagogical innovation. The evidence for success is underwhelming: two-thirds of charter schools perform about the same or less well than traditional schools (Fabricant and Fine, 2012). Further, there is considerable evidence that there are a number of strategies employed by charter schools to ensure their own success,for instance, (1) they cherry-pick students, effectively siphoning off more privileged students from public schools; (2) they under-enroll ELL and special-needs students; (3) they often exclude parents from decisions regarding school closings, charter openings, and governance; and (4) they tend to hire less-qualified, less-experienced, less-well-paid teachers. Finally, charters often described as centers of innovation in reality show no evidence of widespread curriculum or pedagogical innovation and in fact create tension over the use of public funds, resources, and limited space.

As an outgrowth of the small-school movement, and in what was originally imagined as a teacher-driven experiment based upon the principles of social justice, the charter school movement promised to bring multicultural curriculum, effective instruction, and the kind of attention and opportunities traditionally enjoyed by children of privilege to poor children. Instead it has been hijacked and reshaped by corporate special interests, influence, and big money. Labeled the "billionaire boys club" (Ravitch, 2010), philanthropists like Bill Gates, Sam Walton, Eli Broad, and conservative think tanks such as the Heritage Foundation are at the center of this transformation, providing the financial resources, policy support, and the ideological message needed to shift the movement from what Michael Fabricant and Michelle Fine refer to as "an alternative *within* public education to an alternative pitched *against* public education" (p. 20).

The Roots of Deceit

Indeed, public education is under assault (Watkins, 2012). Perhaps it has always rested on tenuous ground: witness the resistance faced by Thomas Jefferson and Horace Mann in their efforts to codify public education in the post-Revolutionary era. The ruse of unprecedented testing, national standards, teacher and student control, and surveillance in our nation's schools has been foisted on the American public using the language of social justice and must be revealed for the ideological Trojan Horse that it is. Over the past century, reform movements have continually cycled in ever-tighter circles, each time squeezing out truly humanitarian ideals and pedagogical models that contain any criticality or resistance.

Historians of education understand reform as happening in three primary waves: from the Common School movement through the development and proliferation of testing in the early 20th century to the Civil Rights Era. There is strong consensus pinpointing 1983 as the launch date of the current era of standards and accountability. After being elected in a landslide in 1980, Ronald Reagan, silver-tongued master of rhetorical conservatism, introduced the first product of his education platform: the report his presidential commission provocatively titled *A Nation at Risk*. This report has been deconstructed thoroughly for its militaristic innuendo and strategic composition as a series of sound bites that were effectively repeated for weeks on television and radio news programs, and for its launching of a new, widely accepted but wholly negative narrative about public education. What is most notable, however, is the degree to which the cooptation was necessary and blatant, coming on the heels of the nation's decades-long struggle to achieve equity for the previously excluded.

If you think about it, there must have been quite an emergency meeting in the conservative war room (after the tremendous spate of legislation passed during the Civil Rights Era), figuring out a way to reframe what must have seemed like a tidal wave of progress in the wrong direction (according to conservatives' reckoning). After all, Keynesian economic policies had effectively flattened out the wealth distribution curve, and ideas that had been relegated to the political left were now infiltrating the federal mandate. The language of social justice has been co-opted, as we have shown, from a period of tremendous social change that—as hard as it may be for some to admit—was short-lived and vulnerable.

The use of soothing language that appeals to people's better instincts about social welfare to enact cruel and brutal social policy is nothing new (Thomas, 2011). Indeed, while the search might take us all the way back to antiquity, a contextual examination of the iterations most intimately linked to the present moment ought to begin in the early 20th century, when the so-called *fathers of curriculum* conceptualized a system of public education through a lens of eugenic ideology (Winfield, 2007). This was an era characterized by utopian visions of society governed by those who proclaimed themselves the fittest, by the promise of science and assurances of objectivity through research-based conclusions about teaching and learning, and by institutions of various stripes designed to punish, reform, train, and house those considered by the visionaries to be not just less "fit" but an outright threat to society. Mandatory sterilization laws were passed in 30 states, the most restrictive immigration legislation in history was enacted, and laws defining whiteness and circumscribing marriage were the norm. Meanwhile, major U.S. corporations were implicitly supporting the rise of the Third Reich, while social reform laws were being duplicated by them as well (Black, 2003)—all this in the name of *bettering society, eradicating poverty and disease*, and *working toward a brighter future*.

These early decades of the 20th century saw public schools as part of a larger model of social control manifest through a proliferation of institutions that kept a certain sector of the architecture community very busy: designers of homes for feebleminded boys and girls, institutions for the deaf and blind, paupers' prisons, and public schools. These buildings are with us to this day and have helped to shape and denote the very boundaries of the reform debate. Surveillance and audit culture (Taubman, 2009) are subsumed unquestioningly into our conversations about achievement—without a thought as to their influence. It was during this period that public schools were most definitively diverted from the meritocratic vision (however limited in scope it may have been—yet another example) articulated by Horace Mann of school as the great equalizer nearly a century before. Industrialization reigned, and schools were reconceived to be in service to the capitalist imperative, while the application of the principles of industry—in the name of efficiency—was used to justify a vision of schools as mechanisms to sort and classify students.

One example comes from father of curriculum G. Stanley Hall (1924), who felt strongly that class divisions were inherited, writing that each child "will be not only tested from childhood on, but assigned his grade, and be assured the place that allows the freest scope for doing the best that is in him" (p. 465). Appealing to the instinct to have your own child's talents seen and recognized is universal, and much of Dewey's philosophy articulates the very best of these ideas. How very instructive it is to see, then, that these articulations could be used to envision a system that places students into levels, grades, and tracks according to a societally preconceived notion of their inevitable place. Hall is very clear that "some are born to be hewers of wood and drawers of water, and are fortunate if they can be made self-supporting; practical slavery under one name or another must always be their lot" (p. 465), and he argued strenuously for a move away from high schools as places for college preparation. Hall's views influenced the field of adolescent psychology and the role of schools for generations.

Of course, the rhetoric to enact what seems in hindsight to be so glaringly undemocratic used glowing language poached from the theories of John Dewey about student-centered curriculum, and the language was aligned to appeal to prevailing views regarding the role of institutions. Furthermore, immigration patterns, the *separate-but-equal* infrastructure defined by *Plessy v. Ferguson*, and the ongoing pathologization of poverty ensured that reformers conceptualized the *public* in public schools to refer to the *great unwashed* in need of surveillance (Kohl, 2009) and control, lest they see fit to rise up. Which leads us to our final contextual consideration of the times, which was the rather robust socialist, anarchist, and Marxist organizing that was yet another facet of the Progressive Movement (shared also by eugenics, suffrage, and temperance movements, among others). In more ways than one, social institutions like public education act as a wad of gum in the dam—a fact not lost on reformers who have the most to lose.

Deception Grows: Working Within an Impossible Tension

Teacher work exists within an impossible tension: the iconic twin images of teacher as the national mother—nurturing, challenging, savior of the poor and downtrodden; and the cruel, less-than-intelligent, power-wielding miscreant—neither of which fares very well under the pressure of exacting, meaningless standards and requirements that rob them of their professional dignity. For Taubman (2009), it is this impossibility that pushes teachers toward an acceptance of the calls for best practice, accountability, and standards-driven curriculum. Having been placed professionally in the bulls-eye of the political media storm for so long, they crave the very thing that has wreaked such havoc on their lives: a measuring stick that will allow them to prove their worthiness. Kozol (2007) understands this deception and argues that it is disingenuous of reformers to decry teacher attrition in urban classrooms and for them to blame it on some fantasized *inability to relate* argument when, in fact, teachers are leaving because of the systematic crushing of their creativity and intellect, the threatened desiccation of their personalities, and the degradation of their sense of self-respect, under the weight of heavy-handed, business-modeled systems of Skinnerian instruction, the cultural denudating of curriculum required by the test-prep mania they face, and the sense of being trapped within a "state of siege." (p. 40)

In an environment where students are cast as "a population of potential victims and perpetrators" (Simon, 2007; quoted in Taubman, 2009, p. 131), teachers carry the weight of responsibility for the manifestations of the entire history of the nation. Indeed, according to Taubman, educator acquiescence is rooted in shame implied in the message that

> racism, poverty, class warfare, political corruption, as well as specific, individual and local problems are translated into a lack of qualified teachers, who can be produced if we just have the right standards and practices in place. (p. 144)

Meanwhile, the tremendous spate of policies, mandates, standards, curricular models, accreditation requirements on all levels, and media portrayals say nothing of the well-documented relationship (Berliner, 2005) between social policy and school achievement or about the egregious wealth disparities in the nation's schools. Instead, the economically driven narrative first put in place after policymakers responded to the Soviet launching of *Sputnik* in the form of the National Defense Education Act, and reinforced in the national mindset by *A Nation at Risk*, has now become the unquestioned focal point of the national debate. So, while teachers are "responsible for keeping the poor and blacks out of prison and out of poverty," reformers have successfully ensured that "class warfare against the poor is recoded as the need to prepare students for the twenty-first century global market" (Berliner, 2005,p. 155).

Harnessing the Public: Using Good Intentions Badly

We find the cooptation of language to be most egregious when it preys on otherwise well-meaning people, who we might hope would be more suspicious of solutions that seem simple, neat, and tidy. District superintendents and principals all over the country must have felt some level of self-satisfaction at their ability to require the objects of their control to sit through professional development trainings that are spurious at best and downright racist and classist at worst—all in the name of supporting children. Take, for example, the Ruby Payne phenomenon as an example of both corporate profitmongering and pathologization. Despite decades of research that has discredited the deficit approach to explaining inequitable opportunity and access in education, Ruby Payne is indoctrinating a generation of teachers with a series of books that contain "a stream of stereotypes, providing perfect illustrations for how deficit-model scholars frame poverty" (Gorski, 2005, p. 8). District superintendents intent on solving the "poverty problem" in their schools are paying millions of dollars to Payne's company, Aha!, Inc., for the textbooks and workshop training for thousands of teachers nationwide.

Payne's overall message is that poor people are slow processors, that they can't be made to think critically, and that the best way to teach them is to know their "culture," which she presents as the most stereotyped, steeped-in-history drivel imaginable. Payne sounds like a eugenicist right out of the 1920s as she explains that "the typical pattern in poverty for discipline is to verbally chastise the child, or physically beat the child, then forgive and feed him/her. . .individuals in poverty are seldom going to call the police, for two reasons: First, the police may be looking for them"(quoted in Gorski, 2005, p. 37). The impact of poverty in this conception, a conception that is being delivered en masse to teachers as we write, is that it is a problem that resides within the people themselves. In other words, the impact of poverty on student achievement needs to be fixed not systemically or through social policy but by changes in the behavior and value systems of poor people—and teachers.

For example, in 2010, the tiny and very poor city of Central Falls in the tiniest state, Rhode Island, became ground zero in the debate over who is to blame for low-performing schools. Teachers became the targets. When teachers balked at a plan to transform the schools in the district, the current superintendent, Frances Gallo, with the endorsement of current Rhode Island Commissioner of Education Deborah Gist and Secretary of Education Arne Duncan (who earlier promised to close over 5,000 underperforming schools), fired the teachers—all of them.

Less than a year later, Secretary of Education Duncan (2011), as part of the ongoing promotion of his federal Race to the Top competitive grant program, revealed his not-so-hidden agenda in a speech delivered to the Rhode Island Public Expenditure Council entitled "Siding with Students." He stated:

> President Obama and I believe deeply that education and the economy are inextricably linked. The key areas of growth in the new economy—fields like health care, technology, and green energy—require us to get much better in subjects like math and science—and do a better job of producing college graduates in these fields. Traditional industries like manufacturing and transportation are also increasingly reliant on a more highly skilled and educated workforce. (p. 1)

So, it is about siding with students only to the extent that they are part of an economic equation.

Reformers have long worked in concert to deliver a message about education that resonates. In order to illustrate the ways in which the power of language has infiltrated the debate and derailed much of the potential for resistance to current reform mandates, a brief digression is in order. During a recent university-wide forum, a well-respected professor of law and member of the Rhode Island Latino community gave a talk that focused on *exclusion and crisis* in Central Falls. The talk began with an accounting of the history of the community, a typical 20th-century urban tale of the rise and fall of industrialization, and the degree to which the largely immigrant community has been vilified and blamed for economic conditions they not only did not cause, but which had in fact hijacked their pursuit of the American Dream. It is what followed that brings to the fore the very crux of the seductive nature of language.

The speaker then proceeded to laud the new Transformation Model that has been forced upon the high school, claiming that thanks to the efforts of Broad Foundation-educated Gist and district superintendent Gallo, the culture of the school had been changed. In fact, the speaker claimed that Duncan's reforms had removed the barrier to community participation in the conversation about school reform. We were shocked. How could it be that this community leader, so deeply aware of inequity in education and the implications of the nation's racist past, could be arguing that Duncan's Transformation Model provided the much-needed opportunity for the indigent, disaffected, and immigrant population to be a part of the conversation? Didn't he see that the reformers were, and had always been, part of the economic and cultural elite, and that the entirety of their rationale rested on the early 20th century's efforts to produce a measurement tool that would prove the intellectual superiority of whites?

None of us wants to hear that just when we think we are the freest, the most liberated to express our outrage, that in fact we are merely actors within a web of hegemony not of our own making. Indeed, to feel such outrage is part of the human experience; identity and allegiance in America are inherently tied to guttural remonstrance of crying for the fair treatment of those who are the least powerful in society. The territory is claimed by the entire political spectrum—from Tea Partiers to liberals, religious zealots to community organizers—we are a nation of people who stick up for the little guy. So why do we live in a country that is so grossly unequal? The answer lies in many places. From rhetorical memes with the capacity to exist within epistemologies that are radically different from one another, to shared moral values that transcend political affiliation (Haidt, 2012), mere terminology is clearly not a safe place to hang your hat when trying to navigate right from wrong.

Perhaps what we are witnessing is some kind of hyperbolic flashpoint, or perhaps it is merely savvy marketing. Make no mistake: the right-wing conservative end of the political spectrum has co-opted the language of social justice to such an extent that it is now possible to side with poor black and brown children at the same time as one sets about constructing a system that disempowers their teachers and wantonly dismantles the key institutions that might provide space for their voices and aspirations to be heard. Throughout this chapter we have sought to reveal the mechanisms by which current reformers in education operationalize historically rooted assumptions about human worth, intelligence, and ability. The role of language as a way of understanding current educational reform agendas is paramount and carries within it imperatives regarding ideology and political economy. We are concerned that the debate surrounding public education reform has become an uninterrupted and unchallenged monologue. Our analysis extends to the proliferation of non-governmental bodies influencing local education agendas nationwide.

Let this be a warning to all current and future member of the profession: there is an underlying movement afoot whose primary aim is a complete dismantling of public education altogether. We hope we have sounded a warning in our effort to expose the extent to which the power elite control the national reform agenda while they harness the substantial membership of long-standing, well-funded, and otherwise well-meaning organizations such as the American Association of Colleges for Teacher Education (AACTE), the American Educational Research Association (AERA), and the Association for Supervision and Curriculum Development (ASCD). Furthermore, the audit culture (Taubman, 2009) extends far beyond K–12 education and includes an attempt to reevaluate the very notion of what it means to be educated, as state departments of education call for K–24 compliance within the new narrative. Our fear is that it may be too late, that the canon has already been rewritten like an Orwellian manipulation of the truth. The language is beyond reproach: it is sweet and smooth but oh-so-deadly.

References

Berliner, D.C. (2005). Our impoverished view of educational reform. *Teachers College Record*.

Black, E. (2003). *War against the weak: Eugenics and America's campaign to create a master race*. New York: Four Walls Eight Windows.

Duncan, A. (2011). Siding with the students. Speech delivered to the Rhode Island Economic Development Council.

Gee, J.P. (1999). *An introduction to discourse analysis: Theory and method*. New York: Routledge.

Gorski, P. (2005). Savage unrealities: Classism and racism abound in Ruby Payne's framework. *Rethinking Schools,21*(2).

Fabricant, M., & Fine, M. (2012).*Charter schools and the corporate makeover of public education: What's at stake*. New York: Teachers College Press.

Haidt, J. (2012). *The righteous mind: Why good people are divided by politics and religion*. New York: Pantheon.

Hall, G.S. (1924). Can the masses rule the world? *Scientific Monthly, 18*, 456–466.

Kohl, H. (2009, January 8). The educational panopticon. *Teachers College Record*. http://www.tcrecord.org ID Number 15477.

Kozol, J. (2007, August 29). Letters to a young teacher.*Education Week,*.

Ravitch, D. (2010, November 11). The myth of charter schools. *New York Review of Books*.

Taubman, P.M. (2009). *Teaching by the numbers*. New York: Routledge.

Thomas, P.L. (2011). Orwellian educational change under Obama: Crisis discourse, Utopian expectations, and accountability failures. *Journal of Inquiry & Action in Education, 4*(1), 68–92. https://journal.buffalostate.edu/index.php/soe/issue/view/11

U.S. Department of Education. (1983). *A Nation at risk: The imperative for educational reform*.

Watkins, W.H. (Ed.). (2012). *The assault on public education: Confronting the politics of corporate school reform*. New York: Teachers College Press.

Winfield, A.G. (2007). *Eugenics and education in America: Institutionalized racism and the implications of history, ideology, and memory.* New York: Peter Lang.
Winfield, A.G. (2012) Resuscitating bad science: Eugenics past and present. In W. H. Watkins (Ed.), *The assault on public education: Confronting the politics of corporate school reform.* New York: Teachers College Press.

12

Spotlight on Failure:
The Mythology of Corporate Education Reform

GORDON D. BAMBRICK

It is easy for teachers in today's rapidly neoliberalizing world to view themselves as victims of a senseless attack that has scapegoated them for all that is wrong with society. The motives for this assault have often been attributed to the naivete, arrogance, and greed of corporate reform leaders, but the problem with such reactions is that they fail to respond to the set of myths that is used to frame thought. While the vilification of teachers is one major component of today's mythology, especially under Arne Duncan's Race to the Top, we need to resist the temptation to attack the credibility of those who blame us on an ad hoc basis, for that, too, is a major distraction from what needs to be understood as a powerful system of rationalizations being used to justify the re-configuration of all aspects of education around profitability. Only when we understand the big picture of how reform works as a powerful and all-encompassing belief system will we be in a position to systematically oppose the real problems, which are political and economic in origin. Herein, we need to recognize that we as teachers are currently operating within a set of expectations that guarantees the demolition of public education.

The Controlled Demolition of Public Education

In 2008 Susan Neuman, former assistant secretary of education, confessed to *Time* magazine that "others in the department . . . saw NCLB as . . . a way to expose the failure of public education and 'blow it up a bit' . . ." (Wallis, 2008). The motive: by Patricia Burch's count, 16 out of 27 high-ranking officials who retired shortly after designing NCLB "assumed positions at for-profit firms selling consultative or other services and products to schools, districts and states linked to the mandates of NCLB" (Burch, 2009, p. 42). The goal of NCLB reform is clearly one of benefiting businesses with a vested interest in educational improvement to be delivered by charter or voucher schools, and through the broader for-profit and non-profit education services industry. In order to justify the need for improvement, the primary lever of corporate reform is a mythology that casts a spotlight on failure, justifying the need for providers from outside the public system. In order to manufacture consent for this diversion of public-sector funding into private-sector profit, what is needed is the production of distrust surrounding the public system's supposed underperformance and lack of accountability. It must be seen to be in need of "discipline" from market forces and competition, for, "if it were a business," Bill Gates says, it "would be bankrupt" (Winfrey, 2006).

Since details of the private sector's own agenda are best kept undisclosed we are never told that we must privatize, commercialize, or profit from education, or that government will be run by corporations; we are told that we must break up the government's monopoly and overturn the status quo.

Using the half-truths of modern spin, the narrative of reform builds on fear and utopian desire; it casts a human drama of heroic, private-sector rescuers clashing with public-sector villains; it offers to lift us from the tragedy of national decline under teacher unions, big government, bloated social services, and red tape, and into a liberation wherein free markets and self-interest rule.

Creating a Useful Crisis

The crisis is a key justification for reform's urgency. In the infamously leaked words of former Ontario Education Minister John Snobelen, what is needed is "a useful crisis" (Cohen, 2001, p. 148). Such a crisis can be created from any number of factors, such as economic recession, debt, low test scores, the need to prepare for the knowledge economy, the underperformance of certain races or ethnicities, and the incompetence of teachers. Reformers frequently heap together selective facts in order to ensure support for what they invariably refer to as real reform, radical change, transformation, liberation, and revolution. In an interview with *Maclean's,* Bill Gates revealed that "parents should be outraged about the state of education in America," not only because of "dropout rates" but also "the number of kids who graduate and then go into remedial courses. . . ." Furthermore, America has "decreasing numbers of people with four-year college degrees [which negatively] affects competitiveness" and leads to unemployment (Whyte, 2010). On other occasions, Gates (2005) has claimed that the crisis is one of low expectations for poor or racially marginalized students; still elsewhere failure is due to schools being "obsolete." Such crisis-mongering has made its way around the world. In Wales, for instance, the education minister cites research from McKinsey, a global consultancy that profits directly from advising how to conduct the very reforms its study recommends. Hence, the company advises on how to build a good crisis:

> Things need to change. And change fast. In their recent report on 'how the world's most improved school systems keep getting better', McKinsey noted that the impetus to start school system reforms resulted from one of three things: 'The outcome of a political or economic crisis, the impact of a high profile, critical report on the system's performance, or the energy and input of a new political or strategic leader.' Well, at least two of those three factors apply to Wales. Never waste a crisis. (Teaching Makes a Difference, 2011)

The Myth of Low Performance

The most important tool of crisis building is concern regarding alleged underperformance. Because tests always provide below-median results for half of the participants, they are the weapon of choice. The manufacture of a crisis in education through standardized testing is such a central justification for privatization that, as Alfie Kohn (2004) notes, whenever schools do improve their results, "The response, from New Jersey to New Mexico, is instead to make the test harder, with the result that many more students subsequently fail."

In order to generate sufficient failure, schools must *raise the bar*, thereby keeping it safely out of reach. In Britain, for instance, "average" is the new "minimum":

> In an attempt to end what he sees as the low-expectations culture in some schools, [the Secretary of Education] will say that by 2015 he expects every secondary school in England to be achieving the current national average. . . . (Wintour & Watt, 2011)

Clearly the goal of failure in the UK is to leverage privatization using similar deadlines to those of NCLB: "The new goal would require 870 of the 3,000 secondary schools in England to improve by 2015 to avoid being taken over by a neighbouring headteacher or academy" (Wintour & Watt, 2011). As teachers, it is essential that we actively and tirelessly debunk the lie that improved standardized test results of any kind can be equated with genuine improvement.

Regardless of the purported causes of the crisis, the solution is mythologized as ever-increasing doses of accountability. On the surface, intensifying accountability builds consent by seeming like an unquestionable benefit. Objection constitutes guilt. "What's there to hide?" asked Arne Duncan when teachers opposed publishing their names and ratings in the *Los Angeles Times* (Felch, 2010). In contrast, reformers offer parents reclamation of the system through tough medicine. As Jim Dueck argues in the *Edmonton Journal*, if we "[s]pare the tests," then we will surely "spoil the school system." Alberta's former deputy minister (now on the panel of Race to the Top) explains that teachers typically inflate grades "so much so that report cards can't always be trusted." It seems that "[t]eachers are against standardized provincial tests not because they're bad policy but because such tests hold teachers more accountable" (Staples, 2012). By characterizing teachers as fundamentally untrustworthy, Dueck can justify testing as the only means to assure that they can no longer dodge accountability. The desired side effect will be to make teachers the official scapegoats for plans that are guaranteed to fail and to leverage in other privatization reforms under the smokescreen of deposing the status quo.

Raising the Bar to Improve Competitiveness

As a global comparison system, the OECD's Program for International Student Assessment (PISA) has come to be regarded as the ultimate global ranking authority. It is this assessment that is being used to create a crisis in human capital, namely, that almost everyone is falling behind in terms of preparing workers to win jobs in the face of global competition. Increasingly, education is mythologized as a kind of international arms race, a patriotic *race to the top* that must be won to secure our future. According to *A Nation at Risk*, one of America's earliest corporate reform manifestos, "If an unfriendly foreign power had attempted to impose on America the mediocre educational performance that exists today, we might well have viewed it as an act of war" (1983). More recently, *Waiting for Superman*, a film heavily promoted by Gates, proclaims that "[t]he fate of our country won't be decided on a battlefield, it will be determined in a classroom" (Ayers, 2010). Ironically, much of this patriotism comes from corporate leaders who export jobs to cheaper countries. Leading the way have been international technology corporations who stand to profit via the replacement of teachers and schools with e-learning. While few push the patriotism button harder than Gates, it is worth noting that he has been a leader in IT job export, especially to India, where competitiveness has more to do with cheaper labor, lower taxes, and less regulation than its education system, which ranks near the bottom of PISA standings (Cowen, 2011). As teachers we have a moral duty to consistently oppose the narrow argument that education is a mere weapon of economic competition; we need to clearly expose the arms dealers in this race for what they are, rather than buttressing their arguments with counter-claims that teachers really are doing a great job of enhancing competitiveness.

Closing the Gap to End Poverty

Against the country-eat-country propaganda of the global race to the top, education must also embrace the philanthropic mission of closing the gap. While this crisis is based on concern over the widening gap between rich and poor, it is presented as yet another useful crisis of educational unaccountability. As numerous studies confirm, low academic achievement correlates most strongly with poverty, yet the goal of reform is to make it seem that poverty was *caused* by school and the failure of teachers.

In order to maintain belief in reform mythology, it is vital, above all else, to convince us that it is fully within the capability of schools to overcome poverty's effects, and that it is only a matter of having better teachers to ensure that schools of the inner cities no longer remain *failure factories*. If schools actually could equalize performance, poverty would supposedly disappear—a strange assumption, considering that almost the entire manufacturing sector was exported to countries with less education and more poverty.

That some people were able to make it from rags to riches in America has always been used to argue that it wasn't one's economic background that determined one's success but strictly virtue. This is at the core of both the Horatio Alger myth and the American Dream. Hence, the miracle schools that overcome the poverty gap are held up as proof that other factors far outweigh poverty. According to education historian Diane Ravitch (2011), claims made about such miracles are "[u]sually . . . the result of statistical legerdemain."

No Excuses. . .for Poverty

Under the "no excuses" slogan, all blame for economic failure belongs to education; conversely, success must be seen to be *caused* by education. Whereas the perceived failure of the public system is a cherished goal of reformers, the success of non-public schools is the Holy Grail. Think tanks and corporate media constantly retell "success stories" of "turnaround" schools, districts, and reformers. The pro-charter Broad Foundation gives an annual award to the inner-city school that shows the greatest gains. Since underperformance is no longer allowed to be attributed to poverty, all blame has to shift to the teachers, a convenient scapegoat when schools inevitably fail to conquer the poverty that causes underperformance.

Much has been invested in research to prove that poverty can be overcome with better schooling, and the quest goes on endlessly for innovations that will supposedly level the playing field. The solution varies considerably. It can be merit pay for teachers based on test scores; it can be parachuting Ivy League teachers into poor areas under the Teach for America logo. Experimenting with pedagogical rather than political solutions to the effects of poverty has become a think-tank obsession, and the children of the poor are the guinea pigs. In some places they are rewarded with cash or prizes. Elsewhere, they are subjected to "the new paternalism," military discipline, or school-to-work programs. In one inner-city school, "First-graders are given $20,000 to invest in a class stock portfolio" (Sanchez, 2010).

According to Gates, with the right education system, "you can take someone in the bottom tier of income and let him compete to be a doctor or lawyer." Thus, public education is characterized as the cause of, and potential solution to, America's economic inequality. Gates explains: "The education system is the only reason the dream of equal opportunity has a chance of being delivered—and we're not running a good education system" (Whyte, 2010).

Of course it's highly debatable whether equalization of educational performance—even if this utopia were possible—would result in a fair start for children. Would it overcome the segregation of the rich in private K–12 schools or exclusive colleges and universities where Gates and his kind are incubated? More importantly, would it compensate for unemployment and reverse the export of jobs?

In fact, the claim that schools with high expectations can overcome the poverty gap guarantees a healthy supply of failure in the inner cities where poverty is highest. Gates, Murdoch, and Duncan depict such schools as failure factories, as if that had been their perverse intent. Britain's secretary of state for education Michael Gove, like many other reformers, argues that people who offer up poverty as an excuse "are more concerned with protecting old ways of working than helping the most disadvantaged children succeed in the future. Anyone who cares about social justice must want us to defeat these ideologues and liberate the next generation from a history of failure" (Shepherd, 2012). Such liberation must come from making every school an academy, says Gove. Consent is manufactured through making change look like parental empowerment. This is why the Eli Broad Foundation bankrolled Parent Revolution, a grassroots movement, to enable parent trigger laws that give parents the right to replace failing schools with charters (Weil, 2009). In the UK, we find the Education Secretary promoting the idea that "[p]arents should help schools root out and sack failing teachers" (Chapman, 2012). It is vital for teachers to understand again that the real issue under debate is not one of their own quality assurance processes, nor the perceived hostility of parents and reformers but rather the absurdity of the claim that schools are the battlefield on which poverty will be conquered. We need to understand and constantly expose the immense strategic value of claiming that poverty is no excuse for failure in terms of how it leverages privatization.

Teachers need to persistently unmask the impossibility of education's contradictory slogans of raising the bar and closing the gap under NCLB and RTTT. The myth that schools, and schools alone, will make America Number One in the world economy and at the same time eliminate its ever-widening gap between rich and poor should not be understood as a mere delusion, but rather as a clever and highly effective neoliberal strategy.

Rewarding Great Teachers (and Firing the Rest)

It is only within this context of guaranteed failure that we can truly understand the significance of the new role of the teacher in corporate mythology. Creating the widespread perception of education as failing gives license to send in the marines and fundamentally change the way education is delivered. The myth of the bad teacher is a perfect way to build fear about what's being hidden from us. The production of this myth is so vital that both the *Los Angeles Times* and *The New York Times* publish teacher ratings along with names; the *New York Post* even hunted down the worst teacher in New York, culminating in a blown-up photo of the culprit, along with quotes from angry parents demanding she be fired and her pay returned (Roberts, 2012).

The myth of a failure in the teaching profession serves a number of key purposes: it can be used to weaken political resistance from unions, to justify corporate takeovers, and to downsize expensive labor. The un-fire-ability of the bad teacher is the key point of attack in today's mythology, especially as hyped by the film *Waiting for "Superman,"* which depicts New York's infamous rubber room where bad teachers are paid as they await hearings, as if the delay were their own fault and they were guilty until proven innocent.

To further undermine job security, think tanks have been preoccupied with demonstrating that—even though the curriculum of reform is dictated from above—variations in teacher quality must account for all underperformance. "If you just say that the bottom 10 per cent of teachers goes away because they don't measure up," Gates claims, "then the U.S. goes back to being one of the best in the world" (Whyte, 2010).

The harvest of bad teachers is self-legitimizing because low dismissal rates imply that "powerful unions" are protecting mediocrity. Job security in the form of unions, tenure, and the right to just cause for dismissal are seen as the only roadblocks to improvement. The notion that teachers are highly motivated and well qualified to begin with, or that predictability of pay scales and seniority works to maintain a quality workforce, is routinely dismissed as "jobs for life." The new ethos of disposability was demonstrated by the mass dismissal at Central Falls, where an entire staff was fired due to low test scores with Obama's blessing (Krause, 2010).

The very goal of the new mythology is to make an obsession out of differences in teacher quality. Typical think-tank propaganda uses formulae to calculate the precise amount of damage being inflicted by the bad teacher:

> The study found that poor teachers decrease the lifetime earnings of their students by more than $1.2 million per class compared to average teachers. If their performance cannot be improved, the authors suggest it would make sense to pay poor teachers enormous sums of money to retire. (Maharaj, 2012)

Similarly, *The New York Times* uses test data, despite their widely acknowledged unreliability, to demonstrate that "Teacher Quality [Is] Widely Diffused" (Santos & Gebeloff, 2012).

Such headlines cleverly solicit more rigorous teacher evaluation. To this end, Jim Dueck also hyperbolizes the difference between teachers: "What happens is that you have a bucket of teachers, and cream rises to the top. As you start to go past the cream, you hire a lot of teachers that you would never have hired in the first place" (Staples, 2012). Such statements need to be understood as a reflection of the immense strategic value of shifting blame for the poverty effect onto teachers.

The myth of the great teacher serves a similar purpose of emphasizing the vastness of the gulf in teacher quality. According to Dueck, "it was found that an average student who had weak teachers three years in a row would drop to the 45th percentile, while average students with great teachers three years in a row would

rise to the 96th percentile" (Staples, 2012). The great teacher is a kind of superman, such as Geoffrey Canada in *Waiting for Superman*. Arne Duncan and Bill
Gates are both obsessed with finding and rewarding great teachers (Mak, 2012).

Dividing teachers among themselves is also a powerful weapon in the broader war on unions. This is why the owners of Walmart, one of the world's most anti-
union corporations, were part of an alliance that donated money to fund extra pay
for teachers in Washington (Abowd, 2010). The Walton Foundation knows that
once teachers have accepted the connection between their worth and tests that generate failure, unions can easily be divided and conquered.

Conclusion

This investigation of the dominant myths being used to undermine the public system reveals how core scripts do not change as they are mouthed from one reformer
to the next. Plots are woven around human dramas. Standard fictive devices depict
a crisis in which heroic reformers overthrow powerful unions, big government, and
their bosses. Accountability crusaders fight on behalf of outraged parents and
innocent children. The world is righted: bad teachers are punished and great ones
rewarded, the poor are saved by the rich, America wins the race to the top, and no
child is left behind.

Questioning these seductive narratives is an act of heresy. Who wants a child
to be left behind? Who doesn't want to raise the bar?

Thus, it will take an act of courage on behalf of educators to consistently expose
the motives of a mythology that scapegoats public education for outcomes that it
neither causes nor can cure. They must recognize that fighting corporate takeover
will require a lot more than resistance to merit pay, standardized testing, or depro-
fessionalizaton on the grounds that it will hurt student achievement or PISA rankings. Unions partnering with foundations in order to fight the gap (and get a seat
at the table) will not help, either.

What is required is a whole new mindset and a much deeper commitment to
educating the broader public about how to disarm mythologies that threaten to
blow up public education. Everyone needs to face up to the fact that it is not the
educational but rather the economic status quo which is failing. Naturally it is in
the interests of those on the high side of the gap to shift blame for poverty to failing schools and teachers. So it should not surprise us to hear Arne Duncan say, "we
actually have over 2 million high-wage jobs that are going unfilled" (Wheeler, 2012)
nor to hear Oprah Winfrey echoing think-tank research that "[m]any companies
are moving their factories to foreign countries and outsourcing jobs because

American workers are lacking basic job skills." (Winfrey, April 11, 2006). It has always been a comfortable illusion of the elite that poverty is a result of ignorance. Now, in order to make education into a profitable site for disaster capitalism, poverty becomes the fault of educators, whose incompetence and culture of low expectations are the whole problem. As Gates explains, "In district after district across the country, wealthy white kids are taught Algebra II, while low-income minority kids are taught how to balance a checkbook" (Gates, 2005). Of course, balancing a checkbook is much harder than algebra when you are struggling to make rent, and having kids learn algebra isn't going to create decent jobs or social supports. Similarly, closing failing public schools and firing unionized teachers won't close the achievement gap, but it may just help to widen the economic gap, which really isn't so bad if you're on the high side of the gap and your kids go to a private school.

References

Abowd, P. (2010, September 4). DC Teachers to vote on privately funded merit pay plan. Retrieved from http://labornotes.org/blogs/2010/04/dc-teachers-gear-vote-privately-funded-merit-pay-plan

Ayers, R. (2010, September 17). An inconvenient Superman: Davis Guggenheim's new film hijacks school reform. Retrieved from http://www.huffingtonpost.com

Burch, P. (2009). *Hidden markets: The new education privatization.* New York: Routledge.

Chapman, J. (2012, January 13). Bad teachers should be sacked 'in weeks': Gove wants parents in classrooms to help drive up standards. *Mail Online.* Retrieved from http://www.dailymail.co.uk

Cohen, R. (2001). *Alien invasion: How the Harris Tories mismanaged Ontario.* Toronto: Insomniac Press. Retrieved from http://books.google.ca/

Cowen, T. (2011, December 27). Why is India so low in the PISA rankings? *Marginal Revolution.* Retrieved from http://marginalrevolution.com

Failing grade. (2006, April 11). *The Oprah Winfrey Show.* Retrieved from http://www.oprah.com/world/Failing-Grade/1

Felch, J. (2010, August 16). U.S. schools chief endorses release of teacher data. *Los Angeles Times.* Retrieved from http://articles.latimes.com

Gates, B. (2005, March 1). What's wrong with American high schools? *Los Angeles Times.* Retrieved from http://articles.latimes.com/2005/mar/01/opinion/oe-gates1

Kohn, A. (2004, April). Test today, privatize tomorrow: Using accountability to "reform" public schools to death. *Phi Delta Kappan, 85*(8) 568–577. Retrieved from http://www.alfiekohn.org

Krause, N. (2010, March 1). Obama weighs-in on CF teacher firings. *Eyewitness News.* Retrieved from http://www.wpri.com

Maharaj, Sachin. (2012, February 29). Ontario teachers deserve to be paid more. *The Toronto Star.* Retrieved from http://www.thestar.com

Mak, T. (2012, January 27). Arne Duncan: Pay great teachers $150K. *Politico.* Retrieved from http://www.politico.com

A nation at risk: The imperative for educational reform. (1983, April). The National Commission on Excellence in Education. Retrieved from http://www2.ed.gov/pubs/NatAtRisk/risk.html

Ravitch, D. (2011, May 31) Waiting for a school miracle. *The New York Times.* Retrieved from http://www.nytimes.com

Roberts, G. (2012, February 26). Queens parents demand answers following teacher's low grades. *New York Post.* Retrieved from http://www.nypost.com

Sanchez, A. (2010, May–June). Disaster schooling: The education "shock doctrine." *International Socialist Review,* Issue 71. Retrieved from http://www.isreview.org

Santos, F., & Gebeloff, R. (2012, February 24). Teacher quality widely diffused, ratings indicate. *The New York Times.* Retrieved from http://www.nytimes.com

Shepherd, J. (2012, January 4). Michael Gove launches attack on anti-academy teachers and councillors. *The Guardian.* Retrieved from http://www.guardian.co.uk

Staples, D. (2012, February 14). Staples: Spare the tests, spoil the school system, former deputy minister says. *Edmonton Journal.* Retrieved from http://www.edmontonjournal.com

Teaching makes a difference. (2011, February 2). *Clickonwales.org.* Retrieved from http://www.clickonwales.org/2011/02/teaching-makes-a-difference/

Wallis, C. (2008, June). No child left behind: Doomed to fail? *Time.* Retrieved from http://www.time.com

Weil, D. (2009, October 5). Say you want a revolution?: Parents Revolution, 'astro turf' organizations and the privatization of public schools. *Daily Censored* http://dailycensored.com

Wheeler, J. (2012, January 22). Reforming education to fill technical jobs in Minnesota. *The Uptake.* Retrieved from http://www.theuptake.org

Whyte, K. (2010, September 21). Bill Gates on what's wrong with public schools. *Macleans.* Retrieved from http://www2.macleans.ca

Winfrey, O. Failing grade. (April 11, 2006). *The Oprah Winfrey Show.* Retrieved from http://www.oprah.com

Wintour, P., & Watt, N. (2011, June 14). Schools told to raise the bar on GCSE exam results. *The Guardian.* Retrieved from http://www.guardian.co.uk

13

More Than Graphs and Scripted Programs:
Teachers Navigating the Educational Policy Terrain

AMY SEELY FLINT, ELIZA ALLEN, TARA CAMPBELL,
AMY FRASER, DANIELLE HILASKI, LINDA JAMES,
SANJUANA RODRIGUEZ, AND NATASHA THORNTON

High-stakes accountability policies and mandates have flooded the educational landscape. There have been unprecedented efforts by state and federal governments to reform the quality and content of instruction in schools. The passage of No Child Left Behind (NCLB) in 2001 paved the way for states to adopt uniform assessments, prescriptive curricula, and negative incentives to achieve Adequate Yearly Progress (AYP). Teachers have responded to these mandates by narrowing the curriculum and focusing on test preparation. These decisions become inconspicuous and commonplace because they quickly become standard practices within schools and classrooms (Palmer & Snodgrass-Rangel, 2011). The consequences of such actions can be felt as teachers struggle to reconcile their own knowledge and experiences about individual students with the overwhelming pressures imposed by accountability policies and mandates.

A number of studies have examined the tensions teachers feel when federal policy messages and implementation intersect (Achinstein, & Ogawa, 2006; Achinstein, Ogawa, & Spiegelman, 2004; Chambliss & Vailli, 2007; Spencer, Falchi, & Ghiso, 2011; Stein, 2001). Extant, however, in the research literature are the voices of teachers as they navigate the educational terrain filled with policies, regulations, restrictions, prescriptions, reforms, mandates, and the like. To fill this gap, we highlight the personal narratives of six teachers who were faced with the unintended consequences of policy as related to language and literacy development.[1] Moreover, in this decade of regulatory practices, we make visible the agentive decisions and practices these educators enacted in their classrooms, districts, and communities.

Conceptual Framework

Educational policies and the messages they carry enter the classroom through a number of different explicit and implicit means, from formal directives to informal conversations and teachers' use of curricular materials. To extend our understandings beyond implementation of policy and to focus on how teachers negotiated and appropriated policy messages, we draw upon two lines of inquiry: sense-making and the role of stories.

Sense-making theory. Policy is typically characterized as a set of laws or normative guidelines that presupposes an implicit view of how things are and should be. To challenge the taken-for-granted perspective of policy, sense-making theorists (Coburn, 2001, 2005; Porac, Thomas, & Baden-Fuller, 1989; Spillane, Reiser, & Reimer, 2002) suggested that action is based on how people notice or select information from the environment, make meaning of that information, and then act on these interpretations. "Sense-making offers a window into how teachers mediate new policies through the lens of their preexisting beliefs and knowledge and, together with institutional theory, helps explain how policies permeate the classroom walls in the first place" (Palmer & Snodgrass-Rangel, 2011, p. 618). Teachers are active negotiators. They select some policy messages while discounting others and negotiate the technical and practical details necessary to translate the abstract into concrete actions (Coburn, 2005). The negotiation of meaning refers to a productive process that is not constructed from scratch. As Wenger (1998) reminds us, "by living in the world we do not just make up meanings independently of the world, but neither does the world impose meanings on us" (pp. 53–54). We make sense in a world we inherit and create.

Telling stories. As noted, we make sense of policies and practices by bringing previous knowledge and beliefs to bear in the construction of meaning in the present environment. One avenue that allows for us to make meaning is through our narratives. The power of narrative is clear and unbridled regardless of one's age, vocation, heritage, or socioeconomic status. Long before humans had the means and ability to use the written form to capture ideas and communicate with others, the spoken word was the main vehicle used to connect with others and make sense of the world.

Becker (2010) described language as "a constitutive force that works to influence individuals in implicit and central ways" (p. 413). He claimed that language helps shape self-perceptions and influences actions. Specifically, he examined how language serves to construct and preserve individual and group identities. It is through an interconnected web of stories, then, that we connect past experiences in order to understand new experiences.

Telling Our Stories

Sense-making of policy and the intended messages occurs across and within various institutional sites where policy flows and takes shape. Meaning is negotiated and appropriated as individual stories are shared in social contexts. In a graduate class focused on the social, cultural, and political contexts of early literacy development, a group of educators found themselves sharing stories of how educational policy influenced practice in both positive and negative ways. They were connected through common experiences and personal beliefs. Each struggled with maintaining integrity in the face of external mandates such as NCLB, Reading First, and Response to Intervention (RTI). In essence, a "community of practice" (Lave & Wenger, 1991; Wenger, 1998) formed whereby the more they shared, the more they uncovered common themes around courage and conviction.

The presented narratives are organized to highlight teachers' sense-making of individual students, school-wide curricular decisions, and community involvement. The stories, constructed through the constellation of "micro-momentary actions" (Porac et al., 1989, p. 398) enabled this group of educators to give form to their experiences. They speak of empowerment, agency, unity, and inspiration. According to Smiles and Short (2006), teachers are uniquely positioned to "document the complexity of classrooms and teaching through making known their insights and experiences [and in doing so] expand the conversations that are necessary if long-term solutions to the complex problems facing schools are to occur" (p. 146). These teacher narratives reveal the lasting contributions individuals and groups can make when they act on their convictions in the face of adversity (Flint et al., 2011).

The first two stories by Linda and Sanjuana illustrate the complexities of meeting children's individual needs that are often not addressed in policy messages. Natasha, Tara, and Danielle situate their stories in the context of the school and the challenges faced when one's own understandings of implementation are different from those of colleagues. And last, Eliza's story highlights community involvement as policies are enacted unfairly. The convergence of policies, practices, resources, and beliefs is evident in and throughout the narratives.

Intersection of Policy and Individual Student Outcomes

On a daily basis, teachers make informed, in-the-moment decisions that contribute to a student's learning trajectory. The particular policy messages and how they are mediated in classrooms have very real consequences for teachers and students.

More Than Graphs. The 2010–11 school year was the most frustrating of my (Linda) 17 years of teaching. I spent the better part of every week running in circles as I tried to get resource services for a student I knew was losing time with every passing day. Lamar² could barely transfer his name to a piece of paper, read eight words per minute, and had no real ability to even use a chair correctly. He had severe deficiencies in all academic areas and social behavior.

My school uses Response to Intervention (RTI) to identify students in need of additional services. Because of the different layers and tiers that the RTI process mandates, I gathered and charted 16 weeks of data necessary to present to the student services team. A day or so before the first scheduled meeting, which occurred in week 12, I was informed the meeting would be postponed 30 days because I did not collect phonics data on Lamar. I found myself in a very passionate debate in which I asked my principal to explain the importance of knowing whether a child could or could not identify digraphs when we already knew that he could barely write his own name and read on a pre-school level. While my principal tried his best to pacify me, he told me that I still had to follow the *protocol.* So, much to my dismay, I began to keep 30 days of phonics data, and we rescheduled the meeting. During this time, Lamar was suspended from school for a total of 10 days on different occasions. Finally, his behavior led to an incident in which he was sent to alternative school for 40 school days. I visited Lamar and found the school to be the most oppressive educational environment I had ever been in and wished I could take him with me when I left.

The meetings continued in Lamar's absence, and I was once again chastised for not keeping enough data. The district evaluator informed me that Lamar would not be eligible for behavior testing because I had not *graphed* a behavior *intervention.* In my disbelief, I thought about how I knew how much Lamar wanted to do the right thing but simply could not. I thought about all the times he had hugged me and told me he loved me, and the bear he bought for me at the dollar store that still sat on my desk. As the meeting closed, I sat there feeling like I was in a trance and said nothing else. I went back to my classroom and cried for the remainder of my planning.

Lamar eventually returned to my school. His time in my classroom remained challenging for him. Lamar finally *qualified* to receive 2 hours and 45 minutes of services daily from our resource department. As teachers, I believe we are to be *advocates* for our students. I often feel that I did not adequately advocate for Lamar, because if I had, it should not have taken 7 months to provide additional services. This is after working daily on his behalf. Given that he had little support in first grade and was made to wait 7 months into his second-grade year, he ended the school year almost 2 years behind grade level. Although I wish for a better outcome, I think Lamar will experience lasting academic and social effects from which he will not be able to recover. The policy message of RTI to prevent unnecessary placement of students in resource and special education had closed the door so tightly that those who needed the support could not get in.

What Is Considered Standard. It was my (Sanjuana) second year teaching in a small town in Northwest Georgia. The student population was predominately Latino, and most students received English as a Second Language (ESOL) services. All but two of the students in my first-grade class carried this distinction. Marcus was one of them. Marcus spoke African American Vernacular English (AAVE), and in the classroom he often switched between formal English and AAVE. Despite being a struggling reader and being labeled an at-risk student, Marcus was an avid storyteller. He loved to talk and he loved to learn. One of Marcus's favorite times of the day was writing workshop. Writing provided him with a forum to share his experiences using his own language.

Over the course of the school year, my goal was to build community through valuing my students' language and culture. We spent countless hours talking and thinking about community. We talked about classroom arrangements and seating. Charts were made as reminders of what our rights and responsibilities were in the class community.

Our community was challenged when a new teacher came into our classroom to provide ESOL support. One day as I was teaching, I overheard her speaking loudly to Marcus. She told him that the English that he spoke was not the *right* kind of English and that if he didn't pay attention, he would never learn to speak English the right way. Marcus looked defeated. Most of my students heard what was happening. They had just witnessed a teacher telling one of their classmates that his language was not good enough.

As I tried to make sense of this event, I thought of the context. What would make a teacher believe this about a student's language? What policies had impacted this teacher's beliefs? I debated in that moment about what I should do. I knew that an instance like this could have a lasting negative impact on Marcus. Language is intimately connected to our identity. Delpit states that "our home language is viscerally tied to our beings as existence itself" (2002, p. xx). I called Marcus to my table and talked to him. I told him how smart he was. I said it loud so everyone could hear, including the teacher who made the comment.

I was aware that my students knew that the rights and responsibilities of being a member of a community also applied to me. What were my responsibilities to this community and to Marcus? I debated for days after that incident about whether I should talk to the teacher. As a teacher of English Learners, I wondered where such a statement fit in with her beliefs about language and learning.

I did not raise my concern with the teacher, and I continue to question this decision. She never expressed those beliefs in my classroom again, but it did make me realize how political movements permeate classrooms and impact students. From this experience, I learned that as a teacher you have to make a commitment to be an advocate for students. I know that I must act when I think something is not right, while always looking through the lens of doing what is best for students.

Intersection of Policy and Teacher Beliefs

Recent educational reforms and high-stakes testing policies have significantly impacted how literacy practices are taught. The experiences of Natasha, Tara, and Danielle exemplify the constant seesaw of policy mandates and teachers' own beliefs about scientifically based reading research.

Sing-Song Baby Stuff. It was my (Natasha) third year teaching, and I remember feeling disheartened because I was asked to submit retention forms for low-performing kindergarten students in October. Before getting to know my students, I had to determine whether they would fail or succeed in kindergarten. It did not occur to me then, but this directive and many others implemented that school year were the result of political mandates stemming from NCLB. Performance standards were the state's focus, and my school district adopted a new reading program that aligned directly with these new standards. We were handed stacks of "Put Reading First" booklets, a publication of the Department of Education, to use as an instructional resource.

The looming task of completing the retention forms was interrupted by our weekly grade-level meeting. I knew that many of my colleagues saw this as another trivial task handed down from the administration, so I decided it was best to be positive. I wanted to talk about the strengths of students I had just completed retention forms for. Two of them, while struggling in reading, were doing really well with a book titled *No, No, Titus!* I explained that my students picked up on the rhyming and repetitiveness of the book and were really engaged in the story. Students used a flannel board and characters to retell the story and participate in a role-play activity. I saw these engagements as a way to increase motivation with text and support phonological awareness. One teacher agreed, saying that she used similar activities, but another teacher chided, "You do that sing-song baby stuff with your students, but I teach-teach!"—emphasizing each "teach" with a clap of her hands.

I was really surprised by her criticisms of my teaching, implying that her phonics-based instruction was the best way to teach reading. Her comments caused me to question what I believed about teaching reading and writing. Was I not challenging my students? Was scripted phonics instruction necessary for foundational literacy development? I wondered what other teachers believed about reading instruction and the students we worked with. I talked to some of my colleagues, and while most of them agreed that meaningful experiences with texts were important for young children, they also felt that the school's reading program was a quick solution for their struggling readers. Some believed that many of the students did not start school with adequate reading skills or literacy practices. Others believed systematic phonics instruction was better for the predominately African American students at this school.

It was evident in my conversations with fellow colleagues that NCLB policies did not align with what many at my school believed about teaching, learning, and literacy development. These tensions became even more apparent as I shared my experiences with others in different schools and districts. I realized that policy not only influenced what instructional materials and programs teachers implement but also their beliefs. Teachers' beliefs and ideas are shaped through the expectations of school districts and administrators—expectations that dictate teaching practices and begin to shape teachers' belief systems.

The remainder of the year was one of discovery. I resisted instructional practices that gave access to some and denied access to others. My beliefs were challenged and at times I did waver, for I was not immune to the pipeline of political mandates that influenced beliefs. Therefore, I worked hard to stay true to what I believed, and that school year, all of my students benefited from a range of meaningful literacy instruction, including sing-song baby stuff.

From Balanced Literacy to Chanting a Script. Rhetoric is powerful, but it does not have to define us. Erickson (2004) wrote:

Anyone who has sung in English cathedral-style choirs of men and boys knows that the boys, angelic-looking at a distance in their ruffs, cassocks, and white surplices, when viewed up close can be seen to be surreptitiously poking one another in the ribs, making faces, and passing notes as they sit in the choir stalls...they can be both inside and outside the ritual order simultaneously. . . .(p. 145)

Rhetoric pervades the education scene: omnipresent, but not omnipotent. In 2001, I (Tara) was scheduled to be a seventh-grade remedial reading teacher in the new environment of NCLB rhetoric; buzz words like "best practice," "scientific evidence," and "every child can learn" dominated staff development and faculty meetings. The discourse was powerful, and when some of it conflicted with our personal philosophies, we teachers began to question our knowledge about how to best teach our students.

As a remedial reading teacher, I had to comply with the prescribed methods recommended by the state. The balanced approach to literacy that we had previously embraced (literature circles, word play, etc.) would be replaced by a more systematic, phonics-based approach. I was dismayed when I opened up the teacher manual and realized that the word "script" was not merely rhetorical and that the lessons were overwhelmingly phonics based, with little regard for comprehension.

Every exiting sixth-grade student took the phonics-based diagnostic assessment. After reviewing the results, I was disturbed to discover that some of my students had already endured their prescribed text 3 years in a row. When I voiced my concerns about this, it was suggested that this is what "those students" needed and that if they still had not mastered the skills, they needed to repeat the level. (After all, it was research-based). The discourse had us in its clutches, so I began to use the discourse of these new policies and mandates to make changes from within, rather than blindly following the script. First, I used data from a variety of sources to move some of "those students" out of the prescriptive program.

Then, for the students who remained in my remedial classes, I implemented the program because of the mandate to do so, but I used it in my own way and to my students' advantage. I started every class by reading aloud from a young adult novel. The students and I negotiated how we would work through the program, using the prescribed materials and supplementing with other texts.

This was certainly not a landmark year in terms of what I accomplished with my students. It was a struggle, but what I learned was valuable. I promised myself that I would never again subject students to a daily regimen, taking for granted that those in power with powerful language know best. I have since given voice to my own philosophies without apology. I am not afraid to counter the prevailing rhetoric with a more open one, embracing a broad view of literacy that emphasizes meaning making as opposed to a strictly phonics-based paradigm of reading. I learned that I can make changes on the local level. I realize now that "the connections of influence between [the local-global] run in both directions—inward to the local encounter from the social world outside it, and outward from the local encounter to actions that take place beyond the temporal and spatial horizon of the encounter itself" (Erickson, 2004, p. 191). As the system shapes me, I can shape it in turn, and like Erickson's choir boys, accomplish goals more appropriate to my students and me as I wear the robe and sing the song.

Taking a Stand. For as long as I (Danielle) can remember, I imagined myself as a teacher. My mom says I get this dream "honestly" because teaching runs through my family's generations. My ancestors and I share a common desire to impact the lives of children by providing positive, meaningful educational opportunities. Yet our teaching stories are unique. Unlike my ancestors, my story as an educator detoured into uncharted territory. While they enjoyed pedagogical and curricular freedoms, I encountered the influences of educational policy.

Like many new teachers filled with inspiration and hope, my days in 2001 were consumed by collaborative planning, teacher-parent conferences, and endless hours of professional training. I made decisions about room arrangement, teaching techniques, learning activities, and materials. The school system required teachers to use quarterly instructional calendars for match and reading, but how we filled the instructional time was ours to decide. I opted to implement the workshop approach to provide students with continuous opportunities to learn and work at their instructional levels. Through the use of whole group mini-lessons, guided small-group instruction, literacy stations, and independent reading and writing opportunities, my third graders not only successfully mastered the required curriculum but also developed a passion for literature.

Surprisingly, my initial year concluded with a system-wide announcement that challenged my philosophical beliefs and changed my career path. I learned that a different language arts program had been adopted for the following year. The program, as described to me in a countywide in-service, was based on a "research-proven formula" to teach decoding, comprehension, inquiry and investigation, and writing. During the required training, explicit instructions were provided in the correct use of the scope and sequence, the three-part lesson plans, and the coding system in the teacher manuals. I knew this program would strip away my decision-making ability and would transform my classroom instruction beyond recognition. Gone would be reading and writing workshops. Thematically based literacy stations, daily read alouds, and word wall activities would also disappear. I realized that the diverse needs of my students might not be met by using these prescribed whole-group lessons. I vowed at this point that this was not the teacher

I would become. As a result, I submitted my resignation shortly after the training. I believed, like Harrison (2006), "Although we are accountable to the state, we also have a moral responsibility toward those we teach" (p. 129). I did not realize it at the time, but this adoption was a direct effect of NCLB, and I had taken a political stand against it.

As the years now pass in a different district with more flexibility and teacher decision-making opportunities, the pressures to conform to mandates and policies from NCLB continue to emerge. Teachers in my district are required to follow rigid instructional calendars, complete endless hours of paperwork for RTI, and routinely assess students using required standardized tests. Luckily, in my current role as an instructional coach, I help teachers to negotiate the "prescriptiveness" of required instructional calendars to provide appropriate, differentiated instruction for their students. We collaboratively analyze instructional calendars, discuss how the instructional objectives can be mixed and matched to provide cohesive, appropriate instruction, and design thematically based lessons that incorporate best practices of teaching. I further support teachers by modeling or co-teaching these collaboratively designed lessons in their classroom. Unlike my experiences early in my teaching career, teachers are not forced to sacrifice their philosophical and pedagogical beliefs, since tools and support are readily available. I have come to believe that teachers can persevere in the current political climate when given the resources and knowledge to work within the established system.

Intersection of Policy and Community Participation

Finally, a powerful story that invites the community to consider the ways in which policies and decisions are in the hands of the few with an impact for the many.

Why Were We Not Included? When the 2011 school year came to an end, my colleagues and I (Eliza) began to hear rumors from teachers at the neighboring middle school that our school would close in order to create a sixth-grade academy. At the next school board meeting we discovered that a committee of 30 members (parents, teachers from other schools, and administrators) had begun to explore how to deal with the overcrowding of our neighboring middle school. There was not one representative from my school on the committee. So what was our response? At first, phone calls and text messages went back and forth among the teachers. Why our school? Why were we not included on this committee? What about the students and how much they have already experienced? Realizing that our "school family" was in jeopardy, we decided to take action to not let an uninformed decision impact our students.

There were three groups we needed to hear from: teachers at the school, parents, and students. The teachers mobilized and began discussing ways to inform parents, the school board, and local community members. Despite possible consequences of losing jobs, teachers commented that they were going to stay steadfast in their convictions that the community should be informed. As a result of these meetings, the following public statement went to the press:

> The staff of Hamilton School considers it an honor to teach for the Montgomery School district, especially at Hamilton School. However, we are concerned about the Montgomery Facility Planning/Study Committee's recommendation to uproot the 715+ students of Hamilton School and reconfigure the facility into a 6th grade academy as a feasible option. There was no staff or parent representation from Hamilton School on this committee which was composed of 30 other Montgomery Public Schools staff, parents, and students. Although the Montgomery Public School Facility Planning /Study Committee began with a total of 39 options, only one is being explored.
>
> In considering the best needs of our students, we believe that our students deserve stability and the same rights of other students in Montgomery's communities. Our main concern is that this decision is being made out of convenience of organizational structures, but not in the best interest of students and families we so honorably serve.

Following the press statement, a community meeting was organized in which over 270 parents and teachers shared information. There was a feeling of urgency among parents to tackle the issue. Teachers and parents voiced concerns that parents from Hamilton School were not included on the committee because of a language barrier. Over 85% of the parents speak a language other than English. Emotions were evident as parents began to take a critical perspective on the lack of inclusion. One parent noted that it was just another way that Latinos in the community "were being walked over." The reference to race being a factor in the process became apparent when another parent commented that "I am concerned that Hamilton was targeted for closing because it is a minority school and they [the school board committee] thought parents would not object"; Michelle Brown, a Hamilton grandparent who is white, said, "I think tonight's meeting shows that they will [object] and that they will show up again."

Although parents and teachers were very active in this process, students played an important role. At the initial community meeting, several students came along with their parents to express their concerns at the meeting. It was these same students who stood on the front lawn on the first Monday afternoon of summer break, wearing their school t-shirts and carrying posters that said, "My School, My

Future, Save Hamilton" and "Let Our Voices Be Heard." The strongest support for being included in the decision-making process, however, came during a follow-up school board meeting. One former student said, "What you all are trying to do to Hamilton has 'wrong' written all over it. You're being greedy and selfish, not thinking of our students' education or of teachers' jobs. You're thinking of yourselves." Another student commented, "I want to keep my school because it's like my family," she said. "I want it to stay the way it is. Please don't change it." The voices of the teachers, parents, and students were heard. The decision to close Hamilton was reconsidered.

Acts of Resistance and Impact

Educational policies and their intended messages take shape as teachers, administrators, and other stakeholders engage with and expand the participatory parameters of what it may mean in particular contexts. The stories shared by the six teachers demonstrated that they were not simply automatons implementing policies without any regard for individual children, their own beliefs about teaching and learning, and the communities in which they work. Rather, the teachers worked to make sense of the conflicting policy pressures and demands in light of their experiences and knowledge. The informal conversations they had with each other each week in class provided a venue for constructing and reconstructing their understandings of policy and the unanticipated impacts. Sense-making, then, was a collective and situated practice (Coburn, 2001, 2005; Spillane et al., 2002) that resulted in sharing of stories. The narratives emerged as a way to critically reflect and engage in dialogue on professional practice, policies, and identity.

The rich complexity of the narratives reminds us that learning and teaching cannot be reduced to the "sameness" of a standardized curriculum or policy. "When teachers are forced to interpret everything that students say or do with reference to 'performance indicators,' 'learning continua' or standardised 'outcomes,' they invariably fail to respond to local difference and diversity" (Doecke & Parr, 2009, p. 68). Constructing stories about professional decisions and practices and sharing them with others can have widespread repercussions. Like ripples from a stone cast in water, the impact of advocacy for children, the profession, and the community can be realized in multiple ways. The narratives revealed the depth of these teachers' commitment to their principles. Moreover, the narratives make visible the teachers' voices and activism as they worked against prescriptive approaches and constrained policies in our current educational climate.

References

Achinstein, B., & Ogawa, R. (2006). (In)fidelity: What the resistance of new teachers reveals about professional principles and prescriptive educational policies. *Harvard Educational Review, 76*(1), 30–63.

Achinstein, B., Ogawa, R., & Speiglman, A. (2004). Are We Creating Separate and Unequal Tracks of Teachers? The Effects of State Policy, Local Conditions, and Teacher Characteristics on New Teacher Socialization, *American Educational Research Journal, 41*(3) 557-604

Becker, K. (2010). American education discourse: Language, values, and U.S. federal policy. *Journal for Critical Education Policy Studies, 8*(1), 409–446.

Chambliss, M., & Vailli, L. (2007). Creating classroom cultures: One teacher, two lessons, and a high stakes test. *Anthropology & Education Quarterly, 38*(1), 57–75.

Coburn, C. (2001). Collective sensemaking about reading: How teachers mediate reading policy in their professional communities. *Educational Evaluation and Policy Analysis, 23*(2), 145–170.

Coburn, C. (2005). Shaping teacher sensemaking: School leaders and the enactment of reading policy. *Educational Policy, 19*(3), 476–509.

Delpit, L. (2002). *The skin that we speak: Thoughts on language and culture in the classroom.* New York: The New Press.

Doecke, B., & Parr, G. (2009). "Crude thinking" or reclaiming our "story-telling rights." Harold Rosen's essays on narrative. *Changing English: Studies in Culture & Education, 16*(1), 63–76.

Erickson, F. (2004). *Talk and social theory.* Malden, MA: Polity Press.

Flint, A.S., Allen, E., Anderson, N., Campbell, T., Fraser, A., Hilaski, D., James, L., Rodriguez, S., & Thornton, N. (2011). When policies collide with conviction. *The Language Arts Journal of Michigan, 26*(2), 13–17.

Harrison, C. (2006). Sustaining myths, necessary illusions, and national literacy policies: Some U.S. and U.K. comparisons. *The Elementary School Journal, 107*(1), 121–131.

Lave, J., & Wenger, E. (1991). *Situated learning: Legitimate peripheral participation.* New York: Cambridge University Press.

Palmer, D. & Snodgrass-Rangel, V. (2011). High stakes accountability and policy implementation: Teacher decision making in bilingual classrooms in Texas. *Educational Policy* 25(4), 614–647.

Porac, J.F., Thomas, H., & Baden-Fuller, C. (1989). Competitive groups as cognitive communities: The case of Scottish knitwear manufacturers. *Journal of Management Studies, 26*(4), 397–416.

Smiles, T., & Short, K. (2006). Transforming teacher voice through writing for publication. *Teacher Education Quarterly, 33*(3), 133–147.

Spencer, T.G., Falchi, L., & Ghiso, M.P. (2011). Linguistically diverse children and educators (re)forming early literacy policy. *Early Childhood Education Journal, 39*, 115–123.

Spillane, J.P., Reiser, B.J., & Reimer, T. (2002). Policy implementation and cognition: Reframing and refocusing implementation research. *Review of Educational Research, 72*(3), 387–431.

Stein, S. (2001). "These are your Title I students": Policy language in educational practice. *Policy Sciences, 34*, 135–156.

Wenger, E. (1998). *Communities of practice: Learning, meaning and identity*. Cambridge: Cambridge University Press.

Notes

1. Earlier versions of the teachers' narratives have been published in the *Language Arts Journal of Michigan* (2011).
2. The names of students, schools, and districts are pseudonyms.

14

Not Bound by Stupid Binaries:
Dismantling Gender in Public Schools Through a New Consciousness and Claiming of Agency

DANA M. STACHOWIAK

Gender is often used to describe a person's sex as male or female, creating a binary that imprisons a rigid definition. Although Butler (1994) argues that "gender is produced through overlapping articulations of power" that force individuals to acquire and perform related social norms, our society operates through a hegemonic and heteronormative discourse that gender is biologically fixed (p. 3). Thus, the gender binary is an institutional ideal that works to separate, rank, and classify individuals, asserting a person is either male or female, but never both, interchanging, or neither (Butler, 1994). This dichotomous thinking encourages oppression and marginalization of not only women, but also those who do not conform to the norms (i.e., genderqueer or gender non-conforming individuals). The gender binary plagues our greater society and is most threatening in our public educational system. Schools serve as the site of both the production and promotion of the binary and, consequently, as a dangerous site of the production and promotion of marginalization and oppression.

My intent for this piece is three-fold. First, I engage in performative writing as a form of inquiry that closely examines my own experiences with gender binaries so that theoretical concepts and ideas can both support my experiences and develop within them. Additionally, I confront the toxicity of our current framings of the gender binary and dislocate normative thinking in regards to gender in educational settings. Next, I use this space to engage in a dialogue between myself and the reader, addressing the importance of agency in relation to debunking gender binaries that traditional norms of schooling currently support. Finally, I attempt to answer the questions of why and how we should even challenge gender binaries in educational settings. Specifically, I encourage the fostering of empowerment and agency through a new consciousness of gender that calls for individual reflexivity and critical dialogue. Empowerment necessarily requires a collective process of the individual and the community in challenging hegemonic assumptions that shape our identity. Critical consciousness and dialogue are vital components of empowerment that people cultivate to be agentic actors in the development of self and community through praxis (Freire, 2000).

Acknowledging, Examining, and Positioning My Subjectivity

My work in this piece is very personal. While I hold to the belief that all of my identities are asynchronous and altogether multilayered, there are positionalities that are important for me to consider when I set forth in my work. First, I am white, and I understand the power and privilege that comes with my whiteness (Johnson, 2006). Where all of my identities overlap and are negotiated, I understand that my whiteness allows for some easier, or possibly not any, negotiations of myself. I am currently a doctoral student, and my primary research interests lie in qualitative studies, queer theory, promoting social justice, and gender studies. I am queer and have a female partner. And, most essential to this work, I am genderqueer. I identify as female biologically, socially, and personally, but my androgynous appearance often gets me labeled as "gender non-conforming" in most social settings. I am hesitant to call myself female, however, based on the social constructs related to femininity. I think of myself as genderqueer because I do not embody femininity. As such, I am constantly working against heteronormativity through continuous self-examination in relation to norms in all of my experiences and social and political contexts. While I believe that this piece of my identity is at the crux of the study, my other positionalities intersect and flow with one another to create my personal frame of reference.

These pieces of my identity are generally thought of as intersecting only, and I want to trouble this only briefly. I struggle with the concept of intersectionality, often trying to find other words to replace it as I write. My argument is that the term intersection is dangerously problematic because it implies that only certain factors must align in order for two or more of our identities to come together and have significance over our situations and experiences. Although we are often encouraged to think of ourselves as being multidimensional (i.e., having intersecting identities) versus just having *an* identity (see, e.g., Tatum, 2003), intersectionality implies that the different aspects of our identity can be turned off, ignored, or simply managed. In my case, it is suggested that I cannot be a queer educator, for example; I can only be a queer *and* an educator, and my queerness needs to be managed differently when I am in the educator role versus when I am in, say, the partner or parental or friend role outside of an educational space. Alternatively, I argue that we come as a package, as an assemblage—my queerness comes with my whiteness comes with my femaleness comes with my Midwesternness; they never just intersect at certain points.

I applaud Jasbir Puar's (2007) call for "a move from intersectionality to assemblage" (p. 211) in our use of language in relation to the identification of the self. Intersectionality encourages difference, separateness, and further marginalization of the "other" when deconstructed. Puar's (2007) definition of assemblage is useful in recognizing and supporting the constant "identification, disidentification, and rearticulation, of constructing a new discourse of self" that all individuals encounter on a daily basis (Britzman, 2010, p. 194). In terms of this current piece about gender binaries, this definition is particularly powerful in asserting that not only do our own identifications come together and, therefore, cannot be separately managed, neither can socially constructed binaries"; an assemblage is more attuned to interwoven forces that merge and dissipate time, space, and body" in a way that challenges current hegemonic thinking and social regulation of identity (Puar, 2005, p. 128). Thinking in terms of assemblages of identity makes space for empowerment and agency. Thus, the conversation about gender needs to shift from identities as compartmentalizable and dichotomous to gender identities as simultaneously multilayered and fluid.

The shifting of the current conversation to the idea of assemblage in terms of gender binaries and related identities can help to expose the realities and emotional violence inflicted upon gender non-conforming individuals who are asked, often expected, to manage their identities to fit social norms. If we begin to understand the inner workings of gender identity navigation in its complete capacity, we can better understand what gender non-conforming students and teachers encounter in educational settings, and we can work to decrease negative visibility and further marginalization of the so-called queer community. I work from an assemblage of my identities and my experiences in this piece.

A Note about Performative Writing

Performative writing powerfully centers the self as a site "to both bear witness to how culture has been experienced, while also situating those experiences within complicated social and political contexts" (Berry & Warren, 2009, p. 604). It offers a space for self-questioning; it is contextualized, action-oriented, imaginative, and dialogic. Performative writing embodies a call for social justice, resistance, and agency. Performative writers find strength in a foundation that is unfinished, fluid, and allows for the colliding and hybridizing of self, social, and political. This dialogical and open space offered through performative writing is particularly helpful in critically analyzing the gender binary because it works as a catalyst for changing the ways in which we think and talk about gender in educational spaces.

With all of its seemingly radical and abstract offerings, performative writing also yields a careful criticism of what Scott (1991) refers to as the evidence of experience. Writers (and readers) of performative pieces need to continuously assess and reassess an experience as a site for the production of self, not as the definition or absolute rationale for the experience and those perceived as directly related (Scott); the experience cannot be written about or read as a privileged insider view of an issue (i.e., genderqueerness, in this case). Rather, performative writing should be seen as an opportunity to dismantle "the consciousness of an identity" (Scott, 1991, p. 785). I use performative writing as a method that works to dislocate institutional and hegemonic investments in framing gender as a binary of either female or male.

Berry and Warren (2009) ask us to consider whether or not writing about our experiences using performative writing "move(s) our scholarship and our pursuit of knowledge forward" (p. 599). I believe the answer is a resounding "yes"; this piece is a testimony to that belief. Performative writing dares both the writer and the reader to take responsibility to critically view an experience as fluid, ever-changing, and necessarily political. Using an experience as a starting point offers a space for critical self-questioning and reflexive pedagogy (Warren, 2011). My hope is that a look at my experiences with gender binaries offers both critical self-questioning and reflexive pedagogy for educators, providing a platform of agency for gender nonconforming students and teachers and their allies.

Not Bound by Binaries

Let's shift our thinking to a public educational space. Can you see it? A typical public school kindergarten classroom with a pink and purple kitchen set and a blue and red tool bench? The boys are playing at the tool bench or encouraged to play with the trucks, and the girls are gathered around the kitchen set or are playing with dolls. A boy walks over to play in the kitchen area, but the well-intended teacher re-directs him, telling him, "Boys don't play with the girls' toys." The little girls in the kitchen area shake their heads in agreement, and eventually the boy accepts this and goes back to the "boys' side" of the classroom. While this may seem a bit extreme, the socially constructed male/female binary is taught and learned at an early age and often in a scene like the one described. If a conversation regarding gender is even generated, it would most likely center on further ingraining and justifying the hegemonic discourse of the male/female binary. This binary is dangerously reinscribed as students progress through our public educational system, but rarely is it challenged as it is in the following scenario.

Conversation with a Fourth Grader (2010)

Scene I: I'm working in my office at a local elementary school. A boy I don't know enters quickly.

1) Hey! Are you a boy or a girl? **2) Me:** Well, hi. (I smile.) Let me ask you, what do you think? **3) Student:** Well, I am pretty sure you are a girl, but you wear, like, pants, and you have short hair. **4) Me:** Oh, I see. So, only boys can wear pants and short hair? **5) Student:** Well, no. But your shirt looks like a boy shirt. If you're a girl, why do you wear stuff that looks like it should be on a boy? **6) Me:** That's a good question…uh…what's your name? I'm glad you have the courage to ask. **7) Student:** My name is Tré. And, well, I see you in the hallways a lot, and other students say you're fun, and that you're a girl. So, I just want to know who you are, ya know? **8) Me:** Let's think about this together, Tré. (He nods in agreement.) Do you like to wear dresses? (He nods vigorously in *dis*agreement, wide-eyed.) Me either! And, I don't like pink. Just because most girls like to wear dresses and like pink, is it fair that I should pretend to like them if I really don't? **9) Tré:** No. I guess not. **10) Me:** Think of it this way: would it be fair if someone made you wear dresses and pretend that you liked them all day long? **11) Tré:** No way! **12) Me:** That's my point: I like to wear pants because I feel more comfortable in them than a dress, just like you. And, I like short hair, mostly because I don't have to do it, which means I get to sleep in! (Tré laughs.)**13) Tré:** Yeah, you're right. (Long pause.) Gotta go! (He runs out my door, but is back 60 seconds later.)**14) Tré:** Hey, is it okay that I tell others that you are a girl, and you are a really cool person? (I nod"yes.") Thanks! (He leaves.)

Scene II: Tré's classroom. I'm in to teach a literacy lesson.

Tré(to classmates): Hey, it's Ms. Stachowiak! Remember I told you about her? She's really cool (he whispers now), and she's a girl, too! Listen to her. She knows about keepin' it real.

Figure 1. Not Bound by Your Stupid Binaries [photograph]. May 13, 2012, from: http://25.media.tumblr.com/tumblr_l4j79r0lP71qzdznuo1_500.jpg

Clearly, my androgynous appearance aided in the commencement of this conversation, so it is important to first wonder if and how a conversation that challenges gender binaries would take place in a public school space. If no one with my genderqueer appearance was around, would this question even arise? I think it would in one way or another. Perhaps in the form of students questioning what makes something for boys only or for girls only. I am not certain, however, that it would be challenged, and this creates and perpetuates the problem of silencing within the gender binary.

Nonetheless, it is equally important to notice how this conversation exposes both danger and hope regarding conversations about gender binaries. The danger is in all of the places where the student asserted that certain elements of dress or accessorizing are male and some are female (Butler, 2004). The student's assertions work to marginalize and oppress those like myself who do not conform to the norms of gender. But there is hope in the simple and innocent question, "Are you a boy or a girl?" raised by the student. This is where questions for educators of why it is important to challenge gender binaries and how we go about it become vital. Here, critical dialogue can fuel individual and group agency of gender through creating a productive visibility of gender that dislocates the gender norms.

Just What *Is* Gender?: A "New Mestiza"

While the intent of this piece is not to seek a solid definition of gender, I aim to encourage critical thinking about gender and to challenge those who might otherwise merely accept the dominant definition. Butler (1994) asserts that "gender is performative" (p. 34), implying that male and female genders are socially constructed, and therefore, it is only the social norms of each gender identity that are "acted out" repeatedly by an individual. Consequently, the compulsory heteronormative society in which we live constitutes and encourages a gender binary that both limits and oppresses (Butler, 1994). This offers a quick explanation for the student who was adamant that certain qualities made me a boy instead of a girl; society insists people must be one or the other, male or female, and any crossing of socially constructed male and female norms is seen as worthy of question and definition. I necessarily think that male and female norms—the gender binary—ought to be and need to be questioned; however, our narcissistic need to establish a related absolute *truth* of gender is problematic in that it offers no fluidity, no space for those who do not fit within the gender norms.

The gender binary becomes a dangerous form of colonization in this way because it acts "by policing. . .legislating and regulating which identities attain full cultural significance and which do not" (Fuss, 1994, p. 21). In our society, men are hierarchically elevated above women and gender-conforming females and males, and these individuals are both regarded more highly than those who are gender non-conforming, androgynous, or genderqueer. This "inherited view of consciousness" inscribes that the differences between gender should be seen as hierarchical rather than interdependent (Alarcón, 1990, p. 357). The gender binary creates an invisible outsider category for those who are gender non-conforming that supports intersectionality and domination over assemblages and agency.

I find myself a part of this outsider position because, although I am biologically female, my inner identity does not fit all the norms of what constitutes female. Just as the student in Figure 1, "Conversation with a Fourth Grader," society has taught me (and most others) that women have long, flowing hair and wear skirts and high heels; men have short hair and wear loafers. According to Mohanty (1991), "women are constituted [by society] as women through the complex interaction between class, culture, religion, and other ideological institutions and frameworks" that is ultimately shaped by their female gender (p. 63).Within this, although I am female, I am not constituted as a woman because my assemblage renders me gender non-conforming or genderqueer. Here I find myself in the borderlands of gender identity. I liken this borderland to Anzaldúa's (2007) "new mestiza" (a person of mixed heritage), where a consciousness of our location on the borderland of our queer identity is an empowering form of agency. This new consciousness disrupts habitual modes of thinking, allowing for new and old modes of thinking to come together and form an assemblage of identity (Anzaldúa, 2007). I urge a new consciousness of gender non-conforming individuals as a means of challenging the traditional paradigms and normative democratic values that work to perpetuate the sadistic cycle of privilege and oppression.

Colonialism via Shape-Shifting Gender Identities

The oppressive nature of the gender binary also encourages a type of performance that is more problematic than the everyday practices of performativity discussed by Judith Butler. Gender performance supports colonization of those who find themselves a part of the borderlands of gender identity. Lee's (2002) writings on women of color occupying the borderlands of Western feminist theory are much like the borderlands in which genderqueer individuals like myself live; it can be a confusing place with constant conflicting emotions and readings of the self and world. Lee asserts that women of color "transform their identity according to their reading of power's formation" (p. 97). Within this, she credits Kimberlé Crenshaw with terming this navigation of identity as "shape-shifting," or "fitting one's shape into those forms already recognized by power formations" (p. 97). This is directly parallel to the work done by genderqueer individuals on the borderlands, because itcreates a tension within the borderlands of a genderqueer individual; shape-shifting creates a "struggle of flesh, a struggle of borders, an inner war" (Anzaldúa, 2007, p. 100) to conform or resist. My performance of "woman" and my queer core are constantly at odds, especially as a queer educator. Shape-shifting is what a queer educator does when s/he moves between performing queerness and performing heteronormativity; this can be done consciously or unconsciously, or in response to fear and powerlessness. I shape-shift between performing queer and performing "straight" on a daily basis as a queer educator, mostly for reasons of privacy and safety.

Today, I embody a genderqueer identity both in and out of public educational spaces, but I have not always done so. I was very closeted when I first began my teaching career, and passing as straight seemed necessary. In most of my roles as an educator, revealing my queer identity has not been safe. I have encountered homophobia in the form of name-calling, derogatory language, verbal threats, physical altercations, and intentional silencing. I was always on the lookout for anyone who might have thought I was queer, and I was always prepared to disprove their suspicions although I was, in fact, queer. In public educational spaces, I shifted my identity to conform to the female gender norms. My long, curly hair and my skirts and heels made my portrayal of straight femininity easy. As the young and single new teacher, several attempts were made to fix me up with my colleagues' sons, grandsons, and male friends. I even went on a few of those dates to increase my chances of passing, but this just further generated an inner struggle. My model, my imprint when I shape-shifted, was any female around who portrayed over-the-top femininity. I did not shift to this extreme, but the blatant identifiable markers of femininity made it easier to mimic, sort of suggesting (even if just in my mind) that I could pass as straight. And when I was not teaching, I embodied my genderqueerness.

Such mimesis, however, is violent because it ensures that dominant power relations and the colonialism of gendernorms work to subjectify and marginalize. Fuss (1994) echoes the work of Frantz Fanon on the mimesis of identity due to colonialism in much the same way. She argues that mimesis is "the most violent and primary mode of subjectification under colonial domination" because the reliance on another individual (i.e., a person of the dominant culture, or gender identity, in this case) to form one's identity virtually removes difference and promotes standardization and dominance (Fuss, p. 29). My shape-shifting from genderqueer at home to the female gender in public educational settings stripped me of my voice and worked to further marginalize myself and other genderqueer or gender non-conforming individuals. Even though I shape-shifted in order to create a safe reality for myself, it was clearly a "strong argument and. . .discrediting" of the reality of the genderqueer community in which I belong (Scott, 1991, p. 7). Shape-shifting became a form of assimilation for me that released opportunities for agency.

This brings us back to forming a new mestiza for the gender binary, a new consciousness for agency and decolonization. I agree with Scott (2007) that "assimilation means the eradication of difference," a fact that is much too violent for us to continue to overlook (p. 12). A new mestiza consciousness of the gender binary calls us to look toward embracing and celebrating the differences between genders and to imagine how these differences are actually interdependent rather than hierarchical (Alarcón, 1990). A new mestiza consciousness encourages assemblages of identities that can be navigated and articulated rather than intersections that force us to silence or ignore parts of our identity. Dismantling the normativity of the gender binary can break down the hegemonic practices so entrenched in our society. Coupling this dismantling with a new consciousness of gender identity(s) will help to locate and shape agency (Butler, 1994). This should be a necessary goal of educators.

Entangled ←→ Unbound

I agree there is no "proper gender" as society would have us believe (Butler, 1994). But, as a product of our gendered society, I still struggle to fully embrace this belief. Deep inside, I still hold on to the thought that because I am genderqueer, and therefore do not conform to social norms of gender, I am inferior and can never be fully human (Scott, 2007). I struggle to find self-agency precisely because of this. My agency today comes in the form of my embodiment of my genderqueerness. Whereas I used to conform to the norms of gender, I now employ my own sense of being human and work to dismantle my own investment of thinking that aligns with the gender binary. Nevertheless, I find myself "entangled in the hegemonic discourse" of the binary at times (Trinh, 1989, p. 52). A clear example of this is when I wear my knee-high boots with two-inch heels.

boots & queens

1. i love my knee-high leather boots with 2-inch heels the way the zipper sounds as i pull it up around my cavles that firm but silenced feel the point on the toe offers me direction i embody a [~~false~~] sense of [~~female~~] identity

2. the sound the heels make as i walk it's unnerving (that's more attention than I want to call to myself)
3. because what if someone realizes i'm wearing heels? *"dykes aren't supposed to wear heels!"* who am i kidding? dykes aren't supposed to wear heels . . .dykes LIKE ME are *not* supposed to wear heels.
4. i only wear men's dress shoes. (right?) with bike toes | or cap toes | or moc toes | or wing tips | or boots | or converse sneakers
5. iam →[caught up in soci-e-ty]← their wants and needs of the queer me
6. But i love my knee-high leather boots with their two-inch heels if only they made me feel like a woman but instead
7. i just feel like a drag queen

In attire that possesses femininity (the boots), I do not feel feminine. Rather, I feel like an imposter, like I cannot and do not embody the female character that society says I should. I don't feel female or male, so I am caught somewhere in between. This is the confusing and emotional space of my gender borderland. It is a look into the word that steals a hidden residence in my soul, but is still somehow visible. Homi Bhabha (as cited in Fuss, 1994), refers to this as a consciousness (or unconsciousness, if it is ingrained enough) "that threatens to split the soul" (p. 29). My soul desires authenticity but also the full acceptance of my peers. In this moment, it is important to stop and break down the parts of this experience (Scott, 1991). When I used to conform to gender norms of femininity, wearing my knee-high boots with two-inch heels felt good, natural. Even though I was embodying a false sense of female identity, nothing on the outside told me that I was not supposed to be wearing those boots. But now, as I embrace being genderqueer, wearing the boots feels uncomfortable, unnerving, pretend—because society tells me that people who look like me should not wear boots that are obviously meant for "true women."

As much as I find agency in disrupting the gender binary (Butler, 1994), I also feel a sense of resistance—resistance in the form of adhering to social norms of gender by not letting myself feel okay about wearing something that is socially feminine. This resistance is "agency that reinscribes domination" (Hartman, 1997, p. 54) because it is exactly what the dominant society *wants* me to feel: I cannot wear the boots because I am not really female. After all, *"dykes aren't supposed to wear heels!"* I can stew thinking about "if only they made me/feel like a woman," but just what does it mean to "feel like a woman" or to "feel okay" wearing the boots? That even though I love my boots but feel like I am not supposed to wear them is oppression hard at work (Butler, 1994). Why can't I just be who *I* am? Is it necessary to put a "truth" on who we are or what a gender is? I do not think so; absolute truths only endorse marginalization and oppression.

Perhaps it is here that I am really looking to be emancipated from the gender binary. But is all my talk and desire of self-agency a feasible reality? Some forms of my self-agency have reinscribed domination, so can emancipation even be at the end of my journey (Hartman, 1997)? I think it is really liberation that I am looking for from agency. Scott (1991) reminds us that "emancipation is a teleological story," a falsehood of freedom and autonomy that the dominant society assures us it is promising. So, I must be careful in the ways I think about agency and emancipation; my thoughts and desires for them need to be constantly and critically questioned. The same goes for educator allies of genderqueer folks. Our society has an ugly history of working to liberate others when, in fact, we are working to naturalize and universalize individuals (Newman, 1999). We often use emancipation in place of liberation, but emancipation requires the other to liberate us. We need to think of agency as the path to liberation instead. Constant questioning of ourselves, our intentions, and our choices in regard to dismantling the gender binary is therefore necessary and especially important for teachers who confront traditional norms of gender in educational settings. We need to constantly monitor how we are working to forge a new democratic value of gender that privileges individual agency versus a universalized form of thinking.

So What and *Now* What?

Gender is made visible and invisible by the complex social construction of it (Cooks & Sun, 2002). Gendered markers and standards, make gender visible. Because of the norms, however, it is rendered invisible; the standards act as rules that go without question. Men and women who ascribe to the gender norms can walk through their lives very seldom having to consider the effect that their gender has on their experiences. On the other side, genderqueer is made invisible because it remains hidden from the discourse. But those individuals who more closely identify as genderqueer are forced to constantly consider how they negotiate their identity in each and every experience, encounter, or situation. This creates a dangerously oppressive, silenced, and marginalized culture for genderqueer folks. The hierarchy instilled by the gender binary places genderqueer folks in a power(less) position behind women, who are behind men. This gender identity on the borderlands is a difficult and confusing place. The toxicity of a dichotomous view of gender is a reason we should dismantle it. And, since public schools are the main producers and retailers of gender constructions, there is no better place to begin a shift in dialogue around gender than in the classroom.

A shift in our thinking as educators requires that we begin with what I have mentioned several times: a new mestiza consciousness about gender. This needs to work not only to deconstruct but also to dismantle the oppressive repercussions of the gender binary. We need to celebrate rather than dismiss the fluidity and in-betweens of gender identities, think of them in terms of assemblages that work together to form all of humanity rather than separate pieces that can be managed, over-powered, and marginalized. This new consciousness requires an "awareness of our situation [that] must come before inner changes, which in turn come before changes in society" because "nothing happens in the 'real' world unless it first happens in the images in our heads" (Anzaldúa, 2007, p. 109). This awareness comes in the form of continuous reflexivity. We need to be able to look at our own selves, our own positionalities, and consider what has shaped and what continues to shape who we are and how we interpret and read both the word and the world (Freire & Macedo, 1987). This involves not only critical reflection but also necessarily critical dialogue and the fostering of agency. This new consciousness of deconstructing and resisting the normativity of the gender binary invokes the start of the enactment of agency (Butler, 1993, as cited in Mahmood, 2005).

Agency always requires careful attention to the possibility of false agency as well as to empowering agentic practices. Agency gained by universalizing or offering a false sense of emancipation is problematic. Dismantling the gender binary is more than rethinking and including a space for genderqueer individuals to claim. A space has limits that seek definitions for identities, not the fluidity and tolerance of ambiguity that is required to break down the binary (Anzaldúa, 2007). Agentic practices (from both allies and other genderqueerfolks) for emancipation do not acknowledge the importance of the individual in their journey toward liberation, because such emancipatory practices put the anti-oppressive efforts in the hands of those who are dominant (gender-conforming males or females, in this case). Aligning with Michel Foucault's thoughts around agency, Mahmood (2005) calls us to locate agency in the self, recognizing that it can look different in different situations and at different times. The bottom line, though, is that true agency is solely in the hands of the individual seeking it. Thus, agency looks different for allies of genderqueer individuals, as they, too, must locate agency in the self. No matter the seeker of agency—a genderqueer individual or an ally—each must begin by forming a new consciousness of the gender binary, one that dismantles, deconstructs, and reconstructs again and again. As educators, we absolutely have the ability and responsibility to demonstrate and encourage a new consciousness of gender for our students. My hope is that more conversations such as the one I will leave you with take place, not only inside the public school spaces, but in and throughout society as well.

Conversation with a Second Grader (2012)

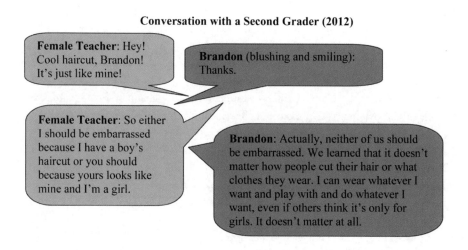

Female Teacher: Hey! Cool haircut, Brandon! It's just like mine!

Brandon (blushing and smiling): Thanks.

Female Teacher: So either I should be embarrassed because I have a boy's haircut or you should because yours looks like mine and I'm a girl.

Brandon: Actually, neither of us should be embarrassed. We learned that it doesn't matter how people cut their hair or what clothes they wear. I can wear whatever I want and play with and do whatever I want, even if others think it's only for girls. It doesn't matter at all.

References

Alarcón, N. (1990). The theoretical subject(s) of this bridge called my back and Anglo-American feminism. In G. Anzaldúa (Ed.), *Making face, making soul.* San Francisco, CA: Aunt Lute Books.

Anzaldúa, G. (2007). *Borderlands: La frontera/new mestiza* (3rd ed.). San Francisco, CA: Aunt Lute Books.

Berry, K., & Warren, J.T. (2009). Cultural studies and the politics of representation: Experiencefl-subjectivityfl-research. *Cultural Studies↔Critical Methodologies, 9*(5), 597–607.

Britzman, D. (2010). What is this thing called love?: New discourses for understanding gay and lesbian youth. In S. Steinberg & L. Cornish (Eds.), *Taboo: Essays on culture and education* (pp. 183–207). New York: Peter Lang.

Butler, J. (1994). Against proper objects. In E. Weed & N. Schor (Eds.), *Feminism meets queer theory.* Bloomington: Indiana University Press.

Butler, J. (2004). *Undoing gender.* New York: Routledge.

Cooks, L., & Sun, C. (2002). Constructing gender pedagogies: Desire and resistance in the "alternative" classroom. *Communication Education, 51*(3), 293–310.

Freire, P. (2000). *Pedagogy of the oppressed.* New York: Continuum.

Freire, P., & Macedo, D. (1987). *Literacy: Reading the word and the world.* Westport, CT: Bergin & Garvey.

Fuss, D. (1994). Interior colonies: Frantz Fanon and the politics of identification. *Diacritics,* 24(2/3), 19–42.

Hartman, S.V. (1997). *Scenes of subjectification: Terror, slavery, and self-making in nineteenth-century America.* New York: Oxford University Press.

Johnson, A.G. (2006). *Power, privilege, and difference.* Boston: McGraw-Hill.

Lee, R. (2002). *Notes from the (non)field: Teaching and theorizing women of color.* Durham, NC: Duke University Press.

Mahmood, S. (2005). *Politics of piety: The Islamic revival and the feminist subject.* Princeton and Oxford: Princeton University Press.

Mohanty, C.T. (1991). Under Western eyes: Feminist scholarship and colonial discourses. In C.T. Mohanty, A. Russo, & L. Torres (Eds.), *Third World women and the politics of feminism.* Bloomington: Indiana University Press.

Newman, L.M. (1999). *White women's rights: The racial origin of feminism in the United States.* New York & Oxford: Oxford University Press.

Puar, J.K. (2005). Queer times, queer assemblages. *Social Text,* 23(3–4), 122–138.

Puar, J.K. (2007). *Terrorist assemblages: Homonationalism in queer times.* Durham, NC: Duke University Press.

Scott, J.W. (1991). The evidence of experience. *Critical Inquiry,* 17(4), 773–797.

Scott, J.W. (2007). *The politics of the veil.* Princeton, NJ: Princeton University Press.

Tatum, B.D. (2003). *Why are all the black kids sitting together in the cafeteria? A psychologist explains the development of racial identity* (5th ed.). New York: Basic Books.

Trinh, M.T. (1989). The language of nativism: Anthropology as scientific conversation of man with man. In *Women, native, other: Writing postcoloniality and feminism.* Bloomington: Indiana University Press.

Warren, J.T. (2011). Reflexive teaching: Toward critical autoethnographic practices of/in/on pedagogy. *Cultural Studies ↔ Critical Methodologies,* 11(2), 139–144.

15

So This Is America:
A Narrative of Becoming and Being a Teacher

GALEN LEONHARDY

Current president of the National Council of Teachers of English (NCTE) Yvonne Siu-Runyan (2011) noted that "telling our stories is one of the most important things we can do for those we teach as well as for our profession." I agree. Offering real-life applications of practice, narratives play a key role in the movement to support and maintain emancipatory educational practices. Telling our stories presents hope for those teaching from a critical perspective and professes possibility for those who would teach critically. This chapter, then, is a critical literary endeavor representing both the hope and the possibility of my becoming and being a teacher.

The story goes something like this: In order to escape poverty, I took a position as an instructor at an alternative school in northern Idaho. I had to leave home and family. This teacher's story began as a letter to my daughters, Sarah and Hallie. They were quite young at the time—too young to understand the burdens of the poverty we endured or the choices adults make. I wanted to write a letter that would let them know why their dad was not home, something they could read once they were old enough. That letter became a journal. The journal became a detailed account of a teacher's day-to-day experiences that I call *The Alternative*. The material in this chapter originated in that larger work, and, consequently, the stylistic outcome combines the visual characteristics of a teacher's journal and that of a more traditional or academic essay.

Becoming a Teacher

From August 14, 2000

When I was in the seventh grade, in 1975, Anne Berlin taught at the junior high school I attended. She retired a few years ago, returning to the field when she noticed an advertisement in the local Kozol Creek paper calling for a school counselor. The same year, the school district separated from a larger district and initiated the process of constructing its own alternative high school. According to Dr. Fairbanks, our superintendent and acting principal, the separation was an act of local resistance against the larger school district, which had been, as he said, " . . . keeping the lion's share of what little funding there was from state and federal sources." Anne became program manager for the district's new alternative secondary-level program. This summer, I noticed the Kozol Creek, Idaho, school district advertisement for an alternative high school humanities teacher, applied, and was hired. My wife and I are poor. I needed the job, though it requires I live fifty-some miles from home. It's my first full-time teaching position.

The Educational Context

Dr. Fairbanks gave us seven days to put together our courses. I have nine classes to prepare.

Anne refused to allow me to construct my own library of free used books for the learner-centered process I proposed during my formal interview. Last month, despite my objections, I was required to order two sets of expensive skill-and-drill textbooks with which Anne was familiar. The first set focuses on building vocabulary and concludes with lessons on grammar and punctuation, all based on multiple-choice testing with no opportunities for students to apply what they are learning in relation to actual writing. The second set is from Glencoe. Even though I have not yet read them, I have been tasked with putting together entire course plans based on the corporate-produced texts. When asked why she is requiring me to use the skill and drill textbooks, Anne responds, "We want a curriculum that can be used by anybody, don't we?"

I told both Anne and Judith O'Leary, the math and science teacher, that I am opposed to the one-size-fits-all approach and pointed out that it would make more sense to move away from the same processes of education that had not allowed access for the youth with whom we would be working at the alternative school. I did not point out my desire to make the classroom a place of social and political transformation, a place where the students could develop beneficial and responsible ways of finding inclusion as well as responsible ways of exercising what Peter McLaren (1989) describes as "moral and political indignation" (p. 202). Nor did I go so far as to explain that using textbooks such as those Anne wants me to use represents a deskilling process that has affected public school teachers and students across the country (Aronowitz & Giroux, 1993, p. 2).

I did, however, say that even John Dewey (1939) was opposed to an educational diet based solely on "predigested materials" (p. 671), noting that Dewey recognized traditional education, with its adherence to a textbook-based process, supported a school environment in which the teacher did not have to become intimately acquainted with the local community or come to understand how those texts might be connected to students' current lived experiences (pp. 668–671). "That is," I continued, "the material the students deserve needs to be connected to their daily experiences as well as their academic needs, and the problem with the textbooks you are asking me to use is that they are not only distanced from the students' local knowledge but, more often than not, they are also distanced from actual writing."

I noted that Aronowitz and Giroux (1993) explain that teachers need control over their work conditions, that teachers need to move away from nationalized testing and standardized curricula while moving toward teaching practices that are contextually relevant, practices that support inclusive opportunities for local knowledge while providing students with the kinds of cultural knowledge that will allow them to gain access to processes of power from which they are excluded (p. 11).

Anne refused to enter into the discussion, concluding her involvement by saying, "Well, you just finish making these courses, and then we can see if what you want to do will work."

I simply have to face the reality that neither Anne nor Judith will support an alternative to the standardized, status quo curriculum they are constructing. It is all they know, and neither seems willing to enter into a scholarly discussion, one rooted in the findings of current studies and the application of that information to the practice of teaching. Neither is prepared to move beyond the reductionistic, myth-based, and intellectually isolated vision of education each maintains.

206 | *Becoming and Being a Teacher*

From August 24, 2000

Today was our moving day. At last, we were ready to move out to the alternative school's location, the Forest Service's Kozol Creek Research Station, a research facility fifteen miles from town and less than a mile from a small wilderness area. Old-growth cedar and white pine surround the area. In addition to the main classroom, the school building has four rooms upstairs and a huge kitchen facility with separate dining and cooking areas.

Being a Teacher

August 31, 2001

This was actually the first day that I had students in the humanities room, and I have made the decision to teach from a critical perspective, despite the risks. I asked the youth, once seated, to touch their pinkies to their thumbs. All of them did that. Right away, there were pinky-thumb gang signs being flashed all over the place. After the students calmed down a bit, I told them that by virtue of being able to touch their pinkies to their thumbs, they were human.

"In this classroom," I added, "the first thing and the last thing we start with is the idea that we are all what Howard the Duck termed 'big talking hairless apes.' You are human. I am human. We are all human. So we can all learn. You can teach me, and I can teach you. We can reason. We can think about where we live. And because we are all human, we can change. In fact, I think we can change the world if we work together."

The rest of the day was spent handing out the texts Anne wanted me to use. In addition to checking out books, I made a point to find out what each student wanted to study. More than half had contemplated possible projects. Perhaps the most aggressive plan came from Gina North, who told me she wanted to graduate by Christmas so she could enroll in a college and get a degree in sociology and counseling that would allow her to support herself and her son without having to rely on money from the welfare system.

A Collaborative Solution

September 18, 2000

Gina North and I have collaboratively negotiated her classes.She will read (or is in the process of reading) Jonathan Kozol's *Amazing Grace* (1995), Niccolò Machiavelli's *The Prince* (1517/1981), Howard Zinn's *A Peoples' History of the United States* (1999), Rius's (the pseudonym of Eduardo del Rio) *Marx for Beginners* (1976), and Karl Marx and Friedrich Engels's *The Communist Manifesto* (1848/1967), among other works. She will keep dialectical journals for each text she reads, communicate online with students in New York about Kozol's work, and write two final research papers. In addition, she will read the introduction to a British literature textbook that Anne Berlin has required me to use.

I contacted a teacher from New York City. Her name is Lori Mayo. We met as members of NCTE-Talk, a listserv for teachers sponsored by the NCTE. Gina wanted to know if what Kozol had written was true. She sent questions about *Amazing Grace* as well as quotations from Kozol's work to the students in one of Lori's classes, and some of those students have replied.

Though the students in New York were interrupted by a fire alarm at their high school, the posts were quite detailed. All the students introduced themselves. Some responded to Gina's initial questions. Among them, one student noted, "There really isn't that much drug dealing around. . .cause police sweep around every night." Several students informed Gina that the city had both positive and negative aspects. But Kozol's claims were ultimately confirmed. One African American student wrote, "It hurts my heart seeing drug addicts on the streets. Being an African American I am destroyed [when I see] my people living in the streets addicted to drugs." Another student told Gina about a friend who had been shot twice in the chest for "looking at someone the wrong way." One student discussed a homeless lady who was "sitting on the sidewalk asking for help and no one would stop to help her."

Lori said that the students in her class " . . .can't believe you have 35 [students] in the school—we have 35 in a class, probably 3500 in the building." She also talked about the fire alarm that had interrupted the class while the students were writing to Gina. I felt lucky to be teaching in a small alternative school in the middle of the woods in northern Idaho, where the only fire drill we had consisted of my booming voice ("Fire! Fire! Fire!") and a ten-minute break—outside—in the woods where birds chirped and a gentle breeze comforted us.

Being in the woods, however, is not always so wonderful. We had enough to deal with in our own small community. Out of 35 students, one had been shot in the chest three times by a cousin. At least ten were involved with meth. One had stolen several cars. Most had dropped out of school. One student spoke of stepping over family members and strangers too intoxicated to stand. At least a third of the female students have communicated experiencing various forms of rape. One, for example, had been raped and left for dead in a ditch. Another student had a brother who had been killed and then dropped down a well. One female student had a brother who had murdered another student's brother. One student had to testify against her father in a child pornography case. And several students had actually been abandoned by one or both of their parents.

Conclusions and Observations

Even though youth at our alternative school have beautiful mountains and forests to walk, wonderful rivers and lakes to swim and fish, and fewer people to crowd them, they still experience horrific forms of violence and poverty. Their poverty is rural poverty. The violence takes place in the country, where people are less likely to hear you scream. This is why I facilitate problem-posing research and student-centered learning. It shows us limited situations, not what textbook companies sell. What the combination of Gina's research, the comments on Kozol's work by the students in New York City, and the experiences of the alternative school students indicate is that poverty and violence are systemic to the American experience. The next question is simple: So what do we do about it?

November 22, 2000 (Wednesday)

> The project of critical pedagogy is positioned irreverently against a pedantic cult of singularity in which moral authority and theoretical assurance are arrived at unproblematically without regard to the repressed narratives and suffering of the historically disenfranchised. (McLaren, 1995, p. 81)

Like many educators, Anne and Judith claim to teach students middle-class values in order to solve systemic problems such as poverty. Both have post-WWII-white-baby-boomer perceptions of what the middle class is. Their pedagogical perceptions produce contradictory results because they are ideologically *webbed in.*

McLaren's (1995) claim in the epigram beginning this section—that the narratives and suffering of the disenfranchised remain subjugated—is true enough. The fact is, I have witnessed educators actually boast of refusing to listen to or accept stories of human suffering, though that kind of selfish denial does not seem the norm for classroom teachers. Rather, as McLaren indicates, the problem is sociological: well-intentioned educators simply enable the continuation of that suffering rather than facilitate liberation, in the end constructing what McLaren describes as a kind of catharsis rather than real liberation (p. 83).

Educators like Anne and Judith are culturally encouraged to act without mindfully questioning their moral authority or theoretical perspectives. There is less resistance, less to fear, when you teach the status quo. There is less to fear when you slam down a Glencoe textbook than when you let the students experience what primary sources might offer. This is escapist education. Educators failing to critically engage their own beliefs, their own ideals, their own theoretical foundations, and the outcomes of their actions are impulsive educators, and the simple fact of the matter is that their unquestioned ideologies confound the potential of students. In fact, educators who rely on predigested materials are, as Aronowitz and Giroux (1993) describe the condition, basically allowing themselves to become deskilled technicians (p. 11). Because they are ideologically webbed in, these deskilled and impulsive pedagogues produce what Dewey (1939) termed "non-educative" experiences. According to Dewey, not adapting material to the needs and capacities of students as individuals is a pedagogical failure (p. 671).

To make matters worse, Anne spends her time and energy rescuing students. She tries to rescue them from emotional, physical, and even economic suffering. She throws life preserver after life preserver out to the students to help ease their suffering. The sorrowful reality is that Anne throws life preservers into spider webs. As a means of rescuing students from economic suffering, for example, Anne gives students money. There is a kindness in such action. She literally hands cash to students. Yet she fails to accept the reality that every student at the school but one lives in or near absolute poverty. She fails to understand that poverty is systemic to the American experience. She fails to see past her nationalistic perceptions and TV-created ideology. Anne's false generosity allows her to dole out money without acknowledging that in a country as rich as America, she shouldn't *have* to give students money. She fails to see that handing out money does nothing to solve the real problems of injustice and inequality. By not allowing her students to see that inequality, she limits them.

210 | *Becoming and Being a Teacher*

Judith teaches students to be successful on state-mandated tests while the students are taking the tests, yet she does not teach students to critically understand the tests. I admire that she teaches students processes for taking a test. Yet that test, like all the rest, means nothing to most of the students and means nothing in the great scheme of learning and will mean nothing to those who grade and read the tests beyond the fact that some group (the test makers and officials of education and overseers of government) has made a test that students across the state *must* take. It is all a kind of lunacy. And by not helping her students to see that lunacy and the oppression it maintains, she limits them.

In terms of middle-class values, what Anne and Judith want is not a stable condition. The middle class of today easily becomes the poor of tomorrow. Moreover, the reality of what middle-class values are shifts from place to place and time to time. Middle-class rural Idaho is different from middle-class Seattle, Washington, and middle-class values in Nazi Germany were still middle-class values. Claiming, as does Payne (1998) in *A Framework for Understanding Poverty*, to teach or transfer the hidden rules and cognitive strategies of the middle class confounds reality. Middle-class values are not reified. Unlike poverty in America, which is systemic, middle-class values shift across geographic spaces, between cultural boundaries, and over time periods. Anne, Judith, and Payne might as well be teaching students to become Reiki masters. Being middle class does not let us magically understand ethical action. Fact is, the middle class can be every bit as combative and disruptive as any other group. It seems far more realistic to acknowledge that "the key to achievement for students from poverty is" creating relationships that do not perpetuate the status quo (see Payne, 1998, p. 142; Baker, Ng, & Rury, 2006; Bohn, 2006; Bomer, Dworin, May, & Semingson, 2008; and Gorski, 2006, 2008).

In order to teach against the status quo, what Anne and Judith should aspire to teach are *reasoned values*. Reasoning allows us to live intendedly. Reason puts us on the moon. Reason allows us to see into space. Reason lets us build skyscrapers. Reason allows us to strive for a necessary principle, a moral imperative. Reason allows us to quest for compassion, fairness, and/or equity. Reason allows us to achieve right action. There is no other way around it. Right action is the necessary consequence of moral reasoning, nothing less, nothing more. Being a teacher means I need to acknowledge that oppression is wrong. After that, I must act accordingly.

My presence at the school exposes the falsehoods of what teachers like Judith and Anne are teaching. I don't bother telling them they are wrong. That doesn't work. My focus is on facilitating students as they grow academically, on helping students talk about oppression and discover how they might commit themselves to the praxis of transforming reality. Neither Judith nor Anne knows how it was for me to be poor and on welfare and taking out loans in order to go to school. Neither Judith nor Anne knows how much my loan payments are. Neither Anne nor Judith understands that the school district is not paying me enough to make my loan payments and support a family.

But the students do.

They have heard those narratives and have contributed their own as well. We name the problems. It's not about *pathoi*, not about emotional appeals. It's about learning how to overcome oppression. It's ethos and logos. It's exemplification and narration and description. It's about real education. It's about learning to identify limiting situations and then determining what can be done to solve those problems. It's about building a future intentedly.

In Gina's case, the solution is education—for the sake of earning a degree in sociology and counseling so she can help other children like herself, children who have had to testify against their fathers in child pornography cases.

The reality is my colleagues and I conflict ideologically. Theirs is the unrecognized ideology of the status quo. For them, handing out money, teaching middle-class values, and creating success on state-mandated tests are the solutions to various forms of poverty, illiteracy, and violence. Yet neither Anne nor Judith can clearly define what they support or believe, nor do they recognize the myth that founds their pedagogical practice because they are unable to escape the fuzzy, semi-unquestioned ideas and ideals that construct their belief systems. As a result, neither really questions the authority of traditional practices. Anne and Judith support those who have power. Both unconsciously espouse the life ways of the class structures and belief systems that web students into the sticky fabric of oppression. I, however, have chosen to become a different kind of teacher.

Dr. Doug Davidson and Richard Harwood have my gratitude for editorial assistance with this journal entry.

References

Aronowitz, S., & Giroux H.A. (1993). *Education still under siege* (2nd ed.). Westport, CT: Bergin &Garvey.

Baker, B., Ng, J., and Rury, J.(2006, June 7). Questioning a speaker's knowledge of poverty. [Letter] *Education Week*, 25(39), 36. Retrieved from http://www.edweek.org/ew/articles/2006/06/07/39letter-2.h25.html.

Bohn, A. (2007). A framework for understanding Ruby Payne.*Rethinking Schools, 21*(2), 13–15.

Bomer, R., Dworin, J.E., May, L., &Semingson, P. (2008). Miseducating teachers about the poor: A critical analysis of Ruby Payne's claims about poverty. *Teachers College Record, 10*(11). [Online]. Retrieved from http://www.tcrecord.org/content.asp?Content sId=14591

Dewey, J. (1939). Philosophy of experience (from *Experience and education*). In J. Ratner (Ed.). *Intelligence in the modern world: John Dewey's philosophy* (pp. 662–673). New York: Random House.

Gorski, P. (2006, February 9). The classist underpinnings of Ruby Payne's Framework. *Teachers College Record* [On-line]. Retrieved December 13, 2006, from http://www.tcrecord.org/ content.asp?contentid=12322

Gorski, P. (2008). Peddling poverty for profit: Elements of oppression in Ruby Payne's Framework. *Equity and Excellence in Education, 41*(1), 130–148.

Huyck, W. (Director), &Lucas, G. (Producer). (1986) *Howard the duck* [Motion picture]. Los Angeles: Universal Studios.

Kozol, J. (1995). *Amazing grace: The lives of children and the conscience of a nation.* New York: HarperCollins.

Leonhardy, Galen (2011). *The alternative: A teacher's story and commentary.* Brooklyn, NY: Noble Press.

Machiavelli, N. (1981). *The prince* (G. Bull,Trans.). London: Penguin. (Original work published 1517)

Marx, K., & Engels, F. (1967). *The communist manifesto* (S. Moore,Trans.). London: Penguin. (Original work published 1848)

McLaren, P. (1989). *Life in schools: An introduction to critical pedagogy in the foundations of education.* White Plains, NY: Longman.

McLaren, P. (1995). *Critical pedagogy and predatory culture.* New York: Routledge.

Payne, R. (1998). *A framework for understanding poverty.* Baytown, TX: RFT Publishing.

Rius. (1976). *Marx for beginners* (R. Appignanesi,Trans.). New York: Pantheon.

Siu-Runyan, Y. (2011). Telling our stories for we must. National Council of Teachers of English. Retrieved December 28, 2011, from http://www.ncte.org/dayonwriting/ teacherstories

Zinn, H. (1999). *A people's history of the United States.* New York: HarperCollins.

Part IV. Being a Teacher: Accountability and the Death of Democracy

16

Neoliberalism and the Filipino Teacher:
Shaking the System for a Genuine Democracy

REGLETTO ALDRICH D. IMBONG

No country is immune from the effects of neoliberal globalization. As "the hegemonic ideology of our time" (Giroux, 2005), neoliberalism has shaped all social institutions over the globe such that even policies and developments in education are not spared from its pressures (Mok, 2006). As "a distinctly US economic model" (Dale & Hyslop-Margison, 2010), its influence extends to the Philippines through U.S. imperialism. Specifically, it has shaped distinctive characteristics of Philippine education—characteristics that are crucial for the fashioning of the Filipino teacher's subjectivity, discourse, and even lifestyle.

An analysis of the current characteristics of Philippine education reveals two important points. On the one hand, it gives us a holistic view of the system and how it produces and legitimizes certain forms of knowledge. This epistemologically related position has three implications. First, it clarifies the issue of the relevance of knowledge. Second, it tries to touch upon the basic relation between knowledge and power. Knowledge is power, but Foucault and other postmodernists have pointed out that power more often determines what stands as knowledge (Krippner, 2011). Third is the transformative or liberating aspect of knowledge. Pedagogy[1] must be transformative in nature (Macedo, 2005). Knowledge must attempt to open new horizons, enabling both teachers and students to see the interplay of the different powers that structure their society, and provide opportunities to develop a critical attitude vis-à-vis the established socio-political realities (Giroux,

2005). These are important points that Filipino teachers must understand if they desire to make their lessons relevant in a postmodern and postcolonial period.

On the other hand, through an analysis of the current educational system, we can make transparent how neoliberalism has reduced the Filipino teacher to a mere commodity and machine, used by U.S. imperialism through its local ruling elites, to preserve a domesticating education that instead of empowering students to transform the world trains them to accept and adapt to it (Freire, 2005; Shor, 1993). In what follows, I shall discuss the nature of Philippine education in the context of U.S. imperialism's drive to maintain power over the Philippines.

Commercialized, Colonial, and Fascist Education

Through the impact of globalization, the concept of public education has been delegitimized in favor of a business-like, commercialized type of education (Mok, 2006).[2] It is important to note that the scheme to commercialize "higher education is basically carried out as part of the 'Washington Consensus,' which includes the privatization of public universities" (Delgado-Ramos & Saxe-Fernández, 2009, p. 36). Describing this kind of phenomenon, Mok—quoting from the World Bank—argued that educational reforms under neoliberal economics must "be accomplished with increased financial inputs from families and individuals and decreased inputs from the state" (Mok, 2006, p. 19). Commercialization of education has been a scheme naturalized under neoliberalism that has eventually placed education in "a context of limited supply and is available for a certain price" (Delgado-Ramos & Saxe-Fernández, 2009, p. 36).

Aside from its *commercialized* nature, education in the Philippines has been and remains *colonial* in orientation. Implicitly or explicitly, it does not so much answer the basic needs of the country but rather encourages its people, through established curricula, both to serve foreign demands and to commit historical and social amnesia. How is this done?

The Philippine government has seen the need to make education globally comparable and competitive (*Commission on Higher Education Strategic Plan for 2011–2016*). Acknowledging that globalization has demanded a lot from Philippine education (Dumlao-Valisno, n.d.), curriculum restructurings have been implemented to meet market demands. The World Bank and other financial institutions serve to influence, if not to direct, these restructurings (Mok, 2006).

Executive Order 358, for example, allowed the integration of vocational qualifications approved by the Technical Education and Skills Development Authority (TESDA) in the early years of higher education programs (Arroyo, 2004). By doing so, courses that are critical by nature are shortened, if not eradicated. This has also been the practice even in basic education, ever since the Department of Education (DepEd) implemented the Revised General Education Program (RGEP) at the University of the Philippines, and the Revised Basic Education Curriculum (RBEC). Common to both curricula is the integration of several learning areas into one subject; the most-affected learning area in these curricula is social studies. Class hours for other subjects such as English, math, and science are increased, while those of history and social studies are shortened. At stake here is the cultivation of a nationalist spirit and critical citizenship among Filipino teachers and students. The problem is that "if we ignore the epistemological issues addressed here and the education they help generate, the most important political values that many of us profess to support—for example freedom, democracy, liberty, etc.—will soon fade from our historical memory" (Kincheloe, 2008, p. 48).

Worse, though history is still taught in classrooms, this is done in the context of either Spanish or American historiography, although the latter is more dominant today. This is a process that eventually devalues and demonizes the role of the Filipino masses in history. As claimed by Tiongson and quoted in Tupas (2008, p. 49),

> [w]ithin standard historical accounts, Filipinos have all but disappeared, as evidenced by the erasure of the Philippine American War and Filipino insurgency against US imperial rule; if Filipinos appear at all, it is usually as objects of derision—savages unfit for self-government, economic threats displacing white labor, sexual deviants obsessed with white women, or ungrateful recipients of US beneficence.

These historical texts are primarily written using the perspective of the colonizers rather than the colonized, of the oppressors rather than the oppressed (Constantino, 1975). In this education, it "effectively transformed the image of the colonizer from conqueror to benefactor" (Constantino & Constantino, 1975, p. 341).

The arm of colonial education reaches even to the issue of the promulgation of English "as the primary medium of instruction in all levels both in public and private learning institutions" (Dumlao-Valisno, n.d., p. 6). Ever since the American colonial period, English has been the language used to teach the colonized people, and today it is used as a very important instrument for neocolonial hegemony (San Juan, 2007). What has been ignored here is the fact that language is a social phenomenon that "cannot be abstracted from the forces and conflicts of social history" (Giroux, 2005, p. 143). Any dominant language is a product of historical and social struggles (Giroux, 2005) and, more importantly, is cloaked in economic neo-colonial purposes. As a matter of fact, as the Philippine government continues to boast Business Process Outsourcing (BPO) as its "sunshine industry" (Danlog, 2005), it continually caters to the needs of U.S. imperialists and other foreign investors in their search for a cheap labor force in the Philippines (Salamat, 2006; Danlog, 2005). Preparation of both teachers and students for this economic agenda necessitates the strong implementation of the English language in all educational levels.

Miseducation is even coupled with control through physical force and violence. As fascist rule continues to dominate Philippine society, so also does it demonize the lives of both teachers and students inside campus gates. On the pretext of conducting "counter-insurgency" programs, schools are haunted by military personnel, demonizing and labeling radical organizations as fronts of the Communist Party of the Philippines–New People's Army (CPP–NPA) (Alliance of Concerned Teachers [ACT], 2007). As these armed men/women preach the so-called "evils" of communism, they call on the leaders of radical organizations and warn them "to stop joining protests as they might be the next 'target'" (Leal, 2006; Campus Repression and Counter Insurgency Section, para. 3).[3] These organizations oppose imperialist intervention in the Philippines and have waged a nationalist and democratic struggle. *Fascism* in the Philippines is nothing more than a war waged against national liberation and democracy.

Commercialized, colonial, and *fascist* education is a system built to further an agenda. But in this case that agenda furthers neither the Filipino people nor national development. Rather, it is a system intentionally established to strengthen the hold of U.S. imperialism in the Philippines. As U.S. imperialism has become more and more strident in its drive to establish hegemonic power over the globe, so, too, have its neoliberal policies intensified in influencing economic, political, military, cultural, and educational policies in the Third World. The Filipino teacher, as an individual shaped by the very conditions of neoliberalism, has been used as a tool for the U.S. imperialist agenda.

The Filipino Teacher in Crisis

The current educational system has serious consequences as to how the Filipino teacher acts/reacts vis-à-vis Philippine social conditions. The *commercialized, colonial,* and *fascist* orientation of education creates specific characteristics of the Filipino teacher that condition his/her pedagogy. Drawing from this argument, we can posit two contradictory types of teachers in the Philippines today. On the one hand, education students, teachers, and academics are forced to perform what has been required of them. This means that they are reduced to becoming both commodities ready to provide whatever the market demands, and mechanical beings ready to transmit and deliver whatever strategies, concepts, and techniques are currently accepted and prepared for them.

On the other hand, there are individuals who have come to realize the rottenness of the system itself and thus hope to transform it and offer an alternative to it. This chapter examines both types and argues for the necessity of adapting the latter attitude among teachers as a precondition for establishing and maintaining a just and democratic Philippines.

The commercialization of Philippine education means the commodification of the Filipino teacher. The Filipino teacher has been turned into a saleable commodity for newly formed markets: schools and universities. Commodification—as a direct consequence of education budget cuts—is clearly reflected through contractualization. Contractualization has demonized not only the working class but even educators. As Tinio, the representative of the ACT Teachers Partylist, argued:

> Contractualization has not spared the teaching profession. There has been an alarming growth in the number of precariously employed teachers in our public schools and higher education institutions. They work on fixed-term contracts, often receive much lower compensation, and are deprived of benefits enjoyed by their regularly employed counterparts. (Umil, 2012, para. 2)

There are 80,000 teachers under contract in all levels of education, 13,075 of whom come from the tertiary level (Umil, 2012). Though contractual on paper, they perform tasks similar to those of regular or tenured faculty. This implies not only economic but professional exploitation. Their skills are tapped, but they are not fairly compensated for them.

Tenured teachers still suffer a different problem. Underpayment is common among Filipino teachers.[4] Among teachers in Asia, Filipino teachers are among the lowest paid in the region (ABS-CBN, 2011). As prices of basic commodities and services continue to rise, their meager monthly salary of P16,000 ($372) does not provide a decent living for the families of these teachers (ACT, 2011).

The phenomenon of commodification has serious economic and professional implications for the teacher. First, unable to secure some of their basic daily needs because of low salaries, Filipino teachers are forced to find alternative sources of income that may augment their pay (Viola, 2009). One solution in public schools is for teachers to become vendors during recess or lunch breaks: they sell foods and snacks to students. Because of financial constraints, quality time may not be devoted solely to teaching preparation, since teachers still need to prioritize their economic needs.

Second, commodification attacks the Filipino teacher's sense of professionalism. One common example that I can cite here is the culture of research among academics and professors in higher education institutions (HEIs). Unlike universities in developed countries that have a strong tradition of research (Salazar-Clemeña & Almonte-Acosta, n.d), "universities in the developing world have retained strong teaching functions and weak research functions" (Sanyal & Varghese, 2006, as quoted by Salazar-Clemeña & Almonte-Acosta, n.d, p. 2). The Philippines is not spared from this situation. Among our educators, only a few continue to do research specific to their fields of expertise. As they get settled in their teaching functions, they abandon research, forgetting that "[t]he work of the faculty in higher education institutions has traditionally been trifocal, consisting of teaching, research and service/extension" (Salazar-Clemeña & Almonte-Acosta, n.d., p. 3).

We can possibly link the contention of Salazar-Clemeña and Almonte-Acosta—that there is a weak culture of research—to declining state and institutional financial support. Researchers need funding and incentives in order to enhance and support research productivity (Salazar-Clemeña & Almonte-Acosta, n.d). The HEIs and CHED could possibly allocate greater financial aid for institutional research, which can serve as good "motivational factors for doing research" (Salazar-Clemeña & Almonte-Acosta, n.d., p. 11). But as long as the commodification of the Filipino teacher continues, this remains an impossible task. Faculty development will be minimal or nonexistent.

The commodification of the Filipino teacher poses serious questions for the quality of education. On the one hand, many of the best teachers prefer to leave their profession in favor of better opportunities abroad (Ramota, 2005), where they could be paid ten times more than their local salary (GMA News Online, 2007). On the other hand, the absence of research, which is considered the life-blood of the academe, hinders the cultivation of academic professionalism and, most importantly, stops the inflow of new and relevant knowledge.

Colonial and *fascist* education has also turned the Filipino teacher into a mechanical being. In relation to the absence of research, for example, knowledge is merely reproduced rather than produced. In the schools, Filipino teachers merely transmit what has been handed down to them. Worse, in the context of colonial education, one specific tradition is even regarded as superior to other traditions. Bloom, for example, as criticized by Giroux and Aronowitz (1991), regarded

Western tradition as superior, because it is not a referent to any culture and is universal. I don't mean to contest its validity or its effectiveness. But the problem in colonial education is that meaning and understanding are already fixed and ready-made according to U.S. imperialist interpretation. This is a clear example of practices "that deskill and disempower teachers" (Giroux, 2005, p. 158). The Filipino teacher's notion of critical consciousness—a precondition for the production of social values and meaning—has been suppressed in favor of a market-oriented (CHED, 2011) and U.S.-supported approach. In this way, the Filipino teacher became no different from the 20th-century *pensionados* who were sent to the United States to be indoctrinated into the "American Way" and returned to the Philippines to be subservient to local compradors and landlords, thus legitimizing U.S. domination (San Juan, Jr., 2007).

At stake here is the relationship of knowledge to the issues of relevance, power, and emancipation. The colonial nature of knowledge raises three points for the Filipino teacher to consider. First, the knowledge that is currently standardized was never something that sprang from the lives and struggles of the Filipinos. In this case, relevance is already forfeited. Second, because of the neoliberal and U.S. imperialist-driven agenda, knowledge/truth accepted under the current system is not legitimized by Filipinos themselves. Foucault has clarified that "[t]ruth is linked in a circular relation with systems of power which produce and sustain it, and to effects of power which it induces and which extend it" (Foucault, 1980, p. 133). Neoliberalism produces colonial knowledge that in turn produces legitimacy and power over subjugated peoples. Third, as a tool for neocolonialism and fascism, it does not wish to emancipate but rather to manipulate people to adapt to a world whose purpose suits the oppressors (Freire, 2005) and dehumanizes the oppressed.

Unite and Resist! We Have Nothing to Lose but Our Chains

Faced with these issues, the Filipino must struggle. This struggle is waged not by Filipino teachers alone. As they rage against the Philippine educational system, they realize that the educational system is a microcosm of a larger system: their wish to radically alter the nature of Philippine education must play out in the context of the larger Philippine society.

This struggle is first and foremost a struggle for liberation. Since 1565, the Philippines has been a colony dominated by foreign powers. By 1946, America granted "independence" to the Philippines—a "bogus independence" (Guerrero, 2005) cloaked in lots of deceptions and irony, "as freedom is acquired by conquest, not by gift" (Freire, 2005, p. 47). From that moment, U.S. neocolonial rule began.

But the struggle for liberation is also linked to a struggle for democracy. As an agrarian country, the Philippines is composed mainly of peasants from the countryside, with only about 15% of workers living in urban areas (Guerrero, 2005). But the problem is that feudalism and bureaucratic capitalism have intensified since the inception of neocolonial rule. Because of its subservience to its foreign masters, the existence of the "ruling bloc of local landlords, compradors and bureaucrats" (San Juan, Jr., 2007) has been legitimized by U.S. imperialism. Since these local rulers "have direct representatives at every level of the reactionary government" (Guerrero, 2005, p. 111), they possess considerable political power. And for as long as this ruling elite holds the bureaucracy, "it will always make use of its political power to serve its interests" (Guerrero, 2005, p. 110), therefore forfeiting the essence of democracy.

The dehumanizing experiences of Filipino teachers extend to the majority of Filipinos. They must unite with other sectors and classes of Philippine society to win national sovereignty and democracy. The Filipino teacher "can join the vanguard of the cultural revolution in shattering the superstructure that stifles the nation and preserve the exploitative system" (Guerrero, 2005, p. 140). In the Philippines, the Alliance of Concerned Teachers (ACT) has already joined the *Bagong Alyangsang Makabayan* (New Patriotic Alliance), coming together with workers, peasants, fisher folk, women, youth, the urban poor, government workers, health workers, cultural workers, and church people. The Filipino teacher is one with the oppressed Filipinos in waging a struggle against neoliberalism and building a genuine government of the people, by the people, and for the people.

References

ABS-CBN News (2011). *Pinoy teachers among lowest paid in Asia.* Retrieved April 1, 2012, from http://www.abs-cbnnews.com/lifestyle/10/05/11/pinoy-teachers-among-lowest-paid-asia

Alliance of Concerned Teachers (ACT) (2006). *Slain teacher activists among hundreds more victims of political killings.* Retrieved March 28, 2012, from http://www.actphils.com/node/22

Alliance of Concerned Teachers (ACT) (2007). *Teachers denounce militarization in college campuses.* Retrieved March 27, 2012, from http://www.actphils.com/node/8

Alliance of Concerned Teachers (ACT) (2011). *Teachers picket the department of education on the unjust delay in the payment of salaries of kindergarten teachers.* Retrieved April 3, 2012, from http://www.actphils.com/node/230

Arroyo, G. (2004). *Executive Order 358: To institutionalize a ladderized interface between technical-vocational education and training (tvet) and higher education.* Retrieved March 29, 2012, from http://elibrary.judiciary.gov.ph/index10.php?doctype=Executive%20Orders&docid=151f808655b334fed1314e789ca9efb9455a487d656c1

Commission on Higher Education (CHED): Strategic plan for 2011–2016. (2011)Retrieved July 10, 2012, from http://www.google.com.ph/url?sa=t&rct=j&q=ched%20strategic%20plan%202011–2016&source=web&cd=1&ved=0CFYQFjAA&url=http%3A%2F%2Fwww.ched.gov.ph%2Fchedwww%2Findex.php%2Feng%2Fcontent%2Fdownload%2F2631%2F13239%2Ffile%2FCHED%2520Strategic%2520Plan%25202011–2016.pdf&ei=Z_38T9yKufLmAXknrGxBQ&usg=AFQjCNG9hmWqXDyTH4wVeMjDmsReE-AEWg

Constantino, R. (1975). *The miseducation of the Filipino.* Retrieved December 23, 2011, from http://www.scribd.com/doc/32721186/Renato-Constantino-The-Miseducation-of-the-Filipino

Constantino, R., & Constantino, L. (1975). *A history of the Philippines: From the Spanish colonization to the Second World War.* New York: Monthly Review Press.

Dale, J., & Hyslop-Margison, E. (2010). *Paulo Freire: Teaching for freedom and transformation.* New York: Springer.

Danlog, A. (2005, April 3–9). Call centers: Boon or bane for new graduates? *Bulatlat, 5*(8). Retrieved April 1, 2012, from http://www.bulatlat.com/news/5-8/5-8-callcenters.html

Delgado-Ramos, G., & Saxe-Fernández, J. (2009). World Bank and the privatization of public education: A Mexican perspective. In D. Hill & E. Rosskam (Eds.), *The developing world and state education: Neoliberal depredation and egalitarian alternatives.* New York: Routledge.

Dumlao-Valisno, M. (n.d). A roadmap to Philippine's future towards a knowledge-based economy. In *Philippine main education highway: Towards a knowledged-based economy.* Retrieved July 10, 2012 from http://www.opae.gov.ph/Philippine%20Main%20Education%20Highway-2008.pdf

Ellao, J. (2010). Aquino's budget cut on education is worse than Arroyo's—Kabataan Party. *Bulatlat.* Retrieved March 28, 2012, from http://bulatlat.com/main/2010/09/14/aquino%E2%80%99s-budget-cut-on-education-is-worse-than-arroyo%E2%80%99s-kabataan-party/

Foucault, M. (1980). *Power/knowledge: Selected interviews and other writings 1972–1977* (C. Gordon, Ed.). New York: Pantheon Books.

Freire, P. (2005). *Pedagogy of the oppressed.* New York: Continuum.

Giroux, H. (2005). *Border crossings: Cultural workers and the politics of education.* New York: Routledge.

Giroux, H., & Aronowitz, S. (1991). *Postmodern education: Politics, culture and social criticism.* Minneapolis: University of Minnesota Press. GMA News. (2007). RP's best teachers are leaving in droves. Retrieved April 1, 2012, from http://www.gmanetwork.co m/news/story/73387/pinoyabroad/rp-s-best-teachers-are-leaving-in-droves

Guerrero, A. (2005). *Philippine society and revolution.* Manila: Aklat ng Bayan.

Kincheloe, J.L. (2008). *Explorations of educational purpose 1: Knowledge and critical pedagogy.* New York: Springer.

Krippner, S. (2011). Postmodern perspectives on the study of consciousness. *Phavisminda Journal, 10*(11) 1–16.

Leal, Z. (2006, July 23–29). Students suffer from high tuition rates, repression under GMA. *Bulatlat, 6*(24). Retrieved March 28, 2012, from http://www.bulatlat.com/news/6–24/ 6–24-seduc.htm

Macedo, D. (2005). Foreword. In P. Freire, *Pedagogy of the oppressed* (p. 25). New York: Continuum.

Mok, K. (2006). *Education reform and education policy in Asia.* New York: Routledge.

Ramota, C. (2005, April 24–30). Education: A low state priority. *Bulatlat, 5*(11). Retrieved March 29, 2012, from http://bulatlat.com/news/5–11/5–11-priority.htm

Salamat, M. (2006, April 2–8). Odd jobs under the Arroyo administration. *Bulatlat, 6*(9). http://www.bulatlat.com/news/6–9/6–9-odd.htm

Salazar-Clemeña, R., & Almonte-Acosta, S. (n.d). *Developing research culture in Philippine higher education institutions: Perspective of university faculty.* Retrieved from http://www.google.com.ph/url?sa=t&rct=j&q=absence+of+research+in+the+philippines&source=web&cd=5&ved=0CEIQFjAE&url=http%3A%2F%2Fwww.oer-africa.org%2FResourceDownload.aspx%3Fassetid%3D347%26userid%3D-1&ei=D MJ6T5zoItGQiQf97rH5Ag&usg=AFQjCNFlV-BYROCo_G7PCCxOIlmoX5-hAg

San Juan, Jr., E. (2007). *US imperialism and the revolution in the Philippines.* New York: Palgrave Macmillan.

Shor, I. (1993). Education is politics: Paulo Freire's critical pedagogy. In P. McLaren & P. Leonard (Eds.), *Paulo Freire: A critical encounter.* London: Routledge.

Tupas T. Ruanni, F. (2008). Bourdieu, historical forgetting, and the problem of English in the Philippines. *Philippine Studies, 56*(1). Retrieved April 8, 2012, from http://courses.nus.edu.sg/course/elcttr/Bourdieu_PhilippineStudies_final.pdf

Ubalde, M. (2007). *Filipino teachers leaving in droves to the US.* Retrieved April 3, 2012, from http://www.gmanetwork.com/news/story/56492/pinoyabroad/filipino-teachers-leaving-in-droves-to-the-us

Umil, A.M. (2012). *Teachers push for bill prohibiting contractualization.* Retrieved April 2, 2012, from http://bulatlat.com/main/2012/03/23/teachers-push-for-bill-prohibiting-contractualization/

Viola, M. (2009). The Filipinization of critical pedagogy: Widening the scope of critical educational theory. *Journal for Critical Education Policy Studies, 7*(1). Retrieved January 20, 2012, from http://www.jceps.com/PDFs/07–1-01.pdf

Notes

1. From the Greek words *pais*, which means "child," and *ago*, which means "to lead," etymologically defined as "to lead a child."
2. This is especially true for the Philippines, where the current president, in his budget message submitted to the 15th Congress on August 24, 2011, stated: "We are gradually reducing the subsidy to SUCs to push them toward becoming self-sufficient and financially independent, given their ability to raise their income and to utilize it for their programs and projects" (Aquino, as quoted in Ellao, 2010). SUC are state universities and colleges.
3. Hundreds of teachers and students have been killed because of their political beliefs and ideologies. Leima Fortu, a public school teacher from Mindoro Oriental and the acting secretary general of KARAPATAN (Human Rights), was shot dead on February 13, 2004, by assassins believed to belong to the 204th Infantry Brigade of the Philippine Army. Napoleon Pornasdoro, a national council member of the Alliance of Concerned Teachers (ACT), was shot dead on February 27, 2006, days after former president Gloria Arroyo declared a State of National Emergency (ACT, 2006).
4. In the case of contractual teachers, kindergarten teachers receive a monthly allowance of P3,000 ($71). Locally paid teachers earn a monthly income of P5,000 ($119). Instructors earn a monthly income of P8,500 ($200). See Umil (2012). Adding insult to injury, salaries are even delayed in most cases. See ACT (2011).

17

Mandated Scripted Curriculum:
A Benefit or Barrier to Democratic Teaching and Learning?

KATIE STOVER AND CRYSTAL GLOVER

John, a fourth-grade teacher, describes how morale is low at his school. With the emphasis on standardized testing and scripted instruction, John feels that his position as a knowledgeable educator has been undermined by the teacher manual placed in his hands and the scripted instruction he robotically disperses to his students. Rather than integrating thoughtful literacy instruction aimed at authentically engaging students in critical thinking, John feels obligated to embrace the scripted reading program endorsed by his school. His resentment of the skills-based literacy program ultimately leaves him feeling robbed of his autonomy as a teacher. Mandated scripted instruction leaves John, and many teachers like him, with a loss of passion for the profession that once brought them joy and satisfaction.

Becoming and being a teacher committed to democratic and critical goals today is particularly challenging in a world of high-stakes assessment, accountability, and mandated scripted instruction. Despite the call for a more student-centered curriculum that fosters critical thinking, creativity, communication, and collaboration (Partnership for 21st Century Skills, 2007), many instructional methods rely on a factory model of scripted instruction and a test-driven curriculum. During the 20th century, John Dewey (1916), a progressive educator, called for a shift from a factory model approach of instruction to one that fosters social interaction and promotes a democratic society. Unfortunately, little has changed over the past century. The wide use of mandated commercial reading programs remains insufficient for 21st-century learners (Shannon & Crawford, 1997).

The call for commercial reading programs as the prominent form of curriculum dates to the early 20th century, when an industrial model was viewed as increasing production and efficiency (Shannon, 2007; Smith, 2002). It was believed that the use of a script increased effectiveness in teaching and learning. Reading textbooks promised to prepare students for an industrialized America with the promise to increase productivity and efficiency in industry and learning (Shannon, 2007). At the turn of the century, the public was concerned about student preparedness for an industrialized nation. A focus on a business model was instilled in order to apply business principles to social institutions such as schools to organize instructional methods and employ economic values of efficiency. The influence of business and science led to the recommendation of efficient, objective methods such as scripted reading programs to achieve higher test scores and, in turn, validate instruction to the public (Shannon & Crawford, 1997). It was believed that basal reading programs met the expectations of the business-oriented public and translated science research into classroom practice.

Scripted reading programs force schools to standardize materials and teaching while publishing companies prosper. Economic factors play a significant role in the adoption of mandated scripted reading programs. The economic and political control placed on scripted programs results in a heavy reliance on the use of commercial reading programs in elementary classrooms. Textbook publishing is big business, seeking to earn a profit. According to Shannon (2007), "publishers recognized that . . .the need for specific supplemental materials would increase their profits" (p. 33). Reading programs became a commodity in a capitalistic market. Apple (1989) laments that reading textbooks constitute a $400 million-per-year industry.

Basal programs have historically been the core materials for reading instruction (Durkin, 1981; Goodman, Shannon, Freeman, & Murphy, 1988; Shannon, 1982; Shannon, 1987; Smith, 2002) and have gained a strong presence with the No Child Left Behind Act and the Reading First Initiative (Allington, 2002). The NCLB law claimed to ensure that all children received equal educational opportunities and that the achievement gap would be closed. This bill proposed that even the neediest children, typically minority and poor children, would receive quality instruction to ensure successful learning. NCLB legislation was used to influence state and local educational practices (Putnam, Smith & Cassady, 2009). To ensure that all children can read, NCLB held teachers and students accountable to higher academic standards. With expectations of higher standards came increased accountability, high-stakes testing, and mandated scripted reading programs.

Policies such as NCLB and its subsequent initiative known as Reading First claim to offer equal education for all children by providing increased funding to public schools. Reading First, a component of NCLB, was enacted to provide additional funding for schools where more than 50% of students receive free or reduced lunch. To receive the funding, states and school districts must ensure that the federal guidelines, such as the adoption and implementation of preselected scripted programs, are met. Current trends suggest the collapse of NCLB legislation as school districts across the country are requesting to opt out of the implementation of its policies.

Implementation of uniform, reliable scripted reading programs that offer systematic and explicit instruction was believed to result in students learning to read and an increase in test scores. Hidden behind claims of scientific authenticity, commercial reading programs entice well-meaning school administrators to indulge in the promise of academic achievement for all students. Lured by the pledge of scientific authenticity, growing numbers of educational institutions have turned to scripted reading programs.

Other factors that influence the decision to adopt reading programs rely heavily on partisan politics. An example of this was seen when McGraw-Hill, a large textbook company, dumped significant funding into George W. Bush's presidential campaign, and later Texas chose McGraw-Hill's materials for mandated use in its schools. This was noteworthy for McGraw-Hill because states such as Texas, California, and Florida account for 40% of the sales market for basal reading programs in the United States (Shannon, 2007). Considerable profits awaited publishing companies as a result of the adoption of reading programs in these three states. Corporations seek compliant workers who serve to efficiently meet company demands and increase profit. The people most influential in making decisions about reading instruction at the national level are often themselves employed by publishing companies (Shannon, 2007). As a result, business interests are valued over meeting the needs of innocent schoolchildren, who become bystanders without any control over their futures.

Policy that derives from business and politics such as NCLB pose mandated instructional reading programs on states, local school districts, teachers, and students. "One-size-fits-all" programs attempt to standardize instruction and reduce teacher instructional variability. Damage results from the use of mandated scripted reading programs. These policies assume that teachers are not effectively teaching children how to read (Shannon, 2007),when in reality, teachers have significant influence on their students' literacy performance. "Researchers investigating effectiveness of commercial reading programs have found that the critical factor in successful reading instruction is not the program, but teacher quality" (Pease-Alvarez & Samway, 2008, p. 27). According to Putnam, Smith, and Cassady (2009), "top-down legislative initiatives that attempt to impose specific pedagogies or curriculum methodologies are typically doomed to failure" (p. 330). Furthermore, critics suggest that NCLB does not produce gains in test scores or close the achievement gap.

Stifling Democratic Teaching

NCLB poses many problems for effective reading instruction despite government claims that the policy narrows the achievement gap and raises students' test scores. The standardization of the teaching of reading reduces teachers' autonomy and professionalism. Following scripted programs with fidelity silences teachers rather than allowing them to tap into their professional knowledge to make instructional decisions based on the needs of their students. Shannon (2007) posits: "In four words, NCLB means the discrediting, reduction, deskilling, and reskilling of teachers" (p. 168). The process of deskilling teachers refers to the limited ability of teachers to use professional judgment and rely only on the materials provided through the scripted curriculum for instructional purposes. Scripted commercial programs dictate what teachers say and how they implement reading instruction. Teachers become robotic as they follow the directives in the manual and present standardized reading instruction to their students. Pease-Alvarez and Samway (2008) contend that the "scripted reading program came to dominate the school day and literacy instruction. Teachers stopped focusing on the needs and interests of children; most of their instruction was decided for them by the teaching manual" (p. 36).

With an overreliance on basal programs, teachers' instruction and routines are controlled. Power is often given to the basal readers as the standard for reading instruction over teacher knowledge. Basal adoptions are similar to factories where machines, like packaged reading programs, "deskill" the worker (Barksdale-Ladd & Thomas, 1993). As a result of deskilling teachers, "many teachers' understandings of effective reading and writing instruction are deemed irrelevant; some of their teaching practices are outlawed, so to speak; and new standardized understandings and practices are to supplant their own" (Shannon, 2000, p. 65).The implementation of basal reading programs standardizes teaching with less subjectivity from uninformed teachers. Equipped with everything teachers need to teach reading, it is difficult to determine where commercial reading ended and where actual instruction began (Smith, 2002).

History, business, and politics reify reading instruction with the use of commercial reading programs by treating an abstract concept as a concrete object (Shannon, 2007). Shannon suggests that scripted commercial programs have negative consequences on reading instruction. First, it becomes easy to neglect the human process that transpires during reading. Second, knowledge is transmitted in only one form as basic skills. Last, reification results in the efficient measurement of knowledge as test scores. Teachers are expected to follow these programs faithfully by reading directly from the script in order to provide more systematic and scientific reading instruction. Moreover, based on the ideology of NCLB, the implementation of mandated reading programs reduce human error and increase productivity in reading instruction fulfilling the interest of big business.

A majority of the research on scripted curriculum points to its ill effects on teachers and students (Duncan-Owens, 2009). Teacher dependency on scripted reading programs can lead to a lack of teacher empowerment in reading instruction (Barksdale-Ladd & Thomas, 1993). Close alignment with the script may lead to feelings of incompetence as well as resistance. According to Barksdale-Ladd and Thomas (1993), teachers harbor negative views and may resist mandated scripted reading programs due to conflicts between teachers' pedagogical beliefs and the mode of instruction through the use of basal readers. The authors noted that teachers relied on scripted instruction as a way of satisfying pressure from administration. Teachers can easily feel trapped and obligated to participate in this type of standardized instruction due to top-down directives and mandates. Many teachers resist the program overtly, but some are more subtle. Teachers who are required to implement mandated, scripted reading programs lose a sense of agency over what they taught and consequently feel undermined and disrespected (Pease-Alvarez & Samway, 2008).

Principals continuously seek methods to improve reading achievement in an age of high-stakes testing and NCLB. The adoption of scientifically based reading programs is a common solution for many schools. "The marks of good teaching are, first, to elicit student compliance to finish the designated part of the scope and sequence during the assigned time period, and then to secure high student scores on basal and other standardized tests" (Shannon & Crawford, 1997). Parsons and Harrington (2009) further the notion that a focus on the use of the "best" program limits the focus to raising test scores instead of teaching meaningful literacy.

Stifling Students' Democratic Learning

Despite claims of improving performance, scripted reading programs have detrimental effects on authentic learning. In addition to dictating how teachers should carry out reading lessons in their classroom, teacher manuals direct how students should act and respond in the classroom. Students become the recipients of the teacher-dispensed knowledge (Freire, 1970/2000; Pearson, 2001). Instructional emphasis on breaking the code of text positions the teacher as an authority figure and drill master who disseminates information and assigns work to students. A one-way transmission of knowledge referred to by Jordan (2005) as the "language of command and obey" (p. 205) is the standard instructional model used with scripted instruction. Teachers monitor students' abilities to recite and memorize information.

The domination of one-size-fits-all

Federal policy promotes one-size-fits-all reading programs that appear to have a plethora of materials but do not meet the diverse needs of a variety of learners. With the use of scripted reading programs, all students tend to use the same materials regardless of reading level, and many selections tend to be above grade level (McGill-Franzen, Amach, Solic, & Zeig, 2006). The use of standardized programs only masks the differences and gaps in reading needs of students. According to Cohen and Spillane (1992), a common curriculum does not necessarily equate to increased student achievement. Furthermore, scripted programs do not promote thoughtful literacy. Allington (2005) defines thoughtful literacy as "engaging the ideas in the text, challenging those ideas, reflecting on them, and so on" (p. 135). In contrast to thoughtful literacy skills, scripted reading programs focus on basic skill instruction that engages students in low-level tasks such as completing worksheets with isolated skill and drill practice. Whole-class, one-size-fits-all instruction, in which teachers control the delivery and the content of learning, provides little opportunity for differentiated learning.

Upper-class dominance

Some research theorizes that textbooks are used to establish and maintain middle- and upper-class intentions. Bloome and Nieto (2001) suggest that basal reading instruction promotes marginalization of some students. Historical biases against poor minorities manifest themselves in the materials and instructional protocol of scripted reading programs. "For three generations now, Americans have been schooled in basal classroom cultures that privilege upper and upper-middle class intentions and values" (Shannon & Crawford, 1997). Shannon and Crawford and Shannon (2007) suggest that basal reading programs manufacture failures among marginalized students by excluding them from effective literacy practices and by establishing and maintaining the ideology of middle- and upper-class values.

The dominant power of society plays a part in the daily lives of children through the use of basal readers. "Basal presence in more than 85% of American classrooms ensures that upper and upper-middle class intentions and values will dominate the continuous negotiations over what kind of knowledge is of most value, what it means to know something, and who has knowledge and knows something" (Shannon & Crawford, 1997). Only the dominant, mainstream student populations are well served in American schools as a consequence of the use of mandated, scripted reading programs. The use of prescriptive reading programs silences students' voices and has the potential to expand inequities among low-income and low-performing student populations (Jordan, 2005; Pease-Alvarez & Samway, 2008).

The use of scripted reading programs contributes to the widening of the achievement gap. Shannon and Crawford (1997) describe the consequences of using basal readers to manufacture failures in students and steer them into low-wage work as a result of the middle-to-upper-class ideals and values portrayed in the basal readers. Power continues to play a dominant role in the lives of children as they are faced with these programs in school (Shannon & Crawford, 1997). Findings from Keller-Cohen and Heineken (1987) suggest that basals and their components focus on preparation for a bureaucratic society over learning to read, with an emphasis on filling out forms over the construction of meaning.

Manufacturing failure

"The standardization of the curriculum—the very politics intended to assure adequate opportunities for children—may, in fact, limit their opportunities to meet grade-level standards" (McGill-Franzen et al., 2006, p. 68). This is shocking, considering that scripted reading programs are mandated for high-poverty schools under the Reading First initiative. Recent research suggests that the use of a scripted reading curriculum does not contribute to the improvement of reading achievement of struggling readers and English language learners (Altwerger et al., 2004; Alvarez & Corn, 2008; Moustafa & Land, 2002; McGill-Franzen et al., 2006; Wilson, Martens, Arya, & Altwerger, 2004). McGill-Franzen and colleagues found that one-fourth of students using state-approved materials did not achieve minimum benchmarks, suggesting that mandated programs may not adequately provide support for struggling readers.

The findings of Wilson and colleagues' 2004 study of three different programs that emphasize systematic phonics instruction reveal conflicting results with the National Reading Panel Report. No statistical difference was found between students' phonics skills after using a scripted reading program that emphasizes phonics skills in comparison to a guided reading approach, in which students were taught to focus more on meaning (Wilson et al., 2004). Data indicated that systematic phonics instruction does not necessarily improve reading achievement. The significant differences that were noted favored students who used guided reading over programs such as Direct Instruction or Open Court. "The blanket adoption of commercial phonics-based programs will not automatically create effective readers" (Wilson et al., 2004. p. 245). Instead, differentiated learning and teaching skills in the meaningful context of literature are recommended.

Currently, commercial literacy programs are widely used in classrooms across the United States. Several factors influence school districts' adoption and mandated use of scripted reading programs in schools. The historical context, along with the influence of business, politics, and policy, plays a significant role in school systems' decisions to mandate a scripted curriculum. The use of reading textbooks dates back to the 18th century; however, the inception of policies such as NCLB have increased the adoption and required use of scripted reading programs.

The mandated use of scripted reading instruction is the subject of much debate among educators, researchers, and policymakers. According to Allington (2005) and Duffy and Hoffman (1999), there is no single best method for reading instruction. Therefore, the adoption of a one-size-fits-all program will not meet the diverse needs of students. As a result of the implementation of scripted reading programs, student learning and teacher professionalism suffer (Parsons & Harrington, 2009). By participating in the use of a scripted curriculum, teachers assist in the manufacture of failure by following mandates without criticism and questioning (Shannon & Crawford, 1997). Nichols and Berliner (2007) argue that a more accurate title for NCLB should be "Most Children Left Behind" (p. 50). While these are harsh words for a policy that ensures equality among all students, educators must consider all perspectives and regularly question in order to determine what is best for individual students.

References

Allington, R. (2002). What I've learned about effective reading instruction from a decade of studying exemplary elementary classroom teachers. *Phi Delta Kappan, 83*, 740–747.

Allington, R.L. (2005). *What really matters for struggling readers: Designing research-based programs* (2nd ed.). Boston: Pearson Education.

Altwerger, B., Poonam, A., Jin, L., Jordan, N., Laster, B., Martens, P., Wilson, G.P., &Wiltz, N. (2004). When research and mandates collide: The challenges and dilemmas of teacher education in the era of NCLB. *English Education, 36*, 119–133.

Alvarez, L., & Corn, J. (2008). Exchanging assessment for accountability: The implications of high-stakes reading assessments for English learners. *Language Arts, 85*, 354–365.

Apple, M. (1989). Textbook publishing: The political and economic influences. *Theory into Practice, 28*(4), 282. Retrieved from Academic Search Premier database.

Barksdale-Ladd, M.A., & Thomas, K. (1993). Eight teachers' reported pedagogical dependency on basal readers. *The Elementary School Journal, 94*, 50–72.

Bloome, D.,& Nieto, S. (2001). Children's understandings of basal readers. *Theory into Practice, 28*, 258–264.

Cohen, D.K., & Spillane, J.P. (1992). Policy and practice: The relations between governance and instruction. *Review of Research in Education, 18*, 3–49.

Dewey, J. (1916). *Democracy and education: An introduction to the philosophy of education.* New York: Macmillan.

Duffy, G.G. & Hoffman, J.V. (1999). In pursuit of an illusion: The flawed search for a perfect method. *The Reading Teacher, 53*(1), 10–17.

Duncan-Owens, D. (2009). Scripted reading programs: Fishing for success. *Principal,* 26–29.

Durkin, D. (1981). Reading comprehension instruction in five basal reader series. *Reading Research Quarterly, 16*(4), 515–544.

Freire, P. (2000). *Pedagogy of the oppressed.* New York: Continuum. (Original work published 1970).

Goodman, K., Shannon, P., Freeman, Y., & Murphy, S. (1988). *Report card on basal readers.* New York: Richard C. Owen.

Jordan, N. (2005). Basal readers and reading as socialization: What are children learning? *Language Arts, 82*, 204–213.

Keller-Cohen, D.,& Heineken, J. (1987). *Workbooks: What they can teach children about forms.* In D. Bloome (Ed.), *Literacy and schooling* (pp. 258–288). Norwood, NJ: Ablex.

McGill-Franzen, A., Amach, C., Solic, K., &Zeig, J.L. (2006). The confluence of two policy mandates: Core reading programs and third-grade retention in Florida. *The Elementary School Journal, 107*(1), 67–91.

Moustafa, M., & Land, R.E. (2002). The reading achievement of economically disadvantaged children in urban schools using Open Court vs. comparably disadvantaged children in urban schools using non-scripted reading programs. In *Yearbook of Urban Learning, Teaching, and Research*, Special Interest Group of the American Educational Research Association (pp. 44–53).

Nichols, S.,& Berliner, D. (2007). *Collateral damage: How high-stakes testing corrupts America's schools.* Cambridge, MA: Harvard Education Press.

Parsons, S.A., & Harrington, A.D. (2009). Following script: When schools and school systems are exploring scripted literacy programs, educators should consider four questions before embracing that approach to teaching. *Phi Delta Kappan, 90*(10), 748–750.

Partnership for 21st Century Skills. (2007). *Learning for the 21st century.* Retrieved May 19, 2011, from www.21stcenturyskills.org

Pearson, P.D. (2001). Reading in the twentieth century (CIERA #01–08). Ann Arbor: Center for the Improvement of Early Reading Achievement (CIERA)/University of Michigan. http://www.ciera.org/library/archive/2001-08/200108.htm

Pease-Alvarez, L.,& Samway, K.D. (2008). Negotiating a top-down reading program mandate: The experiences of one school. *Language Arts, 86,* 32–41.

Putnam, S.M., Smith, L.L., & Cassady, J.C. (2009). Moving beyond legislation to create and sustain intentionality in reading instruction. *The Educational Forum, 73,* 318–332.

Shannon, P. (1982). Some objective factors in teachers' reliance on commercial reading materials. *Reading Improvement, 19,* 296–302.

Shannon, P. (1987). Commercial reading materials, a technological ideology, and the deskilling of teachers. *The Elementary School Journal, 87*(3), 307–329.

Shannon, P. (2000). Politics of reading: You ain't got the ABCs. *The Reading Teacher, 54*(1), 64–66.

Shannon, P. (2007). *Reading against democracy: The broken promises of reading instruction.* Portsmouth, NH: Heinemann.

Shannon, P., & Crawford, P. (1997). Manufacturing descent: Basal readers and the creation of reading failures. *Reading & Writing Quarterly, 13,* 227–244.

Smith, N.B. (2002). *American reading instruction.* Newark, DE: International Reading Association.

Wilson, G.P., Martens, P., Arya, P., & Altwerger, B. (2004). Readers, instruction, and the NRP. *Phi Delta Kappan, 86*(3), 242–246.

18

Schools as Battlegrounds:
Tha Authoritarian Jurisprudence of Clarence Thomas

A. SCOTT HENDERSON

In the field of education, courts have addressed whether public school systems reflect the democratic aspirations found in constitutional and statutory law. Specific issues have included racial segregation (*Brown v. Board of Education*, 1954); the legitimacy and limits of busing as a means to effect school integration (*Swann v. Charlotte-Mecklenburg*, 1971; *Milliken v. Bradley*, 1974); whether education is a constitutional right (*San Antonio v. Rodriguez*, 1973); and the use of publicly funded vouchers to increase educational opportunities (*Zelman v. Simmons-Harris*, 2002).

Courts have also defined the rights of students and teachers. This has been characterized over the past several decades by an expansion of student and teacher agency, which has resulted from broadened definitions of First Amendment protections of speech and assembly, Fourth Amendment protections against unreasonable searches and seizures, Fifth Amendment protections of due process, and Eighth Amendment protections against cruel and unusual punishment (Imber & van Greel, 2010; Mintz, 2004).

Nevertheless, during the past two decades, conservative jurists—exemplified by a rightward ideological shift in the composition of the U.S. Supreme Court—have sought to contain and even reverse this trend (Arum & Preiss, 2009). Among these jurists, Clarence Thomas, an Associate Justice of the Supreme Court since

1991, has been one of the most vocal (Walsh, 2011). This chapter will analyze his opinions in *Morse v. Frederick* (2007), *Safford Unified School District v. Redding* (2009), and *Brown v. Entertainment Merchants Association* (2011). These opinions illustrate a self-contradictory aspect of Thomas's views toward teachers and schooling. While he argues that courts should essentially stay out of the business of educating children, he has no hesitation in supporting a full return to *in loco parentis* (discussed below) as the most desirable educational practice. By doing so, he not only champions an authoritarian model *for* schools, but he also presents himself as an authority *on* schools—an expert whose advice should be followed despite what modern teachers or pedagogy might advocate.

Background and Early Career

Clarence Thomas was born on June 23, 1948, and lived in the tiny town of Pinpoint, Georgia, until 1954, when he moved to Savannah, where his maternal grandparents, Myers and Christine Anderson, raised him. Thomas is a product of private educational institutions, most of which were/are affiliated with the Catholic Church: St. Benedict the Moor Grammar School, St. Pius X High School, St. John Vianney Seminar, Holy Cross College, and Yale Law School. In 1974 he was appointed an Assistant Attorney General in Missouri, and after leaving that post in 1977, he worked for the Monsanto Corporation until 1979, when he moved to Washington, D.C., to become a legislative assistant to U.S. Senator John Danforth. Between that time and his Supreme Court confirmation, he served as Assistant Secretary for Civil Rights in the U.S. Department of Education from 1981 to 1982; Chairman of the Equal Opportunity Employment Commission from 1982 to 1990; and as one of 11 judges on the U.S. Court of Appeals for the District of Columbia Circuit from 1990 to 1991 (Foskett, 2004).

Along with his belief in an originalist approach to interpreting the Constitution (discussed later), Thomas's childhood, particularly the relationship he developed with his grandfather, is reflected in his judicial philosophy. Myers Anderson (whom Thomas called "Daddy") was emotionally aloof and a strict disciplinarian who insisted on patriarchal rule. According to Thomas, he sought "control" over "every aspect" of his life (Thomas, 2007, p. 12) and determined to "mold" him" in his image" (p. 2). He demanded "absolute adherence to all his edicts, however arbitrary they might appear to be" (p. 27). Equally important, Anderson told Thomas that "teachers were always right" (p. 15). For reasons that are still not entirely clear (given Anderson's near-tyrannical behavior toward Thomas), the future Supreme Court

Justice eventually concluded that he had been raised by "the greatest man" he had (or has) ever known (p. 28).

Thomas's admiration for his grandfather has influenced his conception of teachers. For instance, many people believe that they possess insight into schools because they were once students themselves, which is why so many individuals, including elected officials with no background in education, feel free to criticize or otherwise judge teachers. Likewise, because Thomas has come to revere his grandfather, he seems to think that student-teacher relationships should resemble the one that existed between him and Anderson: teachers command and students obey (recall his grandfather's warning that "teachers were always right"). But this is hardly appropriate or pedagogically sound advice for teachers—nor the type of advice that is commonly proffered to other professionals.

Morse v. Frederick

In 2007, the Supreme Court issued one of its most important decisions regarding student speech since the late 1960s. The case concerned Joseph Frederick, a junior at Juneau-Douglas High School in Juneau, Alaska, who was suspended for violating the school district's anti-drug policy. Specifically, Frederick and some of his friends displayed a banner with the inscription "BONG HiTS [sic] 4 JESUS" at a school-sponsored event (a January 24, 2002, gathering outside, and across from, the school where students watched the Olympic Torch Relay). The Juneau School Board had a policy prohibiting "any assembly or public expression that. . .advocates the use of substances that are illegal to minors. . ." (*Morse v. Frederick*, 2007, p. 2623). Frederick filed suit against the Juneau School District, arguing that his First Amendment speech rights had been violated. The U.S. Court of Appeals for the Ninth Circuit ruled in favor of Frederick, and the Juneau School District appealed that ruling to the U.S. Supreme Court.

Writing for the 5–4 majority, Chief Justice John Roberts reversed the Ninth Circuit's decision. The majority concluded that the banner did indeed communicate a message promoting drug use—and that schools, in pursuing their "compelling interest" to deter drug abuse, could legally restrict such speech (p. 2628). Thomas *agreed* with the majority but wrote a separate (lone) concurring opinion. It was as much a manifesto as it was a legal analysis.

Thomas began with the sweeping pronouncement that the "standard set forth in *Tinker v. Des Moines*" was "without basis in the Constitution" (p. 2630). *Tinker* was a landmark 1969 Supreme Court decision clarifying the speech rights of public school students, specifically (but not exclusively) the right of students to engage in political expressions, for instance, wearing armbands to protest the Vietnam War. Because *Tinker* dealt with speech rights, Roberts had cited it in his *Morse* opinion; indeed, both Roberts *and* Thomas quoted one of the best-known passages from *Tinker*: "It can hardly be argued that either students or teachers shed their constitutional rights to freedom of speech or expression at the schoolhouse gate" (p. 2650).Roberts supported *Tinker* but did not believe that it protected the kind of speech at issue in *Morse*. For his part, Thomas thought that *Tinker* itself was fundamentally flawed. His reasoning was based on the assumption that "as *originally* understood, the Constitution does *not* afford students a right to free speech in public schools" (p. 2634; emphasis added).

For Thomas and other conservative jurists (and a few liberal ones, including Supreme Court Justice Hugo Black [1886–1971]), interpreting the Constitution is a matter of discerning how the framers used a certain term or concept. Appropriately enough, this school of jurisprudence has become known as "originalism," which actually refers to more than one interpretive strategy, though they all emphasize the need to determine what the Constitution's authors initially meant or intended by something. Such an approach places a premium on historical context and the putative time-bound nature of the Constitution (Maggs, 2009; Whittington, 1999).

Thomas's unapologetic originalism is what led him, in his *Morse* concurrence, to deny the validity of *Tinker*'s primary contention. Reviewing the history of schooling and pedagogical practices, Thomas argued that students possessed virtually no rights in 18th- or early-19th-century America (of course, there were very few public schools at that time, something that Thomas glosses over). Not unlike Thomas's own grandfather, schools could and did require "absolute obedience." Thomas summarized this historical context epigrammatically: "In the earliest public schools, teachers taught, and students listened. Teachers commanded, and students obeyed" (p. 2631).

The legal doctrine that severely curtailed the rights of students was *in loco parentis*. It emerged as part of English common law during the 17th century and referred to a parent's ability to voluntarily confer authority to a tutor or schoolmaster for the purposes of instructing, supervising, and disciplining his/her children (Imber & van Greel, 2010). Thomas approvingly cited the influential 19th-century American jurist James Kent on the subject: "So the power allowed by law to the parent over the person of the child may be delegated to a tutor or instructor, the better to accomplish the purpose of education" (p. 2631). Over time, American courts focused exclusively on the use of *in loco parentis* to justify *disciplinary* actions (Stuart, 2011). Thomas's own historical interpretation was categorical: "The doctrine of *in loco parentis* limited the ability of schools to set rules and control their classrooms in almost no way" (p. 2636).

If *Tinker* was invalid (which was Thomas's view), then any student speech claims were insupportable, including those made by Joseph Frederick. Because contemporary jurisprudence did not adhere to this extreme position, Thomas warned that it was threatening to undermine (if it hadn't already done so) the power of schools to maintain basic order, something that students would challenge if given half a chance. To support his views, Thomas relied on Justice Hugo Black's dissent in *Tinker*:

> Justice Black dissented, criticizing the Court for "subject[ing] all the public schools in the country to the whims and caprices of their loudest-mouthed, but maybe not their brightest, students." He emphasized the instructive purpose of schools: "Taxpayers send children to school on the premise that at their age they need to learn, not teach." In his view, the Court's decision "surrender[ed] control of the American public school system to public school students." (p. 2634)

By citing Black, Thomas suggested a rather bleak view of schools: they are battlegrounds of continuous conflict between children and adults. The primary role of teachers and school officials is to win those conflicts. They do so by enforcing discipline *and* squelching dissent. In such a model, there is no room for teachers who encourage students to question authority or think for themselves; social *reproduction*, not social *reconstruction*, is the educational philosophy teachers should employ (Dupre, 1996). Thus, despite his statements to the contrary, Thomas's prescriptions would actually diminish the pedagogical latitude of teachers. Instruction would be unidirectional, with teachers filling the empty vessels of students' compliant heads (Bunker & Calvert, 2010).

Safford v. Redding

Courts serve as arbiters in determining whether a student's Fourth Amendment protections against unreasonable search and seizure have been abridged by teachers or school officials. In *Safford Unified School District v. Redding*, the Supreme Court was asked to make such a determination. The facts of the case were not disputed. In the fall of 2003, a 13-year-old student (Savanna Redding) at Safford Middle School in Safford, Arizona, was subjected to a search of her bra and underwear by school officials who suspected (wrongly, it turns out) that she was in possession of prescription-strength and over-the-counter medications, which would have been a violation of school policy and state statutes. Although Redding was not required to remove all of her clothing, the type of search she underwent is usually, if erroneously, referred to as a "strip search." Redding's mother brought suit against the Safford School district, arguing that the so-called strip search of her daughter was unconstitutional under Fourth Amendment strictures.

Writing for the majority in 2009, Justice David Souter ruled that the search had been unconstitutional because "there were no reasons to suspect that the drugs presented a danger or were concealed in her [Redding's] underwear" (*Safford v. Redding*, p. 2637). Specifically, the majority held that "the content of the suspicion failed to match the degree of intrusion," a common criterion for assessing whether a search is or is not "reasonable" (p. 2642). Justices John Paul Stevens and Ruth Bader Ginsburg wrote separate opinions, concurring in part with the majority but dissenting on the issue of qualified immunity (i.e., whether school officials can claim exemption from the consequences attached to conducting a search if it is ruled unconstitutional). As with *Morse*, Thomas wrote a separate opinion, concurring with the majority on the question of qualified immunity but strongly disagreeing over their assertion that the search had been unconstitutional.

As the only one to argue that the search had been constitutional, Thomas accused his other eight brethren of "imposing a vague and amorphous standard on school administrators" (p. 2646). He was most troubled by the fact that the Court's decision would, in his view, extend to judges' "sweeping authority to second-guess the measures that these [school] officials take to maintain discipline in their schools and ensure the health and safety of the students in their charge" (p. 2646). This, in turn, was a problem, because drug use and violent crime in schools had become major problems that were best addressed by deferring to the judgment of teachers and administrators (which echoed his grandfather's dictum that "teachers were always right"). Putting a fine point on the matter, Thomas averred that "preservation of order, discipline, and safety in public schools" was "not the domain of the Constitution" (p. 2657).

According to Thomas, a return to *in loco parentis* would provide school officials with the wide discretion they needed to protect and control students. Once again chiding his colleagues, Thomas noted:

> The Court's interference in these matters . . . illustrates why the most constitutionally sound approach to the question of applying the Fourth Amendment in local public schools would in fact be a complete restoration of the common-law doctrine of *in loco parentis*. (p. 2655)

Thomas's discussion of *in loco parentis* was peppered with quotations from his *Morse* concurrence, which included educational prescriptions found in earlier (state) court decisions. For example, he cited an 1886 Maine decision in which the court had enumerated the various duties for which a teacher/schoolmaster was granted "much discretionary power." They were obliged to "govern the[ir] pupils, quicken the slothful, spur the indolent, restrain the impetuous, and control the stubborn" by making "rules, giving commands, and punish[ing] disobedience" (p. 2657). Unlike Thomas, most modern educators (regardless of their Fourth Amendment views) do not quote from sources that are over 100 years old in order to support contemporary classroom/school management policies. Thomas was compelled to do so because of his originalist judicial views. For him, the only valid guide for deciding cases that involve public schools is to identify what the earliest ones did or did not sanction.

In a brief section toward the end of his opinion, Thomas was quick to add that "restoring the common-law doctrine of *in loco parentis* would not leave public schools entirely free to impose any rule they choose." However, it was not courts, but parents themselves who should decide whether school policies were appropriate. "If parents do not like the rules imposed by [public] schools," Thomas confidently stated, "they can seek redress in school boards or legislatures; they can send their children to private schools or home school them; or they can simply move" (p. 2656). These simplistic and, in some cases, unrealistic assertions removed virtually any meaningful role for courts, suggested that power is shared equally among the public and state actors, and assumed that all families possess significant financial resources. Nonetheless, Thomas concluded his opinion with the hyperbolic admonition that "a return to the doctrine of *in loco parentis* is required to keep the judiciary from essentially seizing control of public schools" (p. 2657).

What Thomas failed to consider was whether teachers were able or willing to embrace a purely *descriptive* concept (*in loco parentis*) as a *normative* one for running their classrooms. First of all, in an era of compulsory schooling, the voluntary delegation of a parent's authority has no meaning. But even if that were overlooked, teachers typically resist the notion that they should react to students as parents do (Stuart, 2011). In addition, teacher education programs and classroom management literature are almost entirely silent on how teachers are supposed to actually act *in loco parentis* (Stuart, 2011). Were Thomas's views to become law, they would necessitate a change in professional preparation programs that teachers themselves would likely resist.

Brown v. Entertainment Merchants Association

In 2005, California passed a law banning the sale of violent video games to minors without parental permission. Representatives of the video game and software industry brought suit against California, arguing that regulation of their products in such a manner constituted a First Amendment violation of free speech. In 2011, in a 7–2 decision, the Supreme Court agreed. Writing for the majority, Justice Antonin Scalia concluded that the types of video games targeted by the legislation did not constitute a "well-defined and narrowly limited class of speech" that the government could restrict. He also argued that there were no demonstrative links between violent video games and their effect on children that might override First Amendment protections (*Brown v. Entertainment Merchants*, 2011, p. 3742).

Thomas and Justice Stephen Breyer wrote separate dissents. Breyer based his on the logical and legal inconsistency of allowing state regulation of obscene materials but prohibiting it when materials contain violence. Thomas, on the other hand, offered an outright rejection of the majority's opinion, stating that "the Court's decision today does not comport with the original public understanding of the First Amendment" (p. 2752). Although *Brown* did not concern schools, Thomas's analysis of it clarified the amount of parental authority he wanted teachers and school officials to possess if there were a full return to *in loco parentis*, which he had advocated in *Morse* and *Safford*.

As with *Morse* and *Safford*, Thomas went to great lengths to describe what he perceived as the original understanding of the right in question, freedom of speech. After surveying developments during the 18th and 19th centuries, he maintained that freedom of speech did not initially include a "right to speak to minors (or a right of minors to access speech) without going through the minors' parents or guardians" (p. 2752). He then described the type of authority that parents had exercised over their children: "The historical evidence shows," he wrote, "that the founding generation believed parents had absolute authority over their minor children" (p. 2752). This was because adults did not believe that children, lacking "reason" and "decision-making ability," were "fit to govern themselves" (pp. 2753, 2754).

Having outlined the nature of parent-child relationships (children were to give unquestioned obedience to their parents, much like Thomas had given to his grandfather), Thomas argued that student-teacher relationships had been viewed the same way. Thomas quoted from James Burgh's *Thoughts on Education* (published in 1749) to make the general point about the importance of teachers: "[T]he souls of Youth are more immediately committed to the care of Parents and

Instructors than even those of a People are to their Pastor" (p. 2766). To underscore the similarities between the dictatorial power that parents and teachers possessed, Thomas quoted Noah Webster's injunction, "The government both of families and schools should be absolute," as well as a similar sentiment expressed by Benjamin Rush: "In the education of youth, let the authority of our masters be as *absolute* as possible" (p. 2756). Admittedly, Rush and Webster had a profound impact on the course of American education. But adducing their statements as the basis for running schools in the 21st century is akin to a non-scientist telling today's scientists to follow Benjamin Franklin's advice on how to run a modern laboratory. Blacker (2009, p. 140) argues that Thomas's opinions on *in loco parentis* reveal an element of "restorative nostalgia" that is highly inaccurate. Yet, as other chapters in this volume attest, Thomas is not the only one who is guilty of "restorative nostalgia" when it comes to educators.

Schools as Prisons, Teachers as Guards

Because Thomas conceives of schools as a primary site for opposition to adult authority, he urges a complete return to *in loco parentis*, justified by an originalist jurisprudence and seemingly modeled on the relationship he had with his grandfather. Although he frames this position as one that would give educators *more* freedom in dealing with students (which is true with respect to teachers' ability to censor speech and conduct searches), it would also paradoxically *limit* the pedagogical repertoire of educators. The authoritarian nature of *in loco parentis* also runs counter to the belief that public schools are democratic institutions where students should be given the opportunity to practice skills associated with an engaged citizenry (Goodlad, Mantle-Bromley, & Goodlad, 2004).

Perhaps worst of all for those who view children and youth more positively than Thomas does, *silencing them* (literally and figuratively) forgoes the possibility of *learning from them*. As Justices Stevens, Ginsburg, and Souter noted in their *Morse* dissent: "Even in high school, a rule that permits only one point of view to be expressed is less likely to produce correct answers than the open discussion of countervailing views" (*Morse v. Frederick*, 2007, p. 2651). For them, the possibility that disagreements might sometimes disrupt school order is no reason to stifle students. Quoting from *Tinker*, they responded to the fear that freedom of speech is inevitably chaotic:

But our Constitution says we must take this risk; and our history says that it is this sort of hazardous freedom—this kind of openness—that is the basis of our national strength and of the independence and vigor of Americans who grow up and live in this relatively permissive, often disputatious society. (p. 2651)

Clarence Thomas is apparently unwilling to take that risk. He would replace a pedagogy of democratic *preparation* with one emphasizing the need to *protect* teachers from students, and students from one another (Gutman, 1987; Kaufman, 2007). That would make schools little more than prisons (battlegrounds for sure) where teachers would be guards, tasked with remaining forever vigilant over prisoners whose intellectual and behavioral obedience was the primary goal of education.

References

Arum, R., & Preiss, D. (2009). Law and disorder in the classroom. *Education Next, 9*(4), 68–76.

Blacker, D. (2009). An unreasonable argument against student free speech. *Educational Theory, 59*, 123–142.

Brown v. Entertainment Merchants Association, 131 S. Ct. 2729 (2011).

Bunker, M.D., & Calvert, C. (2010). Contrasting concurrences of Clarence Thomas: Deploying originalism and paternalism in commercial and student speech cases. *Georgia State University Law Review, 26,* 321–359.

Dupre, A.P. (1996). Should students have constitutional rights? Keeping order in the public schools. *George Washington Law Review, 65,* 49–105.

Foskett, K. (2004). *Judging Thomas: The life and times of Clarence Thomas.* New York: William Morrow.

Goodlad, J.I., Mantle-Bromley, C., & Goodlad, S.J. (2004). *Education for everyone: Agenda for education in a democracy.* San Francisco, CA: Jossey-Bass.

Gutman, A. (1987). *Democratic education.* Princeton, NJ: Princeton University Press.

Imber, M., & van Greel, T. (2010). *Education law* (4th ed.). New York: Routledge.

Kaufman, A.K. (2007). What would Harry Potter say about BONG HiTS 4 JESUS? *Morse v. Frederick* and the democratic implications of using *in loco parentis* to subordinate *Tinker* and curtail student speech. *Oklahoma City University Law Review, 32,* 462–479.

Maggs, G.E. (2009). Which original meaning of the constitution matters to Justice Thomas? *New York University Journal of Law and Liberty, 4,* 494–516.

Mintz, S. (2004). *Huck's raft: A history of American childhood.* Cambridge, MA: Harvard University Press.

Morse v. Frederick, 127 S. Ct. 2618 (2007).

Safford Unified School District v. Redding, 129 S. Ct. 2633 (2009).

Stuart, S. (2011). *In loco parentis* in the public schools: Abused, confused, and in need of change. *University of Cincinnati Law Review, 78*(3), 969–1005.

Thomas, C. (2007). *My grandfather's son: A memoir*. New York: HarperCollins.

Tinker v. Des Moines, 89 S. Ct. 733 (1969).

Walsh, M. (2011, October 19). On students' rights, an originalist stands firm. *Education Week, 31*(1), 20–21.

Whittington, K.E. (1999). *Constitutional interpretation: Textual meaning, original intent, and judicial review*. Topeka: University Press of Kansas.

19

Troubling Traditional Notions of "Prepared":
Two Urban Teachers Ignite the Boundaries of Progressive and Critical Theories

MELISSA WINCHELL AND PATRICIA CHOUINARD

Falling Flat: A Two-Voice Poem

Patricia:	Melissa:
My first year of teaching and I am	
	Secretary Duncan, your words are
falling flat	falling flat.
and am overwhelmed.	
	I hear you laud "professional teachers."
I am angry.	I am angry.
	Angry that you have the
I try to capture the kids'	
attention.	attention
	of a subdued public
The students are not	
	and that we are
sitting quietly and	sitting quietly and
they are not	

Patricia:	Melissa:
	nodding
in unison.	in unison.
And this	And this
complexity	
	tyrannical praise
is not like I was told it would be.	is not like I was told it would be.

As teachers, doctoral students, and university professors, we work with educators who are frustrated by the barrage of polarizing attacks on American public education by educational demagogues. Though we came to the teaching profession in two entirely different ways—Melissa via a four-year college teacher preparation route, and Patricia as a career change via a master of education program—we both felt ill prepared for the complexities of our work and the ways in which we were assumed to be voiceless in our classrooms and in the larger educational conversation. In light of this, we wanted to re-theorize the notion of teacher preparedness and expertise.

Patricia is both an urban high school Spanish teacher and a part-time urban university lecturer. Raised in Mexico and Spain, she moved to the United States at age 18; her cross-cultural experiences inspired her to pursue a career in Spanish education as a middle-aged professional. Melissa is a White educator who began her teaching career after college as an urban high school English and ESL teacher. She is now an instructor of English at an urban community college and an adjunct professor within two college teacher education programs. Both Patricia and Melissa are doctoral students at the same public university.

Throughout our discussion we use a metalogue[1] (Roth & Tobin, 2004) to give expression to the individual and collective natures of our praxis, to emphasize the need for practitioner voices within the national conversation, and to create a social space for our learning. Our theoretical positionalities—Patricia is a progressive educator, and Melissa is a critical theorist—provide us with an opportunity to think with these pedagogues about what "prepared" might mean. We want to ignite the boundaries of pragmatic and critical theories in the hopes of forging a praxis that confronts technocratic notions of teacher preparedness and reframes the discussion of teacher professionalism.

Urban Teachers Survey the Firestorm

Patricia: Education in the United States is in the midst of a heated debate, as traditionalists and progressives war over the state of American schools and how to "fix" them. Traditionalists such as E.D. Hirsch, Jr. (1999) like to blame the progressive movement, which dates as far back as Dewey and the 1930s, for the current state of our schools. But others such as Zemelman, Daniels, and Hyde (2005) contend that the progressive movement has never been fully implemented and that the debate is between the curriculum reformers (progressive educators) and the accountability advocates (traditionalists).

The curriculum reformers are in-school stakeholders such as teachers. Accountability advocates, for the most part, are federal, state, and local politicians, entrepreneurs, testing companies, and conservative think tanks who "believe that schools will improve through tighter controls, more regulation, and frequent high-stakes standardized tests with tough consequences" (Zemelman et al., 2005, p. 3). At the moment, the voices of the traditional, accountability-advocate technocrats, for whom scientific results have become a system of measuring student and school outcomes (Zemelman et al., 2005), are louder than those of the curriculum reformers.

Melissa: Patricia, your description of the debate about public education in the United States illustrates how teachers are thrust into contradiction. This contradiction is far reaching because it simplifies complex purposes of education to just two choices: education for achievement (the traditional model) or education for the whole child (the progressive model). In light of this polarization, teacher preparation becomes a contested choice as educators struggle to prepare students to meet standards *or* to gain self-efficacy. We need to find a third way through this firestorm, as choosing sides will fan the flames of the old debate.

For that reason, I would like to suggest that we ignite the boundaries of a critical-progressive approach to teacher preparation. Progressive theorists have been able to offer an alternative to traditional education; by valuing and validating the individual, they attempt to produce a democratic—equitable for all—education. However, this alternative has reproduced a historical binary: we remain stuck in an either/or dichotomy that frustrates progress. By blending a critical perspective and its socio-subversive notions of power with the pragmatism of a progressive approach (Kincheloe, 2005), we might spark new theory about what being prepared as a teacher might mean. And by doing this as experts inside the field, our work stands in resistance to the technocrats who continue to tyrannize public education as outsiders.

Patricia: For 3 consecutive days, a student has set small fires in my urban high school. As I reflect on these incidents and the corresponding evacuation processes and interruptions to learning, I feel that my understanding of a prepared teacher must change. As his teacher, I felt that we had established a workable relationship. Yet I also felt I was not afforded the opportunity to fully engage with him, because my role as teacher is defined within the current educational milieu as content expert. When I entered the field of teaching, my idea of preparedness was based on the outline given to us by the teacher-training program in which I was enrolled, capped by a semester-long practicum. Prepared meant being licensed, foremost. Next it meant having completed the courses in the teacher-training program, and finally it meant having fulfilled the requirements of the practicum. Nowhere was it mentioned that urban schools are faced with a challenging mix of populations; nowhere was it suggested *how* a teacher might come to know her students individually in order to better serve each one, while teaching to them collectively. Nor was it suggested that a teacher be holistic. But in my experiences, including this one with the youth who set fires, prepared means working with individual students, each one different from another, and some more affected than others by the social ills of poverty, homelessness, and minority status. Educators should be encouraged to embody this other notion of prepared, which I have come to discover along the way.

Melissa: Patricia, your experiences point to the distancing that seems almost inevitable in the traditional model of urban schooling, in which teachers occupy (truly and metaphorically) the front of the classroom as students face, but do not touch, their teachers from many feet away. Contemporary technocrats seem to prefer this model, as standardized testing and scripted curricula push us further away from working *with* students and instead cause us to work *on* or *about* them. Reform efforts are not changing our schools; worse, the technocratic sky-is-falling rhetoric is distracting the American public from deep and historical discussions about the purpose of schooling (Tyack & Cuban, 1995). Certainly this incident with your student demands that we find a way to transform public education—a way that reaches beyond the traditional-progressive debate and ignites new theories.

In addition, your comments point to a troubling binary in the technocratic, corporate reform efforts. This dichotomy suggests that being a prepared teacher does not include a working understanding of complex socio-cultural forces and how we might position and involve ourselves within them. And because so many of the policy makers engendering these judgments are not educational experts or practitioners (Thomas, Introduction to this volume), they fabricate frustratingly simple solutions to complex social inequities. Critical theory has a contribution to make to this oversimplification; it helps us to wrestle with how power impacts our schools and our society (McLaren, 2003). Current political and educational conversation needs to understand the school as a site for reproducing and creating society (Bourdieu, 1977).

I feel as you do—a longing to be more entrenched in issues that are personal *and* academic, emotional *and* intellectual, social *and* educational. The experiences with your student suggest that a reframing of education as school *and* society would be helpful to us.

Igniting Theoretical Boundaries

Patricia: As I evaluate my effectiveness and ineffectiveness with the student who set those fires, I am particularly consumed with the binary of progressive and traditional education; educators have been feeling the heat of the traditional/progressive debate for hundreds of years.

According to Dewey (1938/n.d.), traditional education is defined by a system of "education" in which earlier generations determine what information subsequent generations ought to know, and then educators transmit the information to the students. Dewey (1938/n.d.) also suggested that traditional notions of moral education were limited to habit-forming responses to rules. There are parallels between Dewey's notion of traditional education and today's accountability reform efforts; neither creates a democratic setting.

Progressive education, on the other hand, is poised to establish democratic norms. Student engagement and choice in curricular matters and in negotiation of conflict (Zemelman et al., 2005), for instance, are essential pieces to the progressive model. Dewey's educational vision was characterized by a child-centered curriculum with differentiated instruction. He believed in grading students by academic interest instead of by biological age; he affirmed that all learning be personal and meaningful, and therefore based in experience. Dewey felt that the curriculum ought to be alterable over time, and further advocated for teacher input.

It is important to note that Dewey "did not assume that a child-oriented curriculum meant abandoning traditional subject matter" (Urban & Wagoner, 2009, p. 252) as traditionalists like to suggest. Nor did he intend that progressive education exist at the exclusion of traditional education. As Dewey wrote in *Experience and Education*:

[F]or in spite of itself any movement that thinks and acts in terms of an 'ism becomes so involved in reaction against the other 'isms that it is unwittingly controlled by them. For it then forms its principles by reaction against them instead of by a comprehensive, constructive survey of actual needs, problems, and possibilities. (n.d.)

The 'isms that Dewey wrote about in 1938 are pervasive today. There is so much rhetoric, money, prominence, politics, and perceived success attached to test scores that the implication, created by boisterous technocrats, is that the progressive model is a complete failure.

Melissa: As we re-theorize the notion of "prepared," I think we must consider how to construct a praxis—a theory and practice—of our work as teachers, and to see that praxis as situated in a particular space within the current political debates on education (Freire, 2000). As a beginning teacher, I thought teaching was skills based, and I reenacted the current tensions of public education in the United States:

What dominates the public discourse on the conditions of schools in the popular media is the concern for economic competitiveness. Schools are seen primarily as sites for training workers and consumers who will compete with other workers and consumers all over the world. . .[resulting in schools with] greater control, authority, and discipline. (Stokes, 1997, p. 202)

I became a disciple of this way of viewing education, a perspective that I now consider to be mechanistic and positivistic, inadequate for explaining the sociocultural spaces in which we learn (Kincheloe & Tobin, 2009). I was reproducing one of the first fundamental purposes of U.S. education—to subdue troublemakers and to reproduce a passive public under the guise of democracy (Zinn, 2003). I was enacting a technocratic habitus. And as a do-gooder in an urban school, I was blinded by good intentions and missing the most crucial piece of all, especially in the beginnings of my career—criticality (Kress, 2011).

As I came to know my high school students, they introduced me to many of the ideas of critical pedagogy. From them, I learned that larger structures were at work in the injustices in our city, and I began to see race and class as present and troubling (Freire, 2000; McLaren, 2003). The students taught me to be more thoughtful about how we could position ourselves in relationship to forces of power and marginalization. These early experiences in my career helped me to move away from technocratic views of teacher education and to embrace a notion of praxis.

Patricia: I am constantly plagued by the polarities about which you speak. In fact, Belenky and colleagues (1986) suggest:

> The tendency towards dualism in American society can be seen clearly in its schools. Dichotomous thinking has led to the belief that one cannot develop both intellect and emotion without slighting one. What results is a curriculum that does not value emotional, intuitive types of learning as highly as rational/technical studies. (as cited in Breault, 2003, p. 3)

Based on my experiences in middle and high school classrooms, there is a dissonance in the rhetoric on national and local levels and in actual practice in the classroom. Individualized instruction is the rhetoric of administrations and parents; meanwhile, teachers are controlled by national and state standards.

It is helpful to use Tobin's (2005) model of the macro, meso, and micro levels here. The rhetoric on the macro level (in politics and in government), the teacher mandates and systems of accountability on the meso level (in the schools), and the actual practice on the micro level (in the classroom) often do not work synchronously. Policy is written on the macro level, typically without input from the "players" (Swartz, 1997) on the meso or micro levels.

Bourdieu suggested the notion of "players" and "fields" (Swartz, 1997). Teachers, for instance, are players in the field defined by their school. Players within the same field often do not work cooperatively and therefore are much less apt to do so with players from other fields. Yet, according to Bourdieu, what happens in one field—for instance, in a school—affects surrounding fields—such as the community (Swartz, 1997). Thus, education becomes defined by asynchronous, yet connected, structures. Rarely is education characterized by a democratic synchrony among all of the players involved, across all of the levels and fields. Dewey (1938/n.d.), on the other hand, was hopeful that schools would be the setting where true democracies could flourish, by way of a curriculum constructed by players in all fields.

In my opinion, Dewey's progressive educational theory, in its original intent, may be that third way of theorizing that we so desperately seek. It embodies a personally relevant curriculum, upheld by academic excellence for all. The student who set the fires in my school would have benefitted from a Deweyan curriculum.

Melissa: Critical theory, as expressed by your discussion of Bourdieu, suggests that democratic schooling is not possible within traditional structures of education, and especially not in a technocratic milieu in which students and teachers are primarily data sets. Schools "work against the class interest of those students who are most politically and economically vulnerable within society" (Darder, Baltodano,

& Torres, 2003, p. 11). Technocratic education, as it borrows from traditional educational theory and practice, masks a dominant, oppressive ideology with a claim of an apolitical ideology that discredits the lived experiences of marginalized stakeholders in the school community (Darder et al., 2003; Greene, 2003). Critical theorists are concerned with giving voice to these marginalized experiences even as we challenge the variety of legitimizing myths of dominant American education. As you have suggested, prepared teachers need the pragmatic hope for democracy that Dewey offers. But prepared teachers also need the complexities offered by critical theory, which suggests that teachers working in the current firestorms of polarization must seek knowledge and experience in multiple fields, and connect their praxis to larger, societal issues of economy, race, power, privilege, and class (McLaren, 2003). This is an expertise that cannot be evaluated by simplistic, technocratic teacher accountability measures.

Igniting the Boundaries of Excellence and Care as Rigour

Patricia: An update: The student has had his suspension hearing and is awaiting his expulsion hearing. In the meantime, I have to supply him with the work that he is currently missing. While this young man's education is critically important, I feel like the request was both a formality and an exercise in futility. What continuity would there be for him to finish reading the short story for my class, only to be transferred to a different program later? He needed a personalized program of study right away. I was moved to tears.

Greene's *Releasing the Imagination* (1995) has proven helpful to me as I ponder the events at my school over the last several weeks, and how they might make me a better-prepared teacher. According to Greene, there are two views of education: the larger view that allows for flexibility in approaches and contextualized thinking, and the smaller view, which minimizes the personal and sees the process of education as a system. Sending homework to the suspended student was a small-view educational requirement. The larger view appreciates the magnificence of, and the people involved in, the process of educating. According to Greene (1995), "looking at things large is what might move us on to reform" (p. 16). The student who set fires taught me why this view is important. He taught me that our American public school system needs to do better at personalizing education.

Melissa: What you have done here to trouble the duality of challenge and care is so important. Caring should necessarily involve high academic standards and expectations. We are too often bamboozled by the technocratic rhetoric that conceives of high standards and care as polarities.

Freire offers us some ideas for working among the polarity; he uses the term "rigour" to explain the work that a critical pedagogue must do to become an expert. For Freire, this expertise involves academic knowledge, effective practice, and love (Freire, 1998). Kincheloe and Berry (2004), too, suggest "rigour" as a humanizing, multiplicitous epistemological approach to education; understood this way, rigour challenges notions of academia that are fixed, positivistic, and dead. If we understand our schools as complex and if we embrace our students and our colleagues as humans and not as representative data sets, then rigour expresses the ways we who are developing a literacy of power engage with our work. "Rigour" thus becomes a subversive term that stands in opposition to the technocratic notions of expertise; it empowers us to avoid the duality of excellence versus care, and ignites the intrinsic borders between them.

Your reflections on the small-view approach speak truth to how we "do" school—how fractured and technical it is, how divorced from process and person (Noddings, 1995). Rigour, when re-theorized to embrace the emotional, epistemological, and ethical complexities of our work, characterizes our construction of education as a social-physical space. Prepared teachers care, and we care rigourously.

Patricia: Melissa, the student who set fires at my school was suspended and in spite of his criminal behavior, I truly believe that he was less of a villain than a victim of his world. How might we have helped him? I wrote a letter on his behalf. I do not know where he will end up, and I feel completely helpless knowing that he left my classroom on a bathroom pass to set one of the fires. If anything, the experience highlights my need for a new theory of teacher preparation.

Melissa: I really appreciate the following summary of our politicized environment; it expresses so clearly the tensions of our work amid technocratic notions of expertise. When considered in conjunction with your student's experience, I find myself deeply troubled and imagining new ways to bring justice to bear:

> What conservative reformers demand are new regulations, requirements, credentials, and evaluations that would ensure that teachers have acquired the essential "skills" necessary to fulfill their responsibility to prepare the next generation of workers. . . . The prevailing models are managerial, medical, and scientist; and the language of teacher [preparation] is the language of methods, materials, objectives, skills, schedules, grouping, tracking, discipline, tests, diagnosis, disabilities, deficits, interventions, remediation, and so on. (Stokes, 1997, p. 202)

Your experiences this semester demand that we challenge current, technocratic notions of "prepared"and re-theorize them. We should be prepared to care about students. We should be prepared to care about our content. We should be prepared to teach for social justice. We should be prepared to transform our schools and our society *with* our students.

Forging Praxis from the Flames

Melissa and Patricia: We often hear teachers say that our academic teacher preparation programs did not prepare us sufficiently for the countless unpredictable encounters we have with our students; further, we were not prepared for the political firestorms that surround our work. When we reflect upon the complexities of our urban teaching practices, we realize that we—and other in-service and preservice teachers we know—need more forums for discussing our experiences, for ferreting out the dichotomies that we find (and sometimes unconsciously adopt), for encountering and theorizing the fires of our work. Certainly presenting teaching as a set of technical skills—and teachers and students as technical automatons—does not explain what we encounter when we teach. And so we imagine teacher education programs, professional development, and ongoing collegial conversations as a *praxis* that speaks truth to power and resists technocratic tyranny.

Writing this metalogue has reminded us of the value of a resistant, emancipatory conversation among practitioners. We need these conversations if we are going to create a third way that transforms the polarizing forces of our contemporary public education. Teacher dialogue demonstrates that expertise is developed within localized contexts—including teachers, students, and communities—and not within the meetings of the politically powerful and educationally inexperienced. The firestorm of education, painful though it may be, may yet forge a collaboration of practitioner-experts who are resolved to take back their profession from the technocrats and ignite the boundaries of debate with the flames of justice.

Acknowledgment

The authors would like to acknowledge Dr. Tricia Kress of the University of Massachusetts, Boston for her efforts in providing feedback for this work.

References

Bourdieu, P. (1977). *Outline of a theory of practice.* Cambridge: Cambridge University Press.
Breault, R.A. (2003). Dewey, Freire, and a pedagogy for the oppressor. *Multicultural Education, 10*(3), 2–6.

Darder, A., Baltodano, M., & Torres, R. (2003). *The critical pedagogy reader.* New York: RoutledgeFalmer.

Dewey, J. (n.d.). *Experience and education.* Retrieved from http://ruby.fgcu.edu/courses/ndemers/colloquium/ExperiencEducationDewey.pdf (Original work published 1938)

Freire, P. (1998). *Teachers as cultural workers: Letters to those who dare to teach* (D. Macedo, D. Koike, & A. Oliveira, Trans.). Boulder, CO: Westview Press.

Freire, P. (2000). *Pedagogy of the oppressed* (M.B. Ramos, Trans.). New York: Continuum. (Original work published 1970)

Greene, M. (1995). *Releasing the imagination: Essays on education, the arts, and social change.* San Francisco, CA: Jossey-Bass.

Greene, M. (2003). In search of a critical pedagogy. In A. Darder, M. Baltodano, & R.D. Torres (Eds.), *The critical pedagogy reader* (pp. 97–112). New York: RoutledgeFalmer.

Hirsch, Jr., E.D. (1999). *The schools we need and why we don't have them.* New York: First Anchor Books.

Kincheloe, J. (2005). *Critical constructivism.* New York: Peter Lang.

Kincheloe, J., & Berry, K.S. (2004). *Rigour and complexity in educational research: Conceptualizing the bricolage.* New York: Open University Press.

Kincheloe, J., & Tobin, K. (2009). The much exaggerated death of positivism. *Cultural Studies of Science Education, 4,* 513–528.

Kress, T. (2011). *Critical praxis research: Breathing new life into research methods for teachers.* New York: Springer.

McLaren, P. (2003). Critical pedagogy: A look at the major concepts. In A. Darder, M. Baltodano, & R.D. Torres (Eds.), *The critical pedagogy reader* (pp. 69–96). New York: RoutledgeFalmer.

Noddings, N. (1995). Teaching themes of care. *Phi Delta Kappan, 76*(9), 675–679. Retrieved from web.ebscohost.com

Roth, W-M.,& Tobin, K. (2004). Cogenerative dialoguing and metaloguing: Reflexivity of processes and genres. *Forum: Qualitative Social Research,* apple-converted-space> *5*(3). Retrieved from http://nbn-resolving.de/urn:nbn:de:0114-fqs040370

Stokes, W.T. (1997). Progressive teacher education: Consciousness, identity, and knowledge. In P. Freire, J.W. Fraser, D. Macedo, T. McKinnon, & W.T. Stokes (Eds.), *Mentoring the mentor: A critical dialogue with Paulo Freire* (pp. 201–227). New York: Peter Lang.

Swartz, D. (1997). *Culture & power: The sociology of Pierre Bourdieu.* Chicago, IL: University of Chicago Press.

Tobin, K. (2005). Urban science as a culturally and socially adaptive practice. In K. Tobin, R. Elmesky, & G. Seiler (Eds.), *Improving urban science education* (pp. 21–42). New York: Rowman & Littlefield.

Tyack, D.,& Cuban, L. (1995). *Tinkering toward utopia.* Cambridge, MA: Harvard University Press.

Urban, W.J., & Wagoner, J. (2009). *American education: A history* (4th ed.). New York: Routledge.

Zemelman, S., Daniels, H., & Hyde, A. (2005).*Best practice: Today's standards for teaching & learning in America's schools.* Portsmouth, NH: Heinemann.

Zinn, H. (2003). *People's history of the United States: 1492–present.* New York: Perennial Classics.

Note

1. As Roth and Tobin (2004) explain, metalogue embodies the principles of co-generative dialogue—that is, in a metalogue, the writers maintain their own voices and the product of the discussion is the process, not an agreed-upon conclusion. We are drawn to metalogue because it provides us the opportunity to learn from each other and then (as we re-read and revise the text) to learn from our learning. Metalogue is a powerful tool because we "learn from our own learning processes" (para. 21).

20

Why Accountability Measures Fail:
Practitioner Perspectives on the Role of Teacher Efficacy

DAWN MITCHELL

In the age of teacher accountability in the United States, what successful entrepreneurs say about public education generates far more publicity than what the students' classroom teachers know and say about what matters in their own profession. I've watched *Waiting for "Superman,"* where the public school system and its teachers were criticized, and charter schools with business models and methods were touted as the answer to what ails public education. I've heard politicians promote private school vouchers in attempts to woo their constituencies and manipulate tax dollars for votes. I've listened to well-intentioned colleagues who want schools to succeed in the current system of high-stakes testing and accountability advocate for electronic testing so that teachers can access standardized scores more efficiently in attempts to show student achievement in measureable outcomes. I've heard Bill Gates and other stakeholders in our education system bemoan the current state of public schools, how our country's students are behind in preparing for tomorrow's workforce, and I've seen how this "call for reform" results in the teacher accountability movement that uses high-stakes, standardized testing to hold students and teachers responsible for the teaching and learning that happens in schools.

This is not the answer.

While we are inundated with celebrities who know what is best for our public schools because they went to school themselves or made it in American society by garnering fame and fortune, we rarely hear from classroom teachers, the actual practitioners who day in and day out do the meaningful work of teaching and learning. We see depictions of ineffective and slack teachers in Hollywood movies such as *Bad Teacher*, but we rarely see on the big screen—or any screen, for that matter—effective teachers making a positive difference preparing our students not just for the workforce, but for the world and whatever role they choose in it. In my 12 years of working in the field of education in a variety of roles from fourth grade teacher to teacher mentor, evaluator, and consultant, I have seen first-hand what success in a public school looks like.

I have seen classroom teachers overcome obstacles such as poverty, language barriers, learning disabilities, and inadequate supplies to meet the needs of a diverse group of students in a mere 180 days. I have been a witness to success that is not touted on television or recorded in measureable outcomes on spreadsheets that determine which school gets federal funding and which does not. I have seen success happen in affluent schools and schools labeled Title I because of the socio-economic status of their population that their students and teachers have no control over. I have seen success in classrooms with all the bells and whistles technology has to offer and classrooms that are utilizing traditional teaching methods. I have seen success in teachers who have decades of experience and those who have mere months. What I have witnessed doesn't look the way reformers claim. They aren't "miracle" schools. They are schools that believe and invest in their teachers through providing ownership and autonomy, and those teachers then believe and invest in their students, giving them the same ownership and decision-making opportunities.

What do all these success stories have in common? All of them are related to the practices of their classroom teacher. The current accountability measures target teachers specifically and hold them responsible for measurable student outcomes, more often than not correlated with students' performance on high-stakes, standardized tests. Teachers and public schools in general have become targeted for reform in order to get our country back on track and help us compete in the global economy. Before any educational reform can have a genuine influence in our public schools, we must have real social reform. There are much larger social issues that policymakers cannot afford to ignore, such as our nation's rising poverty levels, our rapidly increasing immigrant population, and the global recession that has decidedly impacted the needs of public school children.

The teachers I know have no problems being held accountable for how their classroom practices meet their students' needs in the classroom. It's what we do. It's why we're here. The whole purpose of teaching is to positively impact a student's academic life individually, and a whole class's growth collectively. I've had meaningful conversations with teachers about how their students have grown and improved in the course of a year. Their conversations don't always include how many points the student improved on a standardized test. Believe it or not, they tend to focus on more meaningful accomplishments such as students having enough confidence to share their writing in front of their peers or the growth that happens over time with support and feedback in students' ability to read independently. You can't measure everything that goes on in a classroom.

You shouldn't always quantify effective teaching. You can't purchase it in a program or in a book. You can't mandate it and reproduce it in mass quantities through legislative mandates. Policymakers as well as the general public understand that classroom teachers are one of the biggest influences in a student's academic life. While their current focus for educational improvement is squarely pointed at the classroom teacher, their methods are definitely missing the mark. While I am advocating that we focus on larger social reform first, if the current reform efforts are going to focus on improving classroom instruction, I argue that teacher accountability is not the answer to improving our students' education and the quality of our public schools. I argue that teacher efficacy is.

Teacher efficacy is a teacher's belief in her/his own ability to positively impact student growth. A body of educational research on the impact of teacher efficacy suggests that "teachers who set high goals, who persist, who try another strategy when one approach is found wanting—in other words, teachers who have a high sense of efficacy and act on it—are more likely to have students who learn" (Shaughnessy, 2004, p. 157). Teachers who have a high sense of self-efficacy truly believe that all students can learn, and they then act on this belief. They believe that what they do each day in the classroom matters; therefore, they believe that they need and deserve ownership over their own classroom practice, and they seek out educational research and theories that are most effective and implement them through reflective practice. Protheroe (2008) highlights some teacher behaviors related to teacher efficacy:

Teachers with a stronger sense of efficacy:

- Tend to exhibit greater levels of planning and organization;
- Are more open to new ideas and are more willing to experiment with new methods to better meet the needs of their students;

- Are more persistent and resilient when things do not go smoothly;
- Are less critical of students when they make errors; and
- Are less inclined to refer a difficult student to special education. (p. 43)

These characteristics have been proven true in my own experience as a practitioner and in the experiences of many of my colleagues. Our voices, our perspectives as classroom practitioners deserve to be heard and included in the national debate on what works in the classroom.

Mastery Experiences: My Story

I have spent the last 12 years teaching and supporting public school. My teaching career began with my position as a fourth-grade teacher, and while I worked very hard, coming to school early and staying late, pouring myself into my plans and preparations, I had no real ownership over what I was teaching. I knew I loved my students, and I knew I wanted what was best for them. I just didn't know what exactly best practice was.

I believed then that my lack of experience and knowledge would be overcome by my passion for this profession and my sincere desire for my students to succeed. I didn't know much, but at least I knew what I didn't know and signed up immediately following my first year of teaching for the invitational summer institute for my area's local National Writing Project (NWP) housed at USC Upstate, the Spartanburg Writing Project (SWP). This decision truly changed the trajectory of my professional career.

I learned through engaging in parallel experiences such as participating in a writers' workshop led by master teachers, watching demonstration lessons taught by my colleagues, reflecting on my own classroom practices, and discovering that what I was doing needed to be led by research and students' needs and interests.

Research suggests that mastery experiences like the ones I shared with my colleagues at SWP's summer institute are one way to increase teacher efficacy (Jerald, 2007). Through the intense professional development SWP provided, I realized that what I do does matter. The more effective I am as the classroom teacher in planning, implementing, and assessing my instruction, the more effective my students could be with their achievement. I entered teaching the following year ready to not only impact my students' success but also to correlate the structures and strategies I used in my everyday practice to achieve it.

As my own teacher efficacy has grown I have worked to find ways to support other teachers' professional growth through my role as an adjunct instructor, teacher mentor, and as a university supervisor working with Furman University's education department to evaluate and support teaching candidates who were completing their senior block clinical experiences in our local classrooms. In my work in each of these capacities I have seen first-hand the correlation between teacher efficacy and teacher effectiveness. I've learned that it can be the missing piece of the puzzle in a classroom, in a grade level, and in an entire school.

Collegiality and Shared Decision Making: Martha's Story

Martha Frye is a teacher with 29 years in our public school system. I had the opportunity to work with Martha as a teacher consultant on an action research project through a partnership her school had with SWP and spent many hours each week in her classroom with her students, working together to improve literacy instruction and implementing a writing workshop. What I learned from Martha and the four other teachers in the grade level is the importance of shared decision-making and how it fosters collegiality.

Teachers report having stronger beliefs about their collective ability as a faculty to help all students succeed when they have more ownership over school-wide decisions related to their classroom instruction (Goddard, Hoy, & Hoy, 2000). Martha and her colleagues had direct ownership over our partnership. They had the support of their school's administration to grow professionally and to conduct action research in an area of their literacy instruction that, as a collective group, they felt they wanted to grow in: writing instruction. Through this shared decision-making process, the five of us met each week to discuss professional readings we chose to inform our practice, plan student-driven units of study, and work through the hard parts of assessment and instruction.

Martha shared that "being equipped to make a difference requires long hours of planning, staying up to date on research and new approaches by attending staff development sessions and taking graduate classes, sharing ideas and resources offered by other teachers on my team and guarding against the 'I've always done it this way' mentality."

This shared decision-making not only provided each of us with ownership over the important work we were doing, but it also fostered a sense of collegiality. We knew that we were embarking on the action research as a team and throughout the course of the yearlong study we relied on each other's perspectives regarding the implementation of a writers' workshop. We shared ideas, resources, and most importantly, the experience of taking a risk and watching it pay off. Our action research resulted in new knowledge gained by all involved—myself, my colleagues, and most importantly, the students.

Social Persuasion: Emily's Story

Emily Perry is a fourth-grade teacher at a rural elementary school in Spartanburg County, South Carolina. I had the opportunity of being her mentor through a partnership her district had with Furman University. Part of my role as a mentor was to encourage Emily to develop a strong sense of efficacy through ongoing support and feedback. In one of our conversations Emily shared how she was supported in taking risks with her classroom instruction. Emily had experience teaching social studies and ELA in a departmentalized classroom prior to her current placement, in which she teaches science and math.

Early in the school year, Emily was not satisfied with the structure of her math block. She began discussing with me and her grade-level colleagues how she wanted to take some risks with her math instruction. Specifically, she wanted to try small-group instruction. Emily shared that she knew a workshop structure worked well in her previous experience teaching reading and writing and felt that this similar structure of a mini-lesson, small group application, followed by support and feedback, could really help increase student engagement and provide her with time to work with students one on one. In reflecting on this experience, Emily shared this:

> As the weeks went on, the stations became more efficient and effective. I learned how to balance the needs of the whole class with the needs of my small group. My students learned how to handle their newfound independence at the stations. I took a risk and with great patience and flexibility, it worked. However, I believed in the risks I was taking and knew my students, therefore I found a way to make it successful.

One of the ways that research suggests is effective in helping teachers take risks and build their own efficacy is through social persuasion. Many factors can contribute to positive social persuasion, such as feedback from superiors, messages teachers receive during professional development, and conversations with faculty (Jerald, 2007).

Emily received similar supportive messages from a variety of sources during her early teaching experiences. Her school was engaged in a professional book study that encouraged teachers to integrate authentic experiences into the content areas. Emily had the research basis for trying out a new structure, and she had the support of her colleagues and her mentor. This social persuasion, along with the elements of shared decision-making and collegiality, really worked to lay the groundwork for Emily's mastery experience with her math stations.

Supportive Leadership: Margaret's Story

Margaret Rosebro is a second-year teacher at a Title I elementary school in an urban setting in Spartanburg, South Carolina. I had the opportunity to work with Margaret during her first year as her university supervisor through Furman University. The biggest part of my role as a university supervisor was the support offered, as both I and her teacher mentor provided her with feedback, strategies, suggestions, and most importantly, the time and space to grow and develop her own sense of teacher efficacy. Margaret's first year of teaching brought many ups and downs. She began her year with the elation of having her first teaching position and worked hard to get to know her students and her school community.

Toward the middle of the fall semester, Margaret began experiencing some frustrations. She was struggling with some unexpected student behaviors, trying to differentiate instruction for several students who needed individual support in math and reading and was searching for consistency in her daily routine and in her planning. That's a tall order for any teacher, veteran or novice; but this is a true picture of the realities of our profession. Even though Margaret was overwhelmed, she had a sincere desire for her students to succeed, and she had supportive leadership from everyone involved in her growth as a new teacher.

As Margaret cycled through some of the common phases induction-year teachers face during that first semester, from anticipation to survival—and yes, even disillusionment (Moir, 1999)—she had continued support from her school, from her district mentor, and from her university, all of whom partnered with Margaret to foster her growth of teacher efficacy. Jerald (2007) suggests that some novice teachers can experience a decline in their sense of efficacy during their first year of teaching and implies that supportive leadership through observations and feedback can be instrumental at keeping these declines at bay.

This proved true with Margaret. Throughout the fall semester, Margaret received ongoing feedback through written observations, informal discussions, and seminars through her induction class. Her school administration knew Margaret's strengths and also knew that her struggles were not uncommon in the induction year. Along with her district mentor, they provided Margaret with the encouragement that is a necessary companion to constructive feedback, giving her the needed time and the support to take ownership of her classroom.

At the end of the first semester Margaret was ready to begin a new phase of her first-year teaching, rejuvenation, and reflection. She says:

> For the first time I felt that I was actually getting to teach effectively. It was all because I needed to find my self-worth. I needed the time to look at what was not working and change it. What caused this amazing change? I did. The more I took control of my classroom and the more that I was confident in what I was doing the more my students were succeeding academically and socially.

Leadership that provides constructive feedback, encourages professional development, and, most of all, provides teachers with ownership over their instructional decisions supports the growth of teacher efficacy, not only in first-year teachers, but teachers of all levels of experience (Jerald, 2007). This type of leadership provided Margaret with the time and support she needed to reflect on her classroom practice, make changes that she believed would increase her students' learning, and then act on them.

Productive Climate: Jessie's Story

Even our prospective teaching candidates can begin to develop teacher efficacy through their clinical experience in a productive climate. Jessie Wolfinger is a teaching candidate in her senior year of study at Furman University. I have had the opportunity to work with Jessie as her university supervisor throughout this year and have watched her grow in multiple ways as she conducted observations, assignments such as her community/school profile, unit work sample, and so on. Jessie has had the support of her university, her co-teacher, her grade-level team, and her school administration throughout, and this has given her the freedom to learn and grow.

One of the biggest factors contributing to Jessie's growth as a prospective teacher is the productive climate of the school that she taught in. Jessie's school has a record of high student achievement, and teachers work collaboratively in grade-level groups to plan their units of study, participate in professional development through monthly meetings with instructional coaches, plan projects and field trips, and work together to meet their students' needs. Jessie's teacher, Mrs. Rosenberger, encouraged her participation in both the grade-level team and in school-wide staff development. Jessie rose to the occasion, contributing to the grade-level group meetings, creating flexible plans that each teacher could modify based on their students and their personal teaching style, and working alongside Mrs. Rosenberger as a co-teacher.

Because Mrs. Rosenberger saw Jessie as a co-teacher and valued her input, Jessie was able to experiment with management techniques and instructional strategies and structures. One particular area that Jessie really grew in was her use of formative assessments to guide her instruction. Jessie was disappointed in her students' performance during a particular lesson and realized that they could have done better with more specific expectations. She wanted to try a different approach, and Mrs. Rosenberger supported her decision. The next day I observed Jessie explain to students what she expected of their writing with this assignment. She used student examples to highlight where a few had done well, and then she modeled what she wanted them to go back and do to make their pieces more effective. Students responded, and this lesson was a turning point for Jessie.

When we talked afterward, Jessie said there is no such thing as perfection in this profession. She says, "Nobody is perfect. As a teacher, you should constantly be striving to improve. Just like we tell our students, we need to learn from our mistakes. Lessons will not go as planned. Management may be off one day. And, it is okay. Feedback allows for you as a teacher to grow. It allows you to see other strategies and techniques. Take risks, try new things. They may not always work out, but that is still okay. You learn from it."

A productive climate where there are shared goals for students and teachers that emphasize learning, support from administrators and colleagues in solving instructional and management problems, and collaboration from colleagues can have a positive impact on teacher efficacy (Jerald, 2007). During Jessie's teaching experience, both the assistant principal and the principal came by to observe Jessie teach and gave her feedback on the practices used. She received support from her co-teacher, Mrs. Rosenberger, and ideas and feedback from her grade level team. This type of climate allowed Jessie not just to experience teaching but also to grow in her sense of efficacy. In her final reflection, Jessie summarized this realization: "As teachers, we need not strive for perfection. We need to strive for growth. In reflecting back on my senior block teaching experience I have definitely learned a tremendous amount from my successes, but I've learned just as much when an instructional decision didn't work."

What We Can Learn from Practitioners

These perspectives from practitioners, from veterans with 29 years of experience to beginning teachers on the cusp of their careers, can teach us how to foster and support teacher efficacy. Teachers who believe that what they do matters; teachers who are purposeful and productive in their teaching; teachers who know that they can make a difference in students' achievement in both measurable and non-measurable outcomes, all possess a high sense of efficacy. These teachers show all of us as stakeholders in public education how we can best support student growth—by supporting the professional growth of each classroom teacher. From the 30-year body of research on teacher efficacy, the majority of the evidence does not support the focus on standardized testing or accountability measures that utilize high-stakes consequences and rewards. What empowers teachers with confidence in their own ability are "mastery experiences" such as the ones described by the practitioners' voices and stories included in this chapter (Goddard et al., 2000).

Participating in experiences such as conducting teacher-driven action research projects within their own classrooms to determine what instructional structures and strategies are most effective in working with a specific group of students, as Martha did, or participating in joint professional development that entails reading professional texts, implementing ideas based on educational research, and then reflecting on the results to make necessary modifications to fit both the content demands and student needs, as Emily did, are ways in which teachers can work together to build their confidence and their effectiveness. How can stakeholders support these kinds of mastery experiences? By understanding that professional development needs to be ongoing and longitudinal. By supporting this development and continued education for our teachers through degree-seeking programs that foster teacher-led action-research and theory into practice. By advocating that instead of focusing on measurable student outcomes, we focus on teacher incomes (both literally and figuratively), having faith that the support we put into our teachers and their professional growth will be reflected in increased student achievement.

Jerald (2007) summarizes the suggestions the research on teacher efficacy offers principals and other stakeholders who want to support the development of teacher efficacy among their educators. He lists providing mastery experiences, reinforcing positive beliefs about student achievement and teacher efficacy through social persuasion, supportive leadership, collegiality, shared decision making, and a productive climate.

Change takes time. As counter-culture as this may be to our fast-paced, want-results- now society, professional development is most effective when it is thoughtful and has ownership from teachers themselves. Efficacy is contagious. When teachers believe in themselves and are empowered to make instructional decisions in their classrooms, they in turn pass that power on to their students, who begin to grow in their own self-efficacy, believing that what they do matters. It is powerful, but it takes time. It takes an investment. It takes an overarching belief that teachers do want what's best for their students. In my experience as an educator, I have met my share of ineffective teachers. I have yet to find one that I felt wanted to be ineffective.

I have a firm belief that is based on over a decade of experience that teachers, regardless of their experience or preparation, want what's best for their students. Many of them don't know how and/or have not yet developed a strong sense of self-efficacy. So what happens is teachers do whatever the current popular opinion or majority tells them to do. That's how my story started. I wanted to do well; I just didn't know what methods were best, and I wasn't driving the bus. I was a passive passenger in my classroom, passively allowing mandates and initiatives to dictate my instruction.

That wasn't effective. It was accepted, but it wasn't effective. It took several mastery experiences, the support of other mentors and professional communities in my field, a school that was willing to let me experiment with my practice, and educational experiences that both encouraged and challenged my thinking to grow my own sense of efficacy. That took time and that's the catch. The old saying that "Good things come to those who wait" is true. It seems that society and educational trends are never willing to wait on the growth to happen. Before the mandates expire for one department of education, a new one is chosen, and we start over with the next trend that is dictated by politicians, influenced by celebrities and entrepreneurs, paid for and backed by lobbyists and special-interest groups such as textbook companies and governor's associations.

What's wrong with this is that, as a profession, our practice is being dictated by people who are not trained as educators and do not have experience in our field. This group creates the mandates by which students are measured, but at the end of the year, they aren't the ones that are taking responsibility for No Child Left Behind or Race to the Top.

We are.

Yes, that's right. As a profession we are letting others not only drive our bus but also use it to run us and our students over. I want to suggest that it quite possibly could be that the practitioners aren't at fault, but the practices and policies used to evaluate them might be. When accountability measures fail, let's look toward methods that support teacher efficacy. From a practitioner's perspective, that is currently where confident teachers make important instructional decisions that positively impact student learning every day in classrooms across the country.

References

Goddard, R.D., Hoy, W.K., & Hoy, A.W. (2000). Collective teacher efficacy: Its meaning, measure, and impact on student achievement. *American Educational Research Journal, 37*(92), 479–507.

Hoy, W.K., & Woolfolk, A.E. (1993). Teachers' sense of efficacy and the organizational health of schools. *The Elementary School Journal, 93*(4), 355–372.

Jerald, C.D. (2007). *Believing and achieving (issue brief)*. Washington, DC: Center for Comprehensive School Reform and Improvement.

Moir, E. (1999). The stages of a teacher's first year. In M. Scherer (Ed.), A *better beginning: Supporting and mentoring new teachers* (pp. 19–23). Alexandria, VA: ASCD (Association for Supervision and Curriculum Development).

Protheroe, N. (2008). *Teacher efficacy: What is it and does it matter? Research report*. Alexandria, VA: National Association of Elementary School Principals.

Shaughnessy, M.F. (2004). An interview with Anita Woolfolk: The educational psychology of teacher efficacy. *Educational Psychology Review, 16*(2), 153–175.

21

Empowerment Through Classroom Cultural Inquiries

MICHAEL SVEC

Since all genuine problems and matters of critical importance are hidden beneath a thick crust of lies, it is never quite clear when the proverbial last straw will fall, or what the straw will be. . . . But the moment somebody breaks through in one place, when one person cries out, "The Emperor is naked!"—when a single person breaks the rules of the game, thus exposing the game—everything suddenly appears in another light and the whole crust seems then to be made of a tissue on the point of tearing and disintegrating uncontrollably.

—*Václav Havel et al.(1985)*

Teachers are, always have been, and will continue to be on the front lines of cultural wars. Schools play a pivotal role in any culture as a means to pass on cultural knowledge to the next generation. E.D. Hirsch, Jr. (1987) declares that literacy is dependent upon being acquainted with your national culture and generously provides a list of what he considers the core body of facts and tradition that are needed to be an American. Yet a tension exists within a culture between maintaining the status quo and adapting to and even creating new realities. John Dewey (1937) reflected upon this tension: "The problem is not whether schools should participate in the production of a future society (since they do so anyway) but whether they should do it blindly and irresponsibly or with the maximum possible of courageous intelligence and responsibility" (p. 236). If culture defines for a community what is accepted behavior, then a change in external forces can alter what behaviors are acceptable. Schools become the battleground where people debate and shape what counts as *our* cultural knowledge, and teachers need to be actively engaged in that discussion.

If you do not like war metaphors, then perhaps another way to think of it is that teachers are on the cutting edge of change. Before the popular media or politicians recognize shifts in the population, teachers will experience them firsthand. Because teachers are engaged with diverse people who live in the community, teachers bear witness to shifts before others are even aware that change is happening.

Schools are important cultural institutions, yet the recognition of the influence of culture on children and teachers is largely ignored in teacher preparation and professional development. George Spindler (1955) explains:

> Educational psychology has clearly dominated the scene, partly because of a historical accident that institutionally wedded psychology and education rather early—at least in America—and partly because of the problems of tests and measurements, principles of learning, and personality development have been naturals for psychological applications. In many teacher-training institutions psychology is still the only behavioral science explicitly recognized in the organization of professional education courses. (p. 10)

The preference for psychology over sociology or anthropology in education is consistent with America's cultural focus on Protestant ideology and capitalism in which success is a result of competition and natural-born intelligence and is thus free of cultural influence. The American focus on the psychology of the individual cloaks the presence of institutional oppression, racism, classism, and sexism.

An anthropological perspective on teaching and schooling can empower teachers and their students. Culture is often perceived as static, monolithic, and even as a level of refinement possessed by some and lacking in others. Those common misconceptions must be challenged and a more accurate and functional understanding of cultures developed. Included in that understanding are the concepts of culture as an integrated system of relationships and parts, the product of history and the physical environment, and dynamic in responding to and causing change. In addition, cultures are composed of and transmitted by symbols; influence and shape individual behaviors and identity; and are complex, with variations within cultural groups.

Assuming that an individual has the most influence on a smaller and local scale, a culture course for teachers needs to explore how large cultural values influence the local but also how the local classroom culture functions. Willard Waller (1932) noted:

> Schools have a culture that is definitely their own. There are, in the school, complex rituals of personal relationships, a set of folkways, mores, and irrational sanctions, a moral code based upon them. There are games, which are sublimated wars, teams, and an elaborate set of ceremonies concerning them. There are traditions, and traditionalists waging their world-old battle against innovators. (p. 96)

This chapter discusses an example of a graduate course on the culture of American schools with the goal of engaging teachers in an understanding of the role of culture in their profession and their classroom. Before examining student cultural diversity, the changing role of teachers under pressure from state and national agencies is explored. One of the primary misconceptions to be challenged is that a culture is static and exists beyond the influence individuals. Through a series of inquiries, teachers develop skills to learn about themselves as well as their students and better understand how to co-create with their students a culture within their classroom that contributes to student and teacher wellness and success.

Why Anthropology?

Education is necessarily cultural in nature, and cultural factors have a profound impact on effective teaching and learning. Considering that worldviews, values, communication styles, language, child-rearing practice, knowledge acquisition, and personal relationships are all culturally bound, it is critically important that teachers be able to examine and understand those variables. Studying the cultural bases of education may give teachers the critical tools they need to better assess their work and facilitate the development of more effective learning. Anthropology provides the discipline, knowledge base, and research methods to begin that analysis.

Two additional concepts are useful when discussing school cultures and help provide a critical lens: wellness and sustainability. Wellness is often understood as an absence of illness. A more accurate definition of wellness is a lifestyle that encompasses a state of balance among physical, mental, and emotional states. Using job satisfaction as an indicator of career wellness, several factors have emerged as significant predictors of a teacher's satisfaction with the teaching career (MetLife, 2006). These factors include being treated as a professional by the community, involvement in team building and problemsolving, the ability to influence policies that affect them, and involvement in shaping the school curriculum. The results of a recent survey suggest that the factors that lead to wellness are becoming increasingly out of balance.

The 2012 *MetLife Survey of the American Teacher* has found that teachers are less satisfied with their careers and their profession, reaching the lowest level in two decades. The survey also shows a large increase in the number of teachers who will likely leave the profession. The economic downturn decreased budgets, and in schools with layoffs, increased class size, and programs being eliminated, teachers felt more insecure and had lower job satisfaction. Teachers with higher job satisfaction were found in schools with higher job security, opportunities for professional development, and more time to collaborate with other teachers.

Low teacher morale is increasingly apparent in graduate class discussions. Teachers are sharing stories of stress and fear—the result of pressures from principals, parents, and other external forces such as the local media. A fourth-grade teacher discussed the expected uniformity and importance of appearance as well as a teacher's being afraid to share opinions at faculty meetings out of "fear for being put on the proverbial 'bad list.'" In the same class, three teachers discussed challenges with parents, two discussed a weak but mandated curriculum, and two described their homogenous school's inability to adapt to increasing school diversity. A private school teacher recounted: "I learned by personal experience that any teacher deemed unprofessional in any area may receive a reprimand that is placed in our employee file. . . . Although never specifically stated, the feeling in our school is that we are to look perfect 100% of the time. . . . With pressure to maintain such an appearance, teaching David [an autistic child in a school with no special education resources] became a hardship." Some teachers will quietly admit to considering the reactions of parents when assigning quarter grades. Teachers feel they don't have the support of the administration, parents, and at times even their peers, thus challenging their sense of wellness.

Sustainability in relation to school culture encourages us to look beyond short-term solutions. Sustainability is defined as the capacity to endure. Incorporating sustainability into the culture of a school encourages a long-term perspective as well as an integrated, interconnected whole. Members of the school should consider and discuss: Does this value or element of our culture help the school to endure?

For example, consider Teach for America (TFA) and whether it presents a sustainable solution to low student achievement. The program is an attempt to address high teacher turnover within low-income rural and urban schools struggling with student achievement by placing committed individuals with minimal teacher training into low-income schools for 2 years. Heiling and Jez (2010) noted that "students of novice TFA teachers perform significantly less well in reading and mathematics than those of credential beginning teachers" (p. i). This result should not be a surprise. If student achievement increases with the experience level of the teacher, how can we expect the school to see improvements in achievement if the teachers are always novices? How can a school community build relationships with its members if one of the key members within the community is transient? If a community is challenged by high teacher turnover, repackaging that turnover as a positive does not address the cause of the poor teacher retention and therefore does not represent a sustainable solution. TFA becomes the equivalent of using an air freshener and closed eyes to cover up the smell of a dirty room, allowing the room to remain dirty. TFA is not a sustainable solution in the long term.

As Gregory and Smith (1987) state, perhaps the most important function of a school culture is the degree to which all the members of the school experience a sense of community. This sense of community must allow the members of the school to see themselves as one group that is collaborating to make the entire school work. Individuals make decisions about joining a community because participating in a group fulfills a basic need for dependence, affiliation, power, achievement, and a sense of belonging. Individuals are most likely to become full members of a community when the culture of the school matches their own beliefs and values. This match occurs when they have had the opportunity to develop and articulate those values.

Unfortunately, traditional school bureaucracy and hierarchy often deny students and teachers the autonomy to co-create school values and beliefs. When school culture is discussed in teacher professional development, it often assumes the audience is the school administration, the implication being that the administrator alone sets and determines the school culture. Consider Deal and Peterson (1999), who argue that "[t]he need for some leader to step forward and take the necessary risks to build positive school cultures has never been greater. If Starbucks' CEO can pour his heart into a cup of coffee, so too can school leaders pour their heart into student learning" (p. 4). Though the administration is a key factor, it is also true that teachers, students, and parents also have a role in creating and sustaining that school's particular set of values in a society dedicated to democracy and freedom.

The lack of a sense of belonging and values-match leaves several options for people who are physically located within the school. Teachers can choose either to leave the profession or seek employment at another school. The students have fewer options. Phelan, Davidson, and Cao (1991) describe the move between two cultures as a border crossing and delineate four types of crossings: smooth, manageable, hazardous, and impossible. Students can withdraw from participating, negate the importance of the school's values and curriculum, or play *Fatima's Rules*. Aikenhead (2000) and Larson (1995) highlight that students often pass through a high school chemistry class with only shallow learning by playing *Fatima's Rules*, named for the student who shared the rules of the game. The rules reflect a passive-resistance approach to school and learning using silence, accommodation to teachers' wishes, ingratiation, evasiveness, and manipulation.

Václav Havel might well recognize *Fatima's Rules* as *living within a lie*. Havel was writing about how a totalitarian government maintains control in part because individuals conform to the system. The individuals, whether citizens, students, or teachers, do not need to accept the lies of the system, but by choosing not to challenge the lies and by finding a means to live within the system, they ultimately help sustain that system.

Empowering Through Inquiries

The first two assignments foster a disposition toward inquiry and build some of the research skills necessary for the final project. Anthropology is distinguished from the other social sciences by its extensive use of qualitative research methods with a clear focus on ethnography. The scientifically based research, standardized testing movement, and focus on value-added measures that dominate current discussions, diminishes the value of qualitative research. But, as Brené Brown (2010) reminds us in her TED talk, "Maybe stories are just data with a soul," and in this time of standardization, teachers need exposure to anthropological research in order to provide a sense of belonging in their school and a connection to the community. Statistics can have the effect of reducing the Rocky Mountains to an average mountain of a certain height and composition, thus ignoring the wide variety of features and variations. Teachers don't teach in an average classroom to a standard child with average background. The South Carolina school report cards provide data on the number of Hispanic students attending a school, but the teacher knows that within that number are represented immigrants as well as multi-generation Americans, any number of regional language dialects, literate and illiterate parents, and numerous other factors that shape the children's classroom success. Just knowing that your new class roster contains Hispanic surnames does little to help you as the teacher anticipate those children as individuals and their needs.

Freire (2005) explains that "[i]t is necessary, for example, to *observe* well, to *compare* well, to *infer* well, to *imagine* well, to *free one's sensibilities* well, and to believe others, without believing too much what one may think about others" (p. 90; emphases in original). Woven into the culture course for teachers are opportunities to observe, infer, and compare their schools and classrooms with others. The classrooms of the teachers in the course provide one set of comparisons, but digital artifacts from European and Chinese schools, as well as historical artifacts, provide another source of data.

Culture courses for teachers need to engage in inquiries. Three types are presented here: surname exploration, artifact analysis, and a cultural inquiry project. By design, the inquiries move the teachers from personal exploration of how culture has shaped their identity to how space and artifacts within a school/classroom express cultural values and beliefs, and to a final project involving better understanding of the students within their classroom.

The focus on ethnography in the teachers' setting has the effect of moving a course away from a recipe approach to diversity. Discussions avoid the "how to teach African American children or people living in poverty" approach, or, in the case of one local school district, "how to teach Russian boys." Instead, discussions emphasize means of learning about the children's home culture and the impact of that culture on the students' identities. In an inquiry approach, caricatures of teachers and of their students are avoided by engaging the people within the physical boundaries of the classroom or school in the inquiries that require sharing and build trust.

Surname Exploration

The cultural journey begins with an exploration of their own surnames. It is important for teachers to be aware of their own thoughts and culture and how they are products of their socialization into their own cultural identity (Hollins, 2008). As part of the assignment, teachers reflect on the impact of their surname on their teaching. One teacher pondered the incongruity between her South Korean ethnic identity and her stereotypically Southern name, concluding: "A person's culture is not only where they are from and what they look like but also how they define themselves." By acknowledging the influence of their history outside the classroom on their teaching, the teachers become more aware of and willing to explore the children's lives outside the school.

One essential element of the surname project is that the writing is shared on a wiki with the expectation that the teachers read and comment on their peers' work. The professor has contributed his surname research in hopes of modeling and building trust. The sharing allows teachers an opportunity to build a connection with each other through similarities in their histories as well as to establish a point from which to start discussing the differences. Comments on the wiki flow into classroom discussions as we explore how we were influenced by our heritage and how our students are influenced by their heritage.

Artifact Analysis

The theory of multimodality allows for ideas to be represented visually as well as in writing. The artifact analysis combines multimodality with ethnography as a method to explore the symbolic and technological expressions of a school or classroom culture. Pahl and Rowsell(2010) articulate a theory of critical artifactual literacy that uses artifacts, spaces, and the stories they tell as a means to leverage more power for the meaning makers.

Teachers, in collaboration with their students, identify several artifacts in their classroom to explore the meaning of those objects. An ESOL teacher shared the power of a globe in her classroom: "When students locate their country, or place or origin, and share their experiences in moving from place to place, their heritage and life experiences are given value." A fifth grader actually "kissed the globe at the location of the Dominican Republic, declaring emphatically, 'I love my country!'"

The teacher then continues to analyze how the objects connect the community, lead to discussions, and convey values and beliefs. A fourth-grade teacher observed: "Upon the simple question of 'What will you remember from our classroom?' my students unanimously agreed that nothing in the classroom that is standard-based or male-centric is nearly as memorable as the student-teacher rapport we have built within the classroom environment." This teacher had used artifacts from his personal life, such as his bicycle and vegan lunches, as a means to share his passions and create a bond of trust and respect with his students. The inquiry concludes with a reflection on how to further engage students in defining the classroom culture in part through the expression of the objects and the stories they tell.

Cultural Inquiry Process

The Cultural Inquiry Process was developed by Jacob (1995) and drew upon Schon's (1983, 1987) idea of reflective practice to create a classroom inquiry based upon anthropology. Typically teachers' knowledge is heavily informed by psychology with a clear focus on individual psychological factors, ignoring cultural factors.

As Jacob and colleagues (1996) note: "From a cultural perspective, a student's behavior might be influenced by institutional norms, the student's definition of succeeding in school, conflicts between the cultures of the student's world, differences in patterns of expected social interactions, and messages in school artifacts such as texts and bulletin boards"(p. 31). The inquiry process leads teachers through a series of steps to identify a classroom challenge or puzzlement that may have cultural roots. The teachers then must develop alternative cultural hypotheses, gather and analyze relevant information, and develop—and, if possible, implement—an intervention. Many diversity workshops provide general information about a particular culture, but this inquiry process takes into account variations within a particular culture and its members.

An experienced middle school teacher shared her transition from 20 years of teaching at a Title I school to a more affluent middle school in a neighboring school district. She began having management issues with her students, only to realize that the other teachers in the school were telling the students that she was only a substitute and that the students didn't need to listen to her. In addition, the teachers seemed to have many misconceptions and biases about the other school district and students attending a Title I school. Her strategy was to first build rapport with her grade-level teachers and then the students. With the support of her peers, she learned what key community events—in this case the high school football game— and community activities were valued. She was able to successfully reach out and gain acceptance from her new school community.

Teacher as Empowered Reformer

Teacher empowerment is the increasing of power and autonomy. Characteristics of the empowerment include the ability to make decisions, access information and resources, improve circumstances, exercise assertiveness in collective decision-making, and take responsibility for their personal growth as professionals. The teaching profession is under assault, and it is now incumbent upon teachers to advocate for themselves by seeking empowerment. Being a teacher concerned with children demands that they must challenge the current discourse.

Teachers and the entire profession have increasingly been oppressed, resulting in classroom practices that further devalue the children and their cultural values. "The oppressed," according to Freire (2000), "having internalized the image of the oppressor and adopted his guidelines, are fearful of freedom. Freedom would require them to eject this image and replace it with autonomy and responsibility" (p. 47). Anthropology can serve as a means to help teachers regain autonomy and responsibility within their classrooms, to help resolve Freire's central problem: "How can the oppressed, as divided, unauthentic beings, participate in developing the pedagogy of their liberation?" (p. 48).

Anthropological knowledge and research methods become another tool to help teachers confront traditional norms and create new democratic realities in their classrooms. It provides a framework for examining neoliberal assumptions about American society and public education. The qualitative research methods enable teachers to gather the evidence needed to examine complex problems in their schools and begin to seek equally complex solutions. Finally, the cultural inquiry process fosters a willingness to learn about and from their students and to use that knowledge in a way that benefits everyone in the classroom community.

Almost two decades ago, Harriet Tyson (1994) called upon the example of Václav Havel when she argued:

> The conditions for a Velvet Revolution in teaching now exist. Teachers are increasingly conscious of assaults on their dignity and of disrespect for their knowledge. Aware of society's pressure on them to perform better, goaded by "choice" plans and other forms of competition, and closer to the woes of society's children than the rest of us are, teachers are increasingly turning to one another to seek ways of doing the one thing that satisfies them most—helping their students succeed. (p. 193)

Becoming and being a teacher requires that teachers and the communities they serve understand and accept teaching as a political act as well as the role that schools place in communicating and defining our culture. The lessons learned in a cultural anthropology class can be one means of helping to achieve Dewey's (1897) vision for teachers: "I believe that every teacher should realize the dignity of his calling; that he is a social servant set apart for the maintenance of proper social order and the securing of the right to social growth" (p. 18). Being a teacher today requires of teachers the willingness and the skills necessary to challenge the lies and ultimately to *live in the truth*.

References

Aikenhead, G.S. (2000). Renegotiating the culture of school science. In R. Miller, J. Leach, & J. Osborne (Eds.), *Improving science education: The contribution of research* (pp. 245–264). Birmingham, UK: Open University Press.

Brown, B. (2010, June). Brene Brown: The power of vulnerability. TEDxHouston, http://www.ted.com/talks/brene_brown_on_vulnerability.html

Deal, T.E., & Peterson, K.D. (1999). *Shaping school culture: The heart of leadership.* San Francisco, CA: Jossey-Bass.

Dewey, J. (1897). *My pedagogic creed.* New York: E.L. Kellogg.

Dewey, J. (1937, May). Education and social change. *Social Frontiers, 3,* 235–238.

Freire, P. (2000). *Pedagogy of the oppressed* (30th anniversary ed.). New York: Continuum.

Freire, P. (2005). *Teachers as cultural workers.* Boulder, CO: Westview Press.

Gregory, T.B., & Smith, G.R. (1987). *High schools as communities: The small school reconsidered.* Bloomington, IN: Phi Delta Kappa Educational Foundation.

Havel, V., et al. (1985). *The power of the powerless.* Armonk, NY: Sharpe Inc.

Heiling, J.V.,& Jez, S.J. (2010). *Teach for America: A review of the evidence.* Boulder, CO, and Tempe, AZ: Education and the Public Interest Center & Education Policy Research Unit. Retrieved from http://epicpolicy.org/publication/teach-for-america

Hirsch, Jr., E.D. (1987). *Cultural literacy: What every American needs to know.* New York: Vintage Books.

Hollins, E.R. (2008). *Culture in school learning: Revealing the deep meaning* (2nd ed.). New York: Routledge.

Jacob, E. (1995). Reflective practice and anthropology in culturally diverse classrooms. *Elementary School Journal, 95,* 451–463.

Jacob, E., Johnson, B.K., Finley, J., Gurski. J.C., & Lavine, R.S. (1996, March). One student at a time: The cultural inquiry process. *Middle School Journal, 30–35.*

Larson, J.O. (1995, April). *Fatima's rules and other elements of an unintended chemistry curriculum.* Paper presented to the American Educational Research Association Annual Meeting, San Francisco.

MetLife. (2006). *The MetLife survey of the American teacher: Expectations and experiences.* Retrieved from http://www.eric.ed.gov/PDFS/ED496558.pdf

MetLife. (2012). *The MetLife survey of the American teacher: Teachers, parents and the economy.* Retrieved from http://www.metlife.com/assets/cao/contributions/foundation-/american-teacher/MetLife-Teacher-Survey-2011.pdf

Pahl, K., & Rowsell, J. (2010). *Artifactual literacies: Every object tells a story.* New York: Teachers College Press.

Phelan, P., Davidson, A., & Cao, H. (1991). Students' multiple worlds: Negotiating the boundaries of family, peer, and school cultures. *Anthropology and Education Quarterly, 22,* 224–250.

Schon, D.A. (1983). *The reflective practitioner.* New York: Basic Books.

Schon, D.A. (1987). *Educating the reflective practitioner.* San Francisco, CA: Jossey-Bass.

Spindler, G.D. (1955). *Education and anthropology.* Stanford: Stanford University Press.

Tyson, H. (1994). *Who will teach the children? Progress and resistance in teacher education.* San Francisco, CA: Jossey-Bass.

Waller, W. (1932). *The sociology of teaching.* New York: Wiley.

Conclusion: "[N]ot the Time... to Follow the Line of Least Resistance"[1]

P.L. THOMAS

In a major journal published by the National Council of Teachers of English (NCTE), a teacher-scholar lamented the then-current state of implementing research in language: "A brief consideration will indicate reasons for the considerable gap between the research currently available and the utilization of that research in school programs and methods" (LaBrant, 1947, p. 87). The discussion of that gap between research and pedagogy led to this conclusion:

> Most thinking persons agree that the existence of civilized man is threatened today. While language is not food or drink, and will not satisfy the hungry and thirsty, it is the medium by which we must do much of our learning and planning, and by which we must think out solutions to our problems if we are not to solve them by the direct method of force. No sensible person believes that language will cure all difficulties; but the thoughtful person will certainly agree that language is a highly important factor in promoting understanding, and a most dangerous factor in promoting understanding between individuals and between the countries individuals represent. . . . *This is not the time for the teacher of any language to follow the line of least resistance, to teach without the fullest possible knowledge of the implications of his medium* [emphasis added]. Before we, either as individuals or as a Council, experiment with methods of doing specific things or block out a curriculum, let us spend some time with the best scholars in the various

fields of language study to discover what they know, what they believe uncertain and in need of study. (LaBrant, 1947, p. 94)

While those of us living our lives as teachers, especially teachers of literacy in K–12 settings or in teacher education, may recognize many points above in our current debate about education reform—including some of the debates that simmer below the surface of the workings of NCTE—these comments are by Lou LaBrant and were published in the January 1947 issue of *Elementary English* (now *Language Arts*). More than 6 decades after LaBrant wrote about the *gap between research and practice*, more than 6 decades after she implored us that "[t]his is not the time for the teacher of any language to follow the line of least resistance," educators across the United States are faced with the failure of leaders, the public, and professional organizations in the face of the promise of universal public education and its promise to drive the great hope we call democracy.

The Locus of Authority: Our Time for Resistance

At the 100th annual convention for NCTE in Chicago in November 2011, I was part of a panel on the council's century of leadership in the field of literacy—reading from the essay above by LaBrant and suggesting how she would have responded to the current calls for Common Core State Standards (CCSS), increased testing, intensified teacher accountability linked to those tests, and accelerating mandates driving teacher preparation and accreditation of colleges and departments of education.

I know from my work as the biographer of LaBrant (Thomas, 2001) that she was a powerful voice for professionalism, scholarship, and teacher autonomy—including for herself and every teacher with whom she interacted. LaBrant, in fact, when enrolled in her doctoral program at Northwestern University in the early 1930s, faced pressure while teaching English to implement required reading lists, textbooks, and benchmark testing, all of which she knew to be flawed practices.

What did LaBrant do? She fabricated lesson plans with her roommate, the foreign language teacher, and submitted them each week while practicing the pedagogy she embraced—student choice in what they read and wrote, holistic instruction and assessment of literacy. At the end of the year, LaBrant and her students (yes, in the early 1930s) faced end-of-course testing, and LaBrant's students received top scores. Consequently, she was praised by the principal in front of the entire faculty for her dedication to the prescribed policies.

This tension between bureaucratic mandates that seek to shift the *locus of authority* (consider Freire's [1993, 1998, 2005] distinction between "authoritarian" and "authoritative") away from the teacher and toward the standards and tests (as proxies for the authorities who mandate both) designed and prescribed by the state is not entirely new (except for the current intensity), but neither is the need for teachers to own their autonomy, their professionalism—to be that resistance.

Also at the 2011 NCTE annual convention, a centennial celebration, Susan Ohanian, Stephen Krashen, Carol Mikoda, Bess Altwerger, Joanne Yatvin, and Richard J. Meyer proposed a resolution: NCTE will oppose common core standards and national tests (Resolution Proposal to Support, 2011).[2] This act of resistance, this act of teacher autonomy and professionalism resulted in what Catherine Gewertz (2011) describes as: "The National Council of Teachers of English was asked by a group of its members to take a strong stand against the common standards, but it declined to do so":

> This year, one of the resolutions called on the NCTE to "oppose the adoption of national standards as a concept," and, specifically, oppose the set of standards drafted as part of an initiative spearheaded by the National Governors Association and the Council of Chief State School Officers. (As you know, all but four states have already adopted thosestandards.)
>
> The resolution was put forth by a group led by activist Susan Ohanian and retired education professor Stephen Krashen. When they introduced the same resolution last year, it passed only as a "sense of the house" resolution, meaning it's not binding policy on the NCTE.

Adoption of the resolution this year would have been at odds with NCTE's current policy, which is officially neutral on the standards themselves, but pledges to support teachers whose states and districts are implementing them. Many of the sessions at the conference focused on helping teachers understand and teach to the new standards.

This is a time when political leaders, the public, and national organizations have abdicated their moral obligation to create and maintain universal public education for all children as a sacred trust between a free people and the promise of democracy. This is a time when becoming and being a teacher is being reduced to a service industry by political and corporate leaders with little or no experience or expertise as educators.

This volume, then, has sought to speak out against that rising tide because *"[t]his is not the time for the teacher of any language to follow the line of least resistance, to teach without the fullest possible knowledge of the implications of his[/her] medium."*

Education grounded in democratic principles must honor the political literacy of the teachers and students collaborating in the pursuit of human autonomy and agency. Silence and stasis are political acts of acquiescence. It is past time for voice and action.

References

Freire, P. (1993). *Pedagogy of the oppressed.* New York: Continuum.

Freire, P. (1998). *Pedagogy of freedom: Ethics, democracy, and civic courage* (P. Clarke, Trans.). Lanham, MD: Rowman and Littlefield.

Freire, P. (2005). *Teachers as cultural workers: Letters to those who dare to teach.* (D. Macedo, D. Koike, & A. Oliveira, Trans.). Boulder, CO: Westview.

Gerwertz, C. (2011, November 21). English teacher's group sidesteps common-core opposition. Curriculum Matters [Web log]. *Education Week.* Retrieved from http://blogs.edweek.org/edweek/curriculum/2011/11/post_5.html

LaBrant, L. (1947, January). Research in language. *Elementary English, 24*(1), 86–94.

Resolution proposal to support: No confidence in United States Department of Education Secretary Arne Duncan. (2011, October 11). Schools Matter [Web log]. Retrieved from http://www.schoolsmatter.info/2011/10/resolution-ncte-will-oppose-common-core.html

Thomas, P.L. (2001). *Lou LaBrant: A woman's life, a teacher's life.* Huntington, NY: Nova Science Publishers, Inc.

Notes

1. Originally posted as and adapted from: Thomas, P.L. (2011, November 21). "[N]ot the time. . .to follow the line of least resistance." Daily Kos. Retrieved from http://www.dailykos.com/story/2011/11/21/1038356/-Not-the-Time-to-Follow-the-Line-of-Least-Resistance

2. Revised resolution passed: Resolution proposal to support: No confidence in United States Department of Education Secretary Arne Duncan. Posted at http://ncte.connectedcommunity.org/CEL/Discussions/ViewThread/?GroupId=1153&MID=5321

Author Biographies

Eliza Allen is a doctoral student at Georgia State University in the Middle, Secondary Education and Instructional Technology department. She currently works as a third-grade teacher. She recently examined the effects of policy on teaching practices in the *Language Arts Journal of Michigan*. Eliza also presents on print-based and digitally mediated multimodal composing practices. Her research interests include the critical language and literacy practices of culturally and linguistically diverse young children and in- and out-of-school literacy practices.

Lawrence Baines currently serves as the chair of Instructional Leadership and Academic Curriculum at the University of Oklahoma. For more information see www.lawrencebaines.com.

Gordon D. Bambrick has been a teacher of English and computers in Barrie, Ontario, for 2 decades.

Tara Campbell is doctoral student at Georgia State University in the Middle, Secondary Education and Instructional Technology Department. She holds an Ed.S. in Curriculum and Instruction and has 20 years' teaching experience in an Atlanta-area middle school. She recently published in the *Language Arts Journal of Michigan* and spoke at the annual NCTE conference about the effects of policy on her instruction. In addition to educational policy, her research interests include the use of young adult literature in the classroom and digital literacies.

Alan S. Canestrari, Ed.D., Boston University, a Professor of Education at Roger Williams University, is co-editor (with Bruce Marlowe) of *Educational Foundations: An Anthology of Critical Readings* (Sage, 2004) and *Educational Psychology in Context: Readings for Future Teachers* (Sage, 2006). *Educational Foundations* was awarded the 2005 American Educational Studies Association Critics Choice Award. He has had a long career in public schools and universities as a history teacher, department chair, adjunct professor at Rhode Island College, and mentor in the Brown University Masters of Teaching Program. He was the Rhode Island Social Studies Teacher of the Year in 1992.

Patricia Chouinard teaches Spanish online at the University of Massachusetts, Boston, as a supplement to her face-to-face teaching in an urban high school. She has co-presented at national conventions on distance learning, the visual learner, and student travel abroad. Her research interests lie in progressive education and Mexican American student achievement. She is a doctoral student in Leadership in Urban Schools at the University of Massachusetts, Boston.

Anthony Cody received his teaching credential at UC Berkeley in 1987 and taught science and math for the following 18 years at a high-needs middle school in Oakland. In 2007, he initiated a district-wide mentoring project in Oakland called TeamScience. He now lives in Mendocino County and authors the popular *Education Week* blog Living in Dialogue, which discusses education policy issues.

Katherine Crawford-Garrett is an Assistant Professor of Education at Ithaca College. Her recent research has explored how first-year Teach for America corps members construct and narrate their impressions and beliefs about urban communities in an effort to illuminate the tensions and struggles that emerge when teachers attempt to work across lines of culture, race, and class in complex socio-political settings. She has published her work in *Children's Literature* and *Working Papers in Educational Linguistics*. Her academic interests include practitioner inquiry, postmodernism, critical pedagogy, and feminism.

Ana L. Cruz, a native of Brazil, received her Ph.D. in Education from the University of Tennessee. She is Professor of Education at St. Louis Community College-Meramec, Missouri. Ana's research interests include critical pedagogy, social justice education, multicultural/international education, and music and deafness. Ana was the chairperson of the AERA Paulo Freire SIG and serves on the Founding Scholars' Advisory Board of the Paulo and Nita Freire Project for Critical Pedagogy. She is involved with the *International Journal of Critical Pedagogy* (IJCP) as International Affiliate, as Brazilian Portuguese Articles Editor, and was Managing Editor.

John M. Elmore is currently an Associate Professor of Professional Education at West Chester University of Pennsylvania and was previously an Associate Professor and Director of Graduate Studies at Medaille College in Buffalo, New York, from 2000 to 2005. Recent publications include "War and the Sectarian Mind," in *Education in a Time of Permanent War* (Peter Lang, 2010), and "Marx and the Foundations of Education," in *Marx Across the Curriculum* (Palgrave, 2012). *Authoritarian Education in a Democratic Society* (Information Age, 2012) is forthcoming. His scholarship and teaching deal primarily with critical pedagogy, Marxism, and education for social justice.

Amy Seely Flint is an Associate Professor at Georgia State University in the Middle, Secondary Education and Instructional Technology department. She has contributed to a number of publications on teacher professional development and critical literacy (*Journal of Literacy Research, Reading Teacher, Elementary School Journal, Language Arts,* and *Teacher and Teacher Education*). Her most recent book is *Literate Lives: Teaching Reading and Writing in Elementary Classrooms* (Wiley, 2007). Amy's recent work examines a generative collaborative model of professional development for teachers working with English language learners in elementary classrooms.

Amy Fraser is a doctoral student at Georgia State University in the Middle, Secondary Education and Instructional Technology department. She holds an Ed.S. in Language and Literacy from GSU and a Master's degree in Special Education from the University of Georgia. Amy has been teaching in a K–8 environment for 11 years. Currently, she teaches fourth-grade students with disabilities at the 4/5 Academy at Fifth Avenue in Decatur, Georgia. Her research interests include classroom discourse and gender identity within K–8 literature.

Crystal Glover is a lecturer and academic advisor in the department of Reading and Elementary Education at the University of North Carolina at Charlotte. She is a National Board Certified Teacher and certified reading specialist. Crystal is currently pursuing a Ph.D. in Curriculum and Instruction with a focus on Urban Literacy. Her research interests include culturally responsive literacy instruction for students of color, urban teacher preparation, and the oral and written language development of children in poverty.

David A. Gorlewski is an Assistant Professor in the Education department at D'Youville College in Buffalo, New York, where he teaches courses in curriculum planning, methods, and advanced curricular issues. He has served in public education as a high school English teacher, a staff developer, and a senior-level administrator in curriculum and personnel. Most recently, he co-authored (with Julie Gorlewski) *Making It Real: Case Stories for Secondary Teachers* (Sense, 2012) and co-edited (with Bradley Porfilio and Julie Gorlewski) *Using Standards and High-Stakes Testing* for *Students: Exploiting Power with Critical Pedagogy* (Peter Lang, 2012).

Julie A. Gorlewski, Assistant Professor of Secondary Education at the State University of New York at New Paltz, taught secondary English for over 15 years. She is the author of the book *Power, Resistance, and Literacy: Writing for Social Justice* (Information Age Publishers, 2011), which was selected for a 2011 Critic's Choice Award by the American Educational Studies Association. In addition, she co-authored (with David Gorlewski) *Making It Real: Case Stories for Secondary Teachers* (Sense, 2012) and co-edited (with Bradley Porfilio and David Gorlewski) *Using Standards and High-Stakes Testing* for *Students: Exploiting Power with Critical Pedagogy* (Peter Lang, 2012).

A. Scott Henderson is currently Professor of Education at Furman University in Greenville, South Carolina. Prior to coming to Furman, he taught seventh- and ninth-grade social studies in Virginia, and was an instructor of English at Yamagata Women's Junior College in Yamagata, Japan. His published scholarship includes works on the history of American housing and education.

Danielle Hilaski is a doctoral student at Georgia State University in the Middle, Secondary Education and Instructional Technology department. She currently works with elementary students as Reading Recovery and ESOL teacher and with teachers as an instructional coach. She recently examined the effects of policy on teaching practices in the *Language Arts Journal of Michigan* and at the National Council of Teachers of English conference. Her research interests include teacher development and early literacy practices that support students' sociocultural diversity.

A former lawyer, as well as a teacher and poet, **John L. Hoben** is a recent graduate of the Ph.D. program at Memorial University's Faculty of Education. John's teaching in the classroom is centered on creating spaces where students can bring imagination and personal experience to their academic work. He and his wife Sylvia and their wonderful daughters, Sophie and Norah, live in Torbay.

Lauren Hoffman is Professor and Director of the Educational Leadership doctoral program at Lewis University in Romeoville, Illinois. Her research interests lie in critical pedagogy and how individuals and groups assert their agency in relation to hegemonic forces. Her current work focuses on human rights and capabilities, social activism, and preparing critical teachers and leaders to reveal and resist injustice.

Regletto Aldrich D. Imbong is currently finishing his master's degree in Philosophy(focusing on critical pedagogy) and is an instructor of the Social Sciences

Department of the Asian College of Technology. He has published articles in local dailies and local periodicals, still connected to the issue of Philippine education and repressed students' rights. He was the representative of the Philippines in a conference in Bogor, Indonesia, where he described the miserable conditions of Filipino students as migrants in other countries. He presented a paper entitled "Philippine Education and Democratic Governance" at the Second Graduate Research Conference of the University of San Carlos, in which the paper is also scheduled for publication.

Linda James is a doctoral student at Georgia State University in the Middle, Secondary Education and Instructional Technology department. She holds a Master's degree in teaching and learning with a concentration in early literacy. She has been teaching for 17 years and has also served as a reading tutor and a sign language teacher. Her research interests include teacher development as it pertains to literacy.

Galen Leonhardy teaches English and humanities courses at Black Hawk College in Moline, Illinois. Galen's greatest joy is spending time with his two daughters, Sarah and Hallie.

Dawn Johnson Mitchell has spent the last 11 years working with both students and teachers of all backgrounds and grade levels as a teacher consultant with the Spartanburg Writing Project, housed at USC Upstate, and as an Adjunct Instructor at Furman University and Spartanburg Methodist College. Dawn conducts action research in public school classrooms in the area, leads book studies, and invests in the professional growth of the teachers with whom she works. She is committed to being an advocate and a source of support for both students and fellow teachers.

Brad J. Porfilio is Assistant Professor of Education at Lewis University in Romeoville, Illinois, where he conducts research and teaches doctoral students to become critical scholars, social advocates, and multicultural educators. He has published numerous peer-reviewed articles, book chapters, edited volumes, and conference papers in the field of education. Dr. Porfilio earned his Ph.D. in Sociology of Education in 2005 at the University at Buffalo.

Thomas Robertine is currently enrolled in SUNY New Paltz's Secondary Education Program. Prior to returning to New Paltz after a 5-year hiatus, he graduated from a 2-year certificate program at the Collective School of Music in New York City. He has had the opportunity to record as a session musician and tour the country. For the past 8 years he has been teaching private and group music lessons. He continues to play and record when he is not in school and teaching. This will be his first opportunity to publish a piece of writing.

Sanjuana Rodriguez is a doctoral student at Georgia State University in the Middle, Secondary Education and Instructional Technology department. She holds a Master's degree in reading education from the University of Tennessee. She currently works as a literacy coordinator for a public school district in Northwest Georgia. Her research interests include early literacy as it relates to English learners and socio-cultural perspectives in education.

Dana M. Stachowiak is a doctoral candidate in the Educational Leadership and Cultural Foundations Department at the University of North Carolina at Greensboro. Her research interests include gender and sexuality, intersections of popular culture and critical pedagogy, curriculum theory, queer theory, and social justice education.

Katie Stover is an Assistant Professor in the Education department at Furman University in Greenville, South Carolina. She holds a Ph.D. in Curriculum and Instruction in Urban Literacy from the University of North Carolina at Charlotte. She has authored a number of publications in the field of literacy in journals such as the *Reading Teacher*, the *Middle School Journal*, and the *Journal of Early Childhood Research*. Katie's research interests include critical literacy, writing for social justice, digital literacy, and teacher education.

Michael Svec is an Associate Professor at Furman University. He graduated from the University of Illinois-Urbana with a degree in physics and earned a Ph.D. in curriculum and instruction (secondary science) from Indiana University-Bloomington. Dr. Svec teaches all levels of science methods, perspectives on American education, and culture of American schools, and supervises field placements. He was a 2005 Fulbright scholar in the Czech Republic.

P .L. Thomas, Associate Professor of Education (Furman University, Greenville, South Carolina), is a former high school English teacher, a column editor for *English Journal* (National Council of Teachers of English), and series editor for Critical Literacy Teaching Series: Challenging Authors and Genres (Sense Publishers). Follow his work at http://wrestlingwithwriting.blogspot.com/ and @plthomasEdD on twitter.

Natasha Thornton is a doctoral student at Georgia State University in the Middle, Secondary Education and Instructional Technology department. She has 8 years' teaching experience in kindergarten and fourth grade. Natasha currently works as a graduate assistant at Georgia State University supporting pre-service middle-grade teachers with integrating literacy in content area instruction. She is a Southern Regional Education Board Doctoral Fellow, and her research interests include teacher development and literacy instruction in urban settings.

Lisa William-White has authored/co-authored chapters focused on critical race theory, gender studies and multicultural education, autoethnography, and spoken word scholarship. She has been engaged in educational equity work since 1991 and has been employed as a high school English teacher, as a college recruiter and academic counselor, and as an educator in the University of California, California State, and California Community College Systems.

Melissa Winchell is an Instructor of English at Massasoit Community College in Brockton, Massachusetts, and an Adjunct Professor at the University of Massachusetts, Boston, and Gordon College. A doctoral candidate in the Leadership in Urban Schools program at Boston's University of Massachusetts, Melissa's research interests include teacher education, cultural competence, critical pedagogy, critical race theory, coteaching, and coresearch.

Ann G. Winfield has a Ph.D. in Educational Research and Policy Analysis with a concentration in Curriculum Studies. She is Associate Professor at Roger Williams University in Bristol, Rhode Island, and is the author of *Eugenics and Education in America: Institutionalized Racism and the Implications of History, Ideology, and Memory* (Peter Lang, 2007). Dr. Winfield's work examines the role of early 20th-century eugenic ideology on social policy, past and present.

Index

CRITICAL STUDIES

 in DEMOCRACY   PAUL R. CARR, SERIES EDITOR

 & POLITICAL LITERACY

Why do so few people vote? What is political engagement? How does education intersect with democracy and political literacy? What can be learned from interdisciplinary studies on democracy? How do we cultivate political literacy? What is the relevance of elections in light of war, poverty, discrimination, social inequalities, etc.? What are the alternatives to the traditional electoral, representative, party-politics models that have characterized our societies? Is the mainstream media holding government to account, disseminating propaganda, or fuelling the need to pacify the population? How do international systems, approaches, and realities related to democracy compare, and what can we learn from others? These are some of the questions addressed through this book series.

Seeking to fill an important gap in the literature, the series takes on the theme of democracy in a multi-/inter-disciplinary, comprehensive, and critical way. Some of the leading research in the field indicates that the scope, depth, and quality of educational materials available is limited, and can lead to a relatively apolitical, non-critical understanding and assessment of what democracy is, and what it should be. Some books have democracy in the title but do not make it the focus, and often books that address more directly, for example, multiculturalism, media studies, or school reform may delve into the area of democracy without fully deconstructing what it is, how it functions, how people can shape and intersect with it, and how it is used (or misused) to distort power relations, which is at the base of teaching, learning, and action. The need for critical analyses, perspectives, and resources offering a broader range of understanding of the multiple, nuanced, and complex realities of democracy is, therefore, clear.

Critical Studies in Democracy and Political Literacy seeks authors, voices, and perspectives to more concisely and critically explore the meaning and essence of democracy within contemporary realities, either from theoretical, conceptual, and/or empirical perspectives. The overlapping and interdisciplinary nature of the study of democracy bleeds naturally into the areas of media studies, sociology, political science, peace studies, multiculturalism, feminist studies, and cultural studies, all of which have a natural and inextricable relationship to and within education. With democracy as its focus, the series presents a broad range of materials specifically tailored to teacher education and scholars within the education field.

To submit a manuscript or proposal for editorial consideration, please contact:

Paul Carr, Series Editor
Youngstown State University
prcarr@gmail.com

To order other books in this series, please contact our Customer Service Department:

(800) 770-LANG (within the U.S.)
(212) 647-7706 (outside the U.S.)
(212) 647-7707 FAX

Or browse online by series:

www.peterlang.com